ROYAL NAVY TRAWLERS
Part One: Admiralty Vessels

By Gerald Toghill

Dedication

To the men of the Royal Naval Patrol Service
Who went down to the sea in their little ships
To meet the foe.

First published in the United Kingdom in 2003 by Maritime Books, Lodge Hill, Liskeard, Cornwall, PL14 4EL

CONTENTS

AUTHOR'S NOTES

Naval history and in particular ship's histories have always been a passion with me, so much so that when I served for a number of years in the Training world at GANGES at Shotley and RALEIGH at Torpoint I frequently lectured to the trainees on the subjects. There really wasn't anything clever about it because if I wanted to make notes for a lecture there was always a wealth of books to look up. Until one day I wanted to know about Trawlers. To my amazement, there was virtually nothing available to draw on. It took months of delving to get enough information to talk for even half an hour on the subject.

When I retired from the Royal Navy and began to follow my hobby more extensively I came back to the subject of Trawlers time and time again. Eventually I was driven to the conclusion that, there being nothing in print, I would have to do something about it. Thus was born the two volumes comprising this work.

Trawlers served in the Royal Navy in both World Wars and stood the Navy in good stead carrying out many tasks for which, at the outbreak of both Wars, the Navy was ill equipped to cope. Minesweeping, Convoy escorts, Anti-Submarine patrols, Auxiliary Patrols, Boom Gate Vessels, Barrage Balloon Vessels - the list of tasks they undertook is almost endless. Most of them were taken up from Trade - existing Trawlers in the fishing industry requisitioned, purchased or hired (See Volume II), but others were specifically built by the Admiralty and it is these vessels with which this first volume deals.

Frequently referred to as "The Destroyers' poor relations" they were not as glamorous as their big brothers, but there was no lack of the "derring-do". Witness the gallant little ARAB in the Norwegian Campaign in 1940 when her CO won the VC (See Vol.II) or HMT JUNIPER, of the Tree Class, also in the Norwegian Campaign. Escorting a tanker in Norwegian waters she sighted a whole German squadron comprising two Battleships, SCHARNHORST and GNEISENAU, the cruiser, ADMIRAL HIPPER, and four destroyers. She couldn't escape, so she hoisted her Battle Ensign and, with her diminutive little pop-gun turned into 530 tons of spitting, fighting fury, a David taking on seven Goliaths all at the same time. Incredibly she survived for an hour and a half before she finally sank beneath the waves leaving just four survivors. It was this sort of action, which compelled me to write these Volumes.

In doing so I have resorted to many abbreviations and for this I apologise, but there are only so many times an author can laboriously write out in full names like Cook, Welton and Gemmeli, Barrage Balloon Vessels, Boom Gate Vessels, etc. so they become CWG, BBV and BGV and so on. Lest any non-naval readers should become a little confused I have included a List of Abbreviations on page 223 and I sincerely hope this will help.

Obtaining photographs of Trawlers has been a big headache and despite extensive searching by both the publishers and myself I regret that there is an absence of pictures in one or two of the Classes in this Volume. Those that have been obtained are fully credited, once more with abbreviations: IWM (Imperial War Museum), NMM (National Maritime Museum), PRNM (Portsmouth Royal Naval Museum, keepers of the famous Wright & Logan Collection), and MPL (Maritime Photo Library). All others are fully credited below each picture.

By the same token, information has often been impossible, in some cases, to come by despite very extensive research and I apologise for any omissions such as Pennant Nos. and armament. Armament in particular has been a bug-bear mainly because from the very outset they were at the back of the queue and had to take what was on offer. As the Wars progressed they sported a motley collection of weapons which ships' companies scrounged from any source available.

The Acknowledgements page is fairly extensive and I make no apology for it. The help I have received in information gathering has been enormous from a wide diversity of people including the fishing industry and not least members of the RN Patrol Service. I thank them all profusely and if I have inadvertently missed anyone out please accept my most sincere apology.

Someone who merits a huge vote of thanks is my Editor, Steve Bush of Maritime Books, without whose untiring help in licking my writing into a book, these Volumes would never have come to fruition.

There is a popular misconception that Minewarfare is an invention of the Twentieth Century when in fact it goes back much further. It took 20th Century technology to bring the sea-mine into its own, but as far back as the 16th Century when Drake and his colleagues were busily making life difficult for the Spanish, the Dutch, who were also having trouble with the Dons, employed mines (of a sort) in the defence of Antwerp in 1585. There is no accurate record as to how successful these "mines" were but it would appear that they were not overly effective because there is nothing else recorded of the device, whatever it was.

It took nearly 200 years before they cropped up again in the American War of Independence. This time the idea caught on and only 20 years later, in the bloody French Revolution of the late 18th Century, both sides made use of mines. A little later, in 1814, when ships of the Royal Navy attacked Long Island in the fledgling United States of America, mines were used unsuccessfully against the English ships. This was followed by a number of instances during the 19th Century when they were used with increasing efficiency both in European and American waters. The technology that went into their design and construction improved - and so did their effectiveness. The culmination of this period of design and experiment came in 1904 in the Russo-Japanese War.

The Early Twentieth Century Mine

At this stage, and all the way through WW1, there was only one type of sea-mine in existence and that was the contact mine. The quite basic design was nevertheless representative of the technology of the time. Comprising of a cylindrical drum containing the explosive and the simple mechanics of the device, it was attached to a heavy sinker by a length of wire cable. The cable could be adjusted to the required length before being dropped according to the depth of the water in which it was being laid, so that the mine itself floated, just below the surface of the water, anchored by its sinker. Having been carefully laid all it had to do was to lie in wait for a passing ship to bump into it. Around the outside were a number of contact points or "horns" which were connected to the exploding mechanism inside. When an object such as a passing vessel touched one of the horns the mine was designed to explode.

This, then, was basically the early 20th Century mine. During WW1 it was laid in vast numbers in the waters around the shores of the UK where shipping could congregate, particularly in the areas surrounding anchorages, the entrances to harbours, and the routes taken by coastal convoys.

Obviously it was impracticable to lay them too far out to sea simply because of the depths of water involved, but the shallow coastal waters were ideal and before long they made their mark on naval warfare by indiscriminately claiming any victim which came within their reach.

The Advent of the Minesweeper

As with the case of that other new innovation, the submarine, so it was with the sea-mine. Their Lordships at the Admiralty frowned upon such "ungentlemanly" weapons, dismissing them as the "weapons of the weak" and therefore to be ignored by such a powerful navy as theirs. However, in reply to a few voices of warning within the Navy, they did take some notice and in 1900 a directive went out to the C-in-C of the Mediterranean Fleet to provide the fleet with mines, but it was a half-hearted affair and heels were dragged to the extent that 3 years later the order was rescinded. However, there were events afoot which, over the next few years, were to change the Admiralty's thinking.

In 1904 Japan went to war with Russia. It was not a long war and ended with the ignominious defeat of the Russians the following year. When the intelligence reports of the naval conflict between the two protagonists were read and digested at the Admiralty they began to sit up and take notice. The ships involved in this war were Dreadnoughts very much like the British battle-fleets, and looking at the reports it became obvious that these Leviathans didn't like mines one little bit. In fact they gave up and sank remarkably quickly when encountering them. It became obvious that it was time for something to be done and so thinking-caps were donned. Suddenly the Royal Navy was very much aware of the mine and there were many conjectures as to their use. More importantly, in line with the philosophy that they were the "weapons of the weak", much thought was being given to methods of combating them.

In 1907 command of the prestigious Channel Fleet was in the hands of Lord Charles Beresford. Beresford's importance in the world of mines and minesweeping stems from the fact that in 1907 he put forward a plan to the Admiralty whereby fishing trawlers could be utilized to experiment with minesweeping methods and equipment.

Why Trawlers? It appears that when, earlier, the subject of mines and the methods of counteracting them had been bandied around the Fleet someone had been shrewd enough to notice the similarities between trawling for fish and trawling for mines, a coincidence that obviously needed further investigation. Lord Charles caught hold of the idea and held it in enough esteem to go to Grimsby himself to take a closer look at these strange un-navy-like vessels. He was sufficiently impressed to make representations to the Admiralty suggesting that the idea be followed up.

Undoubtedly one of the factors that crossed his Lordship's mind was the fact that, should they prove satisfactory, there would be the advantage that this type of vessel was prolific and, therefore, available. There were hundreds upon hundreds of them dotted about the shores of Great Britain, mostly congregated in the main fishing ports. They were also, by contemporary standards, cheap. The fishing trade was not renowned for its concern over the comfort of its men and the vessels they used were equally not renowned for their luxury. They were built in a spartan manner, best suited to the job they were required to perform. In the basic vein they were small, reasonably handy and cheap to run and maintain. Above all they were remarkably seaworthy.

Now there are degrees of seaworthiness. There is seaworthy and there is seaworthy and the trawlers were seaworthy!! Time and again in the annals of two World Wars mention is made of the how they were able to stand to their tasks in the most atrocious weather when destroyers, frigates and even larger ships were obliged to run for shelter from the fury of the elements. Hardly surprising! Trawlers brought a whole new meaning to "occupying their business in great waters". The 'great waters' in which these sturdy little craft were occupied were, in the main, above the Arctic Circle around Greenland, Iceland and Bear Island and in the White Sea where the Beaufort Scale frequently had little meaning and if it had, a Force 8 or so could almost be likened to a summer breeze. These sturdy little vessels could weather just about anything that those inhospitable latitudes could hurl at them and still carry on the business of supplying the nation's tables with fish. Usually they were away for weeks at a time, the duration governed only by how long it took to fill their holds with silver fish and how long their fuel, which was coal, lasted.

These, then, were the ships that Lord Charles had in mind when he put forward his ideas to the Admiralty. That they liked and approved of the notion is evidenced by the fact that within a year - a surprisingly swift action on the part of the Admiralty - the order went out for the purchase of two trawlers for conversion to minesweeping duties. Commander Booty of the Channel Fleet Battleship KING EDWARD VII was despatched to Grimsby to select the vessels. He chose ALGOMA and ANDES. In February 1908 these two diminutive additions to His Majesty's Fleet arrived at Portland and began minesweeping trials. They were classified as Auxiliary Minesweepers and they were so successful in the trials that they secured a place for trawlers and drifters in the two great conflicts which were to come in the 20th Century. Others were to follow. SEAFLOWER, SEAMEW, SPARROW and SPIDER were purchased in April 1909 and converted for minesweeping trials, and the ROSE followed in 1910. When war broke out in 1914 these ships were sent to the various Port Divisions to act as Training ships for the Fishery Reserve - men called up to man the requisitioned trawlers. ROSE was at Devonport, SEAMEW and SEAFLOWER went to Chatham/Sheerness, whilst SPARROW and SPIDER were based at Portsmouth.

At the same time, the Admiralty designated a number of smaller warships to join in this newly developing discipline. These ships, Torpedo Boat Destroyers, all built in the 1880/90s and weighing in at 700/800 ton displacement, were now obsolete and a number of them had already made their weary way to the breakers yards. Those remaining were granted a new, if short, lease of life, and joined the purchased trawlers at Portland to carry out trials and experiments with minesweeping equipment.

These were the vessels which developed the method of minesweeping which was to be employed at the outbreak of the Great War. This very basic method employed two vessels steaming side by side, a short distance apart, and dragging between them a length of cable to which was fitted a steel cutter. The principle was that when the cable snagged a mine's mooring wire it would be dragged along the cable into the jaws of the cutter. Once the wire was severed the mine would float free to the surface where it would be destroyed by rifle fire. Basic, but for the times, reasonably efficient. There was, however, no lack of danger involved in this operation as this method was good only for mines which fell into the area between the two ships. It took no account of those which could be in the direct path of the vessels. A little later the addition of kites and otters (methods used in the fishing industry for keeping open the mouths of trawl nets) were incorporated and this eased the danger to the sweepers, but not entirely.

The Requisitioning system

At the Admiralty, more serious thought was being put into the question of minesweeping and trawlers. It was obvious that, after the initial snags and teething troubles had been ironed out, these ships were very well suited to the task, so negotiations were opened between the Admiralty and the trawler owners. Plans were formulated for the creation of a facility for requisitioning vessels from the fishing fleets in the event of war. Originally arrangements were made for the chartering of 80 vessels but before long this number was increased to 150.

The Trawler Section, RNR

Equally important would be the "calling-up" of the men to man such ships and so, in 1910, a special division of the Royal Naval Reserve was created known as the "Trawler Section" to cope with this requirement. Open to sufficiently experienced fishermen it required, for officers, trawlermen in possession of a Board of Trade certificate of competency who had held a command for 2 years or more. These officers were given the rank of Skipper, RNR, which was equivalent to the regular RN rank of Commissioned Warrant Officer. The requirement for ratings was to be filled by trawlermen who had attained the qualifications of Second Hand, Engineman, Deckhand or Trimmer and their equivalents in the regular service were Seaman Petty Officer, Stoker Petty Officer, Able Seaman and Stoker. To recruit trawlermen to the cause was one of the jobs of the little fleet of minesweeping trawlers, which paid courtesy visits to the major fishing ports to "show off" their expertise and interest and encourage trawlermen to enlist in the RNR.

Conditions of employment for the volunteers were established. The age limits imposed for crews were between 25 and 45 years and they were required to engage for terms of 5 years at a time up to a maximum of 20 years for officers and 25 years for ratings. They were paid an annual retainer and were required to spend at least 2 weeks each year training in the minesweeper fleet for which they received the pay equal to their regular service equivalents. These incentives were enough and from the major fishing ports the fishermen joined up to become minesweeper crews.

THE FIRST WORLD WAR

The Call-up commences

The system was hardly in place before it was required to perform in earnest. The First World War was rapidly approaching.

When Europe erupted in 1914 in what was to be hopefully termed "the war to end all wars" the carefully arranged plans of the Admiralty were put into action. From the fishing ports of the UK the well-weathered trawlers made their way to the designated ports and dockyards for conversion to warships. In accordance with the previous negotiations between the Admiralty and owners, 150 vessels were requisitioned and converted and to man them a total of 1200 specialist Reservists were called up.

The system worked well. Vessels were taken in hand, and refitted to suit their new role. Guns sprouted from their fore-ends and, as they became available, other armaments were added. Fish holds were converted into messdecks, a space was created for a magazine and, of course, the sweeping gear was installed. Fortunately extra room could be found by taking over some of the bunker space. Designed originally to spend long periods away from home, usually in the inhospitable northern lattitudes where bunkering facilities were unavailable, their bunkers were really quite generous, but in their new role they were unlikely to be very far from bunkering facilities as they would be operating, in the main, off the coasts of the UK, so some of that space could be utilised for other stores.

Armament - WW1

Generally the larger trawlers of WW1 mounted a 12-pdr gun on the forecastle and this was the 12 cwt Mk.1 mounting. Aft there would be a 6 or 3-pdr. The smaller vessels mounted only 6 and 3-pdrs. At the outbreak of war there were insufficient of these weapons to cover the requirements but, as and when, further weapons became available they were mounted as the vessels were refitted. All the guns were Quick Firing (QF) and later there was an increasing availability of Dual Purpose (DP) models capable of firing at both high and low angles. (HA/LA) The high angle capability enabled them to fire at aircraft and these were fitted primarily to vessels operating in the Channel and North Sea where they frequently came into contact with Zeppelins and other enemy aircraft. There was not, however, the scramble for AA weapons which was to be a feature of the Second World War as there was not the preponderance of aircraft that was to be encountered in all theatres of that war. To prosecute the fight against submarines a number of trawlers were fitted with 7.5-inch or 3.5-inch bomb throwers. These, together with the "Listening Hydrophones" which were also fitted to a large number of trawlers, were the rudimentary forerunners of the A/S weapons which were to be developed in the Second World War.

The minewarfare strategy

This was to be the first war in history in which the mine was to play such an important part. As has already been mentioned mines of one sort or another had been around for a very long time, but it was not until the "Great War" that the proliferation of minewarfare came into its own and the reason for this was simple. The High Command in Germany was not slow to appreciate that Britain was an island and relied for her very existence on trade, and that trade came via the sea from all over the world. Almost everything that Britain required to sustain her war effort had to come from overseas or, in the case of carrying the war to the enemy, had to be sent overseas. Even the short distance from England to France involved crossing the Channel. Whatever Britain did it had to be done by sea. The answer to Britain's downfall was therefore quite simple. Deny them the use of the sea. Accomplish that and in a matter of weeks the nation would, for one thing, be on the brink of starvation. The prosecution of the war would be of very low priority if the government was faced with a starving population.

To help them solve the problem of closing the seas to the British the Germans needed only to look at the British themselves and the tactics they employed in the last conflict of sizeable proportions. In the Napoleonic wars which had ravaged Europe only a century before, the Royal Navy had employed a tactic which had, for the most part, denied Napoleon the freedom of the seas and had certainly counteracted any ideas he had nourished of invading Britain. That tactic had been the blockade. At the approach of every major French harbour the British stationed a blockading squadron which sat off shore patiently awaiting any move by the ships in those harbours to leave or any ships on the outside to enter. The tactic was highly successful as witnessed by Napoleon's often uncomplimentary remarks directed at the stretch of water which separated him from "perfidious Albion". It also had another important effect. It caused the Emperor to lose confidence in his navy and it was not long before he diverted funds, supplies and men from the French navy to his armies, where, as far as he was concerned, they were of infinitely more use.

All this would be the fate of the Royal Navy in the present conflict if the Germans could but find a way of blockading Britain's harbours. Technology in the form of modern ships, weaponry and warfare had moved on a great deal in the intervening one hundred years since the Napoleonic wars, and despatching squadrons to sit outside British harbours was no longer an option, but those harbours needed to be closed. The answer, of course, was the mine. Sow the harbour entrances with these cheap to produce, silent, deadly and most importantly invisible weapons and effectively the harbours are closed! Any vessel, large or small, attempting to enter or leave a harbour so treated would be in deadly peril. Britain's lifeline to the Empire - and to the rest of the world - would be cut and the Islands would grind to a halt in a matter of weeks.

The minesweeping trawlers

This was the situation which faced the trawlers when they entered the War. From the outset the task allotted to trawlers was that of minesweeping. They were embraced under the category "minor war vessels" though the task of keeping the nation's harbours open could hardly have deserved the epithet "minor". Quickly, efficiently and effectively they were organised into Command areas, then into Groups within those Commands and allotted areas of responsibility, - harbours and coastal shipping lanes. Usually a Group comprised four vessels under the direction of a Senior Officer and they went about their dangerous work as a team, laboriously sweeping a stretch of water and marking it clear of mines and therefore safe for shipping to pass over. Unfortunately the enemy were in the habit of laying mines overnight so that the area swept on the previous day and declared safe had to be swept again next morning. And so the minesweeping trawlers settled into the soul-destroying but deadly routine of their part of the war at sea.

The very first shots of the naval war were fired on the 5th August, 1914, just one day after war had been declared, when the destroyers LANDRAIL and LANCE encountered the German KONIGIN LUISE just 30 miles off Aldeburgh Napes on the East Coast. The ship was a minelayer! The destroyers sank her, the first warship to be sunk in WWI, but she had already laid her deadly cargo in nearby waters. The following day, 6 August, the 3,440 ton Scout Cruiser AMPHION, Senior Officer of the 3rd Destroyer Flotilla of the Grand Fleet, entered the freshly laid minefield 35 miles east of Aldeburgh and struck one of the mines. When she sank 148 of her 325 ship's company were lost.

In almost no time at all vulnerable places like the entrance to the Moray Firth, the gateway to Invergordon (which at that time was the main anchorage of the Grand Fleet) were peppered with mines.

One enemy armed raider, the WOLF, in a daring sortie sailed as far as the Pacific and back, scattering a total of 450 mines in the focal shipping areas of the South Atlantic, Indian Ocean, N. and S. Australia, around New Zealand and as far as Fiji. Thus minesweeping capabilities were soon needed on a global scale. In the Dardenelles, the scene of major operations in 1915, the Turks employed the mine to devastating affect. On just one day, 18 March, the Royal Navy lost two battleships, the 15,000 ton IRRESISTABLE and the 12,950 ton OCEAN while the 17,250 ton Battlecruiser INFLEXIBLE was badly damaged, all three having run foul of Turkish mines. Trawler minesweepers were rapidly despatched to the Mediterranean for operations in the Dardenelles.

Before the 1914-18 conflict was more than a few weeks old, it became painfully obvious that the minesweeper force was completely inadequate, numerically. Minewarfare had arrived in a big way and the Admiralty had the foresight to realise that it was here to stay. They were also quick to realise that they desperately needed an enormous increase in their tiny little minesweeper fleet. So the orders were quickly put into operation for the requisitioning of more, and yet more, trawlers. From the four corners of the Islands they came together with a number from the continent which had escaped the advancing German hordes, and a number of prizes captured from the enemy too.

There was, however, a limit to the number of trawlers which could be taken up from trade. One of the trickiest tasks facing the Admiralty was striking a happy medium between the number of vessels taken up and the number left on the fishing grounds to carry on the equally vital work of helping to feed the nation. Even with the requisitioning of other types of vessels to swell the numbers, - tugs, barges, paddle steamers and motor launches - the insatiable thirst for more and yet more 'sweepers was not slaked.

Miscellaneous Trawlers

Unfortunately not all the trawlers which went to war were up to the task of minesweeping. Quite often when a "called-up" vessel reached the dockyards for conversion it was found that she was not up to the task with which the Navy wanted to burden her. The creaky, the leaky, the cranky and the just plain worn out were usually returned to the fishing fleet, but some were employed as ferries, stores carriers, and on the thousand and one jobs a navy generates for small vessels in keeping a fleet at sea. The less weary were given a gun and a crew, turned into Auxiliary Patrol Vessels and given the job of patrolling the coasts and also protecting the fishing fleets. These vessels went to sea with the fishing fleets into the North Sea and frequently further afield to protect them as they went about lawful their business.

Minelayers

Fourteen requisitioned trawlers became Minelayers. ERNA, HERO, KATE LEWIS, KING EMPEROR, OSTA, OSTRICH II, PITFOUR, RUSSELL II, ST. MAURICE, SCOTT, SHACKLETON, STRATHCOE, THE NORMAN and WELBECK were converted to each carry 24 mines. All bar one, SCOTT, survived the war and 2 of them, KATE LEWIS and STRATHCOE were subsequently puchased and attached to the Mine School at Portsmouth. Two of their number, ST. MAURICE and SHACKLETON started out as minesweepers and then crossed over to the other side of minewarfare when they were converted into minelayers, whilst several others became poachers turned gamekeepers when in the later stages of the war they too were converted to minesweepers. A number were requisitioned again in WWII and were all converted to minesweepers.

The Admiralty-Built Trawlers

Eventually, by the end of 1916, the Admiralty realised that they were facing a famine of trawlers and were obliged to do the only thing left open to them. They went into the building business. They had already dabbled in this area. At the outbreak of the war the builders Smith's Dock & Co.Ltd of Middlesbourough were in the process of building a number of vessels for the trade. The Admiralty bought ten of them whilst they were still on the stocks, had them completed to their own specifications and called them the Military class. Now they turned again to Smith's Dock together with three other main builders, Cook, Welton & Gemmel of Beverley, Cochrane of Selby, both in Yorkshire, and Hall Russell of Aberdeen, and asked them to forward to the Admiralty the plans of the vessels for which they had become justifiably famous. With a few adjustments to the plans the Admiralty placed orders with those yards and others for large numbers of trawlers to be designated as the "Strath", "Mersey" and "Castle" classes. The yards worked furiously turning out these vessels laying down keels and seemingly in very little time sliding the finished hulls down the slipways and towing them off to the fitting out basins. At the same time the Admiralty purchased most of the vessels of comparable size being built in the yards for the fishing trade and designated them as "Non-Standard" versions of the class they resembled closest. However, by the time the Armistice was signed in 1918 and the requirement had ceased, a large number of them were cancelled before they had been laid down. Those which were in the process of building were completed as fishing vessels and sold off by the Admiralty whilst others were handed over to the builders who also completed them as fishing vessels and sold them.

By the time the Armstice was signed, the RNR Trawler Section, originally a little force of 1200 men and 150 vessels for sweeping UK waters, had expanded to a massive 39,000 men, manning more than 700 vessels at home and abroad. The bulk of these ships were deep-sea trawlers, and their crews were representative of every fishing port in the UK, from Newlyn to the Shetlands. More than 200 of these ships were sunk during the war by mine explosion, surface attack or heavy weather, the greater proportion from being mined. Minesweeping was not a fine art and tragically the hunter was often bitten, fatally, by the quarry. Nearly half of these sinkings took place in East Coast waters and casualties among crews were high.

The minesweeper men, free and easy sailors who did not take kindly to naval discipline, did a splendid job of work in their own element. Tough, hardy, used to the bitter conditions and wild seas of the far northern latitudes where, in minutes, a chilly breeze can become a howling Force 10. They went out daily in all kinds of weather to sweep the war channels clear of the mines scatterd so assiduously by the enemy. During the four years of war the Germans laid a total of 43,636 mines - most of which were sown in Britain's Coastal waters. Every harbour of consequence, every fairway, channel and anchorage was laced with them - again and again. Throughout the year 1917, for example, more than 70 mines a month were laid in the Dover area alone, and up to a score a day in the approaches to Harwich. In 6 months one flotilla of minesweepers pounding up and down their allotted area swept a distance equivalent to steaming 3 times around the world.

The Fishery Reserve

As has been mentioned, one of the things the Admiralty had to keep in mind when they were gobbling up vessels from the fishing fleet was that of striking a balance between the trawlers "called-up" into naval service and those left behind for fishing. Early in 1917 they were acquainted with the fact that they had failed dismally. At the outbreak of WWI there had been some 1900 vessels in the fishing fleet but by 1917 no less than 1400 of them, nearly three quarters, had been requisitioned! Those that were left to pursue their trade had been decimated by "the dangers of the sea and the violence of the enemy".

If the Admiralty had wanted confirmation of this parlous state the British housewife could have easily and succinctly obliged them. As the flow of fish available for the table diminished owing to the shortage of trawlers, the price of a visit to the fishmonger spiralled. This was evidenced by the fact that pre-war a trawler could look forward to turning a profit of between £5,000 and £7,000 in a year. By late 1916 that had risen astronomically to the region of £30,000 to £40,000 p.a. Understandably, the government was not too happy with this situation any more than the housewife, and looked to the Admiralty to do something about it. Their Lordships were also faced with the fact that unless they did something fairly quickly about the rate of war losses sustained by those still fishing, they would soon cease to exist. Unarmed and unescorted, fishing vessels at sea paid a heavy price, particularly at the hands of U-Boats.

In May 1917 a War Order requisitioned all remaining trawl fishing vessels with immediate effect. There were, at that time, a number of foreign trawlers - mainly Belgian - fishing out of British ports which had escaped the Continent for the safer harbours of the UK. These were exempted from the Order unless their owners specifically agreed and it can be seen from the lists that not a few of them readily gave their permission.

Unlike other requisitioned trawlers, the vessels in the Fishery Reserve were not issued with Admiralty Numbers but a number of them were armed. To operate these new additions the RNR Trawler Section set up a sub-section known as the Fishery Reserve. Each vessel was commisioned and wore the White Ensign and a number of them, about a quarter, were armed with whatever was available. With the passage of time it is difficult, not to say impossible, to identify exactly which of them were armed except for those few which had been previously requisitioned and armed for other duties. It is safe to assume that these trawlers retained their armament when they were reduced to the Fishery Reserve. It is another safe assumption that these latest additions to the Navy were as far down the priority list as it was possible to get, therefore those which did mount an armament were obliged to make do with whatever was at hand and could be spared. As the Minesweepers and APVs were rearmed with any 12-pdrs becoming available, their smaller guns were passed down to the fishing trawlers - usually a 3 or 6-pdr. The operational plan decreed that they would fish in groups of approximately 20 vessels and, of these, five or so would be armed to protect the others.

Rates of pay were worked out with the owners and men. The owners received the hire rate of 1 shilling per month per vessel and another shilling for each man. This may seem somewhat parsimonious at first sight, but the vessels were to carry on fishing under the control of their owners just as they had before. Running costs, victualling, bunkering, repairs etc. were still the responsibility of the owners, but the men were paid the same as those in the rest of the RNR Trawler Section, a considerable come-down from the sums they had been receiving before, so to ease the burden they were also paid a 5% bonus from their fishing profits.

With the cessation of hostilities the Fishery Reserve were amongst the first ships and men to be demobilised. They returned to their original fishing routines although, even during the period of their requisition, they had none-the-less enjoyed unrestricted fishing rights.

The End of the Great War

With the cessation of hostilities the victorious allies turned homewards to a well-earned peace. The soldiers and sailors who had fought and suffered in France and Mesopotamia, the Mediterranean and Africa, the Atlantic and the wild wastes from the Arctic to the Antarctic came home and were demobbed in vast numbers. But the task of the trawler minesweepers had not come to an end with the Armistice of 11 November

1918. The thousands upon thousands of mines sown by all protagonists during the conflict were still there lying in wait. Of these, nearly 17,000 British and American mines had been sown in a vast belt stretching for 230 miles between the Orkneys and the Norwegian coast. Known as the "Northern Barrage", the object of this lethal underwater fence was to deter U-Boats and surface raiders from breaking out into the Atlantic by the northern route. The English Channel, the gateway for a large amount of the country's - and Europe's - commercial shipping was peppered with mines, both enemy and "friendly". These floating packages of death and destruction recognised no Armstice, appreciated no peacetime, and had no cognizance whatsoever of "friend or foe". There was only one answer to them. They had to go. So for another weary 12 months the little ships went out with their sweeps to clear not only the enemy-laid minefields but those of the Allies as well.

There was, however, not such great urgency in the business. When an area had been swept it remained swept. There was no longer an enemy to creep in under cover of darkness to sow replacement mines and so undo all the previous day's hard work. The sweeping of the sea-lanes went on quietly, safely and efficiently all through 1919. There were no losses to the minesweeping trawlers in that year and by early 1920, when the purpose built minesweepers of the Royal Navy were able to finish the clearing-up operations, the requisitioned trawlers had all finally returned to occupying their proper business in great waters, the business for which they had been designed - on the fishing grounds.

Slowly the great fishing ports of the UK began to fill up with the returning ships and men. Grimsby, Hull, Fleetwood, Aberdeen, Milford Haven, Harwich and in a host of other ports, owners, friends and families went to the quaysides over the weeks and months of 1919/20 to welcome back the battle-scarred veterans, both ships and men, and to mourn for those which would never return - the empty berths and the empty chairs at the fireside.

Nevertheless, life went on and gradually everything returned to normal with the trawlers sailing and returning with their catches but all the while the fishermen continued to enlist and train in that special section of the Royal Naval Reserve set aside for the training of fishermen in the art of minesweeping. Although they had just fought and won the "war to end all wars" who could tell what the future held?

Between the Wars

By the end of 1919 or early 1920 the last of the requisitioned trawlers had been returned to their owners and their crews resumed their normal business of wresting a living from the sea under peaceful conditions. The War had been a very testing time for the Trawler Reserve and it had risen to that test by proving beyond all doubt that they had the ideal vessels and men for the jobs they had been called upon to do. This applied not only to minesweeping. During the conflict trawlers had been called upon to perform a number of other jobs. As Auxiliary Patrol vessels they had been very successful in patrolling the coasts and in escorting coastal convoys. A number, too, had been employed on harbour service running as ferries, liberty-boats and shunting stores from shore to ship. Others again had been employed on harbour defence duties acting as boom gate vessels. There were the Barrage Balloon Vessels and several of the APVs had even been fitted to carry aircraft. These were seaplanes, which took off from the water when hoisted outboard by derrick. On return they taxied alongside and were hoisted back inboard. They were employed in the North Sea on Anti-Zeppelin patrols. Everything they had been asked to do they had done and, what is more, they had done it in an exemplary manner.

So many undertakings had been prescribed for the trawlers that when the dust settled and the Reserves organisation at the Admiralty were able to take stock of just what had been achieved by these diminutive ships, it became apparent that further re-organisation was going to be necessary. Along with the other naval reserves, the RNR Trawler Section was reconstituted. It was renamed the RN Patrol Service, and to serve it a keen eye was kept on the trawler fleet for the vessels which could be requisitioned at short notice. Bearing in mind the rapidity with which the first requisitioned vessels had been allocated at the outbreak of the previous conflict the allocation of 150 vessels was increased to 300. It was not too long however, before the Director of Torpedoes and Mines at HMS VERNON, Portsmouth, with whom the responsibility lay, was pushing the Admiralty to increase this allotment to 400. Unfortunately he was unsuccessful and the outbreak of WWII found the RNPS just as short of vessels as the Trawler Section had been in 1914.

Nevertheless, 300 vessels were earmarked and arrangements for their manning were put in place. The call continued to go out to the fishermen to join the Reserves and they continued to answer the call, undertaking the two-week training period each year. In the regular Navy personnel dwindled throughout with the coming of peace and a mere handful of trawlers were retained to continue to wear the White Ensign and glisten with naval grey paint. These were eventually formed into a tiny flotilla and based on the shore establishment, HMS BOSCOWAN at Portland, and to them the RNR Patrol Service volunteers went each year to earn their retainer and keep up with the advances in minesweeping technology.

Also situated at Portland and a close neighbour of HMS BOSCAWEN was HMS OSPREY, a training establishment of special importance. Part of its work was concerned with a new and potent device which had been added to the Navy's anti-submarine armoury, the Asdic. Since trawlers both could be, and had been, used as convoy escorts, an essential part of whose task was the hunting and destruction of U-Boats, it was eventually decided to allocate some of the vessels due to be taken up from the fishing industry in any future emergency as anti-submarine craft. A number of Patrol Service ratings were selected to begin training as Submarine Detector Operators.

The strength of the permanent RN Patrol Service at the time when the Director of Torpedoes and Mining was endeavouring to obtain approval for the increase in the number of trawlers to 400, was 454 Skippers and 3,733 ratings. The overall size of the RNPS was based on a minimum complement of officers and ratings required to man each individual vessel in wartime, this figure then being multipled by the number of ships the Service was allocated. To the total thus calculated, a further percentage of the whole was added to allow for wastage due to sickness and other causes. Needless to say, at the outset of WWII the RNPS, even though still based on the original approved figure of 300 ships, was considerably under strength for both officers and men. When was it ever different?

Development of the Sea-Mine

Throughout the period from 1918 to 1939 there was slow but steady development of mines for use at sea, but it is very difficult to obtain information on this subject. As Maurice Cocker says in his admirable book Mine Warfare Vessels of the Royal Navy - 1908 - to Date, ".....although the facts and figures of fission weapons and missiles are surprisingly easily available to the layman - even up to the latest devised items of devastation - particulars of the sea mine are harder to acquire, for reasons best known to the powers that be".

Certainly, at the beginning of WW2 there was still the familiar contact mine only somewhat updated from WW1. These mines were profusely laid in coastal waters around the UK by both sides from 1939, by the Germans in harbour mouths and estuaries, and by the British, defensively, in the Channel to hinder the progress of enemy warships. (There can't be many people who have not seen one of these mines. After the war large numbers of redundant casings were bought up by a well-known charity and placed as collecting boxes on piers and esplanades around the British Isles). The war was well under way before more sophisticated mines began to appear on the scene.

THE SECOND WORLD WAR

The conflict of 1914-18 had ended with the sea-mine being almost identical to the one that had been used at the beginning. The technology employed had progressed but little and the "horned" contact mine was still the only type used.

The next global conflict was to see a massive change in this state of affairs with sea-mines being honed to refinements inconceivable in the Great War. The contact mine was still employed, but joining it came new and ingenious proliferations. Mysteriously technical words began to be bandied about the minesweeping world, words like "magnetic" and the even more mysterious and frightening, "acoustic".

Several years prior to the outbreak of the Second World War the Admiralty had already been taking up trawlers from trade and converting them into men o' war. The Abyssian crisis in 1935 had spurred the Admiralty into action and in that year they purchased 20 modern trawlers. These were split evenly into two Groups. One, named after Gems, was converted for Anti-Submarine duties and the other, named after Trees, was converted for Minesweeping. Also purchased in 1935 was MASCOT which, renamed VULCAN, was converted to a Depot Ship for Coastal Forces.

Early in 1939 a further 20 trawlers were purchased. This time they were divided into 3 Groups. Ten were converted to A/S vessels and added to the Gem Group, 6 to M/Ss and added to the Tree Group whilst the remaining 4 were converted to Boom Defence Vessels and renamed JENNET, PUNNET, QUANNET and RENNET.

The experience gained from these conversions was to stand the Admiralty in good stead within a very short time.

In pre-war days British fishing trawlers were built for the primary purpose of catching fish and returning with it as soon as possible since they were not then equipped with refrigeration plants. Little space was squandered on the provision of crew amenities in the shape of spacious cabins and luxurious messdecks, although these were comfortable enough. Periodically throughout the season the vessels sailed for the fishing grounds which might be anywhere from Iceland to the White Sea, trawled until their holds were full, and then hastened back with their cargoes, spurred on by the knowledge that the catch from the first ship home would fetch the highest price. Back in port and the fish disposed of, Skipper and crew packed their gear and went to their homes until they should be required again.

In 1939, as in 1914, the Admiralty put into operation the plans that had been laid for requisitioning, hiring and purchasing trawlers. They cast their net not only over the fishing fleets of the UK but as far afield as the USA in order to bring up to strength the requirement for small vessls. Large numbers were taken up - especially when war was finally declared and the demand increased dramatically.

The organisation required to "call-up" and then convert, man, and allocate so many vessels was enormous. The conversion work alone was a mammoth task. Taking a trawler fresh from the fishing fleet and turning it into an armed man o' war was a task not to be undertaken lightly, but in the the first two years of both wars this operation was carried out, perhaps not completely smoothly, but sufficiently well to provide the help so desperately needed by the beleaguered RN.

The fitting-out yards swung into a smooth routine to transform the fishing vessels into men o' war. Stores and materials piled high on jetties as trawlers came alongside for the "treatment". Strengthening was added to the hull, deckheads, and frames to enable them to bear the weight of the guns and sweeping gear. The fishhold was scrubbed clean in an attempt to get rid of the smell of fish - it was never wholly successful - and then fitted out as the ship's company messdeck with hammock hooks, mess tables and benches. Usually the fishing gear had been landed in the home port before despatch for fitting out, but any gear that had not been landed, together with the winches, were unshipped and landed on the jetty. In the after part of the superstructure was the galley with its provision store of almost entirely tinned and dried foods. Of fresh foods there was precious little as rare indeed were those vessels which could boast possession of a refrigerator. A miniature wardroom for the two or three officers was constructed underneath the wheelhouse complete with bunks and a table and chairs. Stores were fitted in wherever space could be found. The ship's safe containing any moneys, documents and Confidential Books was housed in the Wardroom whilst the ammunition was stowed in a specially constructed magazine underneath the messdeck.

One ingredient in the transformation scheme which was never considered or included in the equipment piled high on the jetty waiting to be taken into the ship, was comfort. There was no bathroom or shower and "dhobeying" of body and clothes was via a bucket with limited hot water by courtesy of the coal-burning galley range when it was alight. Home comforts were very few and far between. All in all, life on board was cramped and anything but luxurious. Due to the peculiar motion of a trawler in a seaway, since she rides the waves instead of punching through them like a heavier vessel, the normal functions of daily existence were often apt to be severely curtailed in even moderately poor weather. On those occasions when cooking could be carried on, eating the meal was no easy feat. Washing was difficult, shaving impossibly dangerous and bathing, even out of a bucket, was out of the question. There was no recreation space as such - a mere few feet of upper deck upon which to stretch the legs, no canteen, and not even the modest domestic comforts of a corvette or a destroyer.

As each Trawler was completed in its new garb of war, the men flocked down to the yards to man them. The organization required to feed the demands for man-power was immense, but the plans laid down during the twenty years of peace between the wars flowered into practicality. The Headquarters of the Royal Naval Patrol Service was set up on the east coast at Lowestoft. For some time the Admiralty had had their eye on the town's theatre known as the "Sparrow's Nest" and which stood proudly in the Corporation's Pleasure Gardens. It was here, in this building, and surrounding hastily set up temporary buildings, that the brain of the RNPS took shape. The theatre was commandeered whilst it was still in full swing. Among the artistes appearing there at the time was a famous ladies duo known as "Gert & Daisy". Imagine their suprise when the lorries rolled into the Gardens containing the men and all the paraphenalia for setting up a Naval Establishment!

Quickly and efficiently the routine of the Establishment began to take shape. In the early stages there was choice in the matter of forming ship's companies. It was possible to take a few seasoned trawler men, some of whom had minesweeping or ASDIC knowledge, add a scattering of unseasoned, untried and hastily trained volunteers who had been "called up", and there you had a fighting Trawler's crew. This ideal situation was, however, not to last long. As the demand increased and Trawlers and their crews were lost, the percentage of the of the untrained and untried increased. Even the volunteer quota quickly ran out and men were channeled into the RNPS direct from the General Service Training Establishments.

Armament - WWII.

In WWII the arming of Trawlers followed much the same pattern as at the outset of the First World War but in a short time there was a general melee involving individual trawlers in an effort to obtain extra armament. As a result rarely were any two trawlers alike in armament as a hotchpotch of weapons were "won" by an ever-eager ship's company to add to their firepower, particularly in respect af AA weapons. A typical example of this was HMT ALEXANDER HILLS which mounted an Italian Breda gun. This weapon was "won" by the scavenging sailors who found it in an abandoned Italian gun emplacement in the desert behind Tobruk in 1941, and somehow it "found" its way back to the trawler. Similar to the Oerlikon in general service with the RN, it is probable that standard Oerlikon ammunition fitted the Breda.

The largest weapon, usually a 12-pdr, or a 4-inch if one was available, was mounted on the forecastle, and an Oerlikon, Bofor, or a pair of 0.5-inch machine guns on a special mounting aft of the funnel. Lewis or Hothchkiss guns were also mounted in the bridge wings for defence against air attack. In ships destined for anti-submarine duties, Asdic gear was installed and depthcharge throwers and rails were fitted aft.

In some ships there was a Holman Projector. This rather bizarre weapon - a sort of steam-powered mortar - was the brainchild of Mr Treve Holman of the Camborne firm of Holman Bros. In 1939 he came up with the original idea of using compressed air to launch Mills Bombs (handgrenades) through a metal tube. A prototype used in trials achieved the remarkable feat of sending a grenade to a height of 650 ft. By 1940, under the auspicies of the Department of Miscellaneous Weapons Developement, the weapon was in the fleet, mounted in vessels as diverse as submarines and merchantmen. Numerous claims were made as to its success, one of which came from a trawler which claimed to have damaged a low-level attacking Heinkel bomber!

Certainly there must have been some success as very soon the Department came back to Holman with the request that he develop the weapon to operate using steam-power. This led to a Cornwall County Council steamroller being trundled onto the moors near Porthtowan to provide the power source for trials.

Before long the steam-powered version was up and running and installed in numerous vessels including trawlers. Within a year of service it was credited with having accounted for no less than a dozen or so enemy aircraft.

It quickly became highly popular with trawler crews when it was discovered that it was equally adept at firing potatoes and of considerable use in battles between friendly trawlers and so became known as "the potato gun". The weapon was not, however, very popular with the Chief Engineer particularly when he was not warned the weapon was being fired. The resultant sudden drop in steam pressure was an engineers nightmare.

Pennant Numbers

By the outbreak of the Second World War communications had progressed beyond all recognition from those in operation in the previous conflict. Radio was universal and so it was essential that individual ships possessed their own recognition signal. Trawlers were no exception and carried Pennant Numbers accordingly. As a general rule their Flag Superior, the letters or number at the beginning of the Pennant Number, indicated their employment, although this was not necessarily a hard and fast rule. With changes in their employment demanded by the urgent requirements of war there was often no time to observe the nicities of changing numbers so the old ones were retained in their new employment. This situation excepted, the Flags Superior for trawlers were as follows:

Flag   B   Air Sea Rescue vessels (ASR)

FY	The vast majority of M/Ss, A/S, D/Ls, De-Gausing (DGs), Mine Wiping (M/Ws), and Mine Recovery vessels (MRVs). This Flag was also worn by a small number of ASRs, APVs, BBVs, and ABVs.
J	Dan Layers of the RN and RAN, and M/Ss of the RCN
M	Controlled Mine Layers
T	Admiralty-built A/S and M/S trawlers and A/S and M/S trawlers of the SAN
U	A small number of A/S trawlers
Y	Supply vessels (Essos, Water Carriers, Store Carriers etc.)
Z	BDVs and BGVs. (These vessels wore Flags FY until 1940 when Flag Z was introduced)
4	APVs, BBVs, WDVs, WLVs, Examination Service, and a few M/Ss and A/S trawlers

US Navy's entry into WWII

In December 1941 the war escalated when Japan attacked the USA at Pearl Harbour and Japan's allies, Germany and Italy also took up arms against the Americans. The USN had been studying the A/S warfare operations of the RN long before they entered the war and they thought they had it fairly well taped. Unfortunately they were wrong. They had assumed that Anti-submarine warfare was purely one of technology and that all they had to do was to provide the vessels and equipment together with the men to operate them. They quickly came to appreciate, however, that what they lacked and without which it was impossible to operate, was the Royal Navy's enormous operational and organizational skills.

Early in 1942 the far-sighted German U-Boat chief, Admiral Donitz, had sent half a dozen of his submarines to operate in the USA's eastern coastal waters. They had a field day! The U-Boat Commanders found their new adversaries totally unprepared. Peering through their periscopes at the American shoreline, ablaze with normal peacetime lights, they must have pinched themselves to make sure they were not dreaming. Even the American navigation beacons were operating to give the Germans their bearings. If they surveyed the sky to judge the weather they needn't have bothered. All they had to do was to tune in to the local radio wavelength to get an up to date forecast provided with the compliments of the broadcasting networks. They really couldn't believe their luck. With virtual impunity the Germans sank scores of Allied merchant ships during January - March with barely a threat from the American anti-submarine operations.

It was obvious that this state of affairs could not be allowed to continue and the American President approached Prime Minister Churchill for assistance. The outcome was that the Royal Navy despatched a number of Trawlers, Corvettes and Whalers together with their crews, on loan to the USN to train their new allies in anti-submarine warfare. Twenty-four trawlers were sent for A/S and patrol operations off the American east coast. HMTs ARCTIC EXPLORER, BEDFORDSHIRE, CAPE WARWICK, COVENTRY CITY, HERTFORDSHIRE, KINGSTON CEYLONITE, LE TIGER, LADY

ELSA, LADY ROSEMARY, NORTHERN CHIEF, NORTHERN DAWN, NORTHERN DUKE, NORTHERN FOAM, NORTHERN ISLES, NORTHERN PRINCESS, NORTHERN REWARD, NORWICH CITY, PENTLAND FIRTH, ST. CATHAN, ST.LOMAN, ST.ZENO, SENATEUR DUHAMEL, STELLA POLARIS and WELLARD were accompanied by 10 Corvettes and 2 Whalers. Half a dozen of these trawlers were fated never to return to home waters again. NORTHERN PRINCESS didn't get as far as the USA having run foul of a U-Boat whilst on passage off the Grand Banks, and five others came to grief whilst on operations and their hulls lie beneath the sea off the American coast from New York to South Carolina.

WWII Admiralty Built Trawlers

As they had in 1916, the Admiralty turned to the major trawler-building yards, Cook, Welton & Gemmel, Cochrane, Smith's Dock, Hall Russell etc. These yards had put a great deal of work into their designs during the peacetime years with the result that the trawlers of the 1930's were much improved in both design and efficiency. Still coal-burning, they were capable of 10 - 12kts, had increased in size to between 115 - 170 ft in length with a beam of between 22 - 26 ft, and weighed in at between 275 and as much as 590 tons (gross). A single funnel abaft the bridge structure was universal and with the progress made in communications - radio was by now considered an essential piece of equipment - they often shipped two masts to carry the required aerials. The building companies were asked to forward their designs to Admiralty and after a few basic alterations to particularly suit their new role, orders were placed. However, this time the Admiralty had not left it until well into the conflict, as they had in the First World War, before they went into the building business.

In 1935 builders Henry Robb of Leith launched the first Admiralty prototype of the "Basset" Class. HMT BASSET was of 460 tons and capable of 12 kts. With her larger foc's'le and bridge moved amidships she was exactly what the Admiralty wanted. There was only one more addition to the class built in the UK, the MASTIFF also built by Robb and launched in 1938, but orders for a further 44 of the class were placed with Indian yards, 4 in Canada and 4 in Burma. Unfortunately only 21 of the Indian vessels were completed for reasons stated later and all 4 of the Burmese vessels were lost on the stocks when Burma was overrun by the Japanese in 1942. The Canadian trawlers were completed and served successfully, surviving to to sold off to the mercantile after the war. However, such was the success of the Basset design that all subsequent classes of trawlers were based on it with only small alterations to the original plans.

To compliment those vessels purchased for the RN in 1935 and again in 1939, the Tree Class had wet their keels by the end of 1939. The Dance Class started taking to the water in 1940 together with the Shakespearian Class and the first of the 145 vessels of the prolific Western Isles Class (later shortened to the Isles Class). By 1941 the Hills, Fish, Round Table, and Miliary Classes were rolling down the slipways. Abroad, in Portugal, the 12 Portsdown Class trawlers were launched. In India the Basset Class was being launched and in New Zealand they were building the Castle Class although these remained with the RNZN. In Brazil a class of 6 trawlers was being built for the RN but, in the event, these vessels were transferred to the Brazilian Navy for work off the East Coast of South America.

With one exception - the Portuguese built vessels - all Admiralty-built Trawlers of this period were coal burners. The reason for this was logistical. Although the vast majority of warships built during the Second World War were oil-fired, a much more efficient fuel than coal, the Admiralty had, nonetheless, to take account of the fact that all oil had to be brought into the country by tankers via the precious and costly convoy system. On the other hand, the coal mines of South Wales were producing what was, probably, the finest steaming coal in the world. At the same time there were a number of very able engine manufacturers in the country who had vast experience of producing engines for trawlers. These companies, C.D.Holmes, Amos & Smith, Plenty, Aithchison Blair, Whites etc. were more than able to rise to the task of producing the coal-burning engines required. The only difficulty to arise with this policy was the despatching of sufficient engines overseas to fit to those trawlers which were being built in foreign yards. The Portuguese trawlers were all fitted with single shaft deisel motors, but the Brazilian vessels all received their coal burning engines. India, on the other hand, was less lucky. It was considered just not sufficiently viable to ship out engines for the building Basset Class in the sub-continent and building was suspended for several years and cancelled altogether by 1945.

The war ground inexorably along taking its toll of both the ships and the men of the Patrol Service. The backbone of the Service, the requisitioned and purchased trawlers, paid a heavy price and by 1943 too many of them had been sunk. The gaps they left in the prosecution of the war were now filled by the specially designed Admiralty built trawlers which had been coming off the stocks in a steady stream. 1942 had seen the largest number of these new vessels entering service and eagerly entering the fray.

There were only a few minor differences between these classes. With displacements up to 650 tons and measuring 164ft x 27 ft x 12 ft 6 in they were coal-fired with a speed of 15 kts and a range of 3,000 miles. Fitted with radar and Asdic, with a complement of 33, they were armed with a 4-inch DP gun on the bow supplemented with 4 x 0.5-inch machine guns (2x2) and, as was the custom with trawlers, anything else that came to hand. With the exception of the few which were designated, at building, as Dan Layers, they were all classified as A/S - M/S being capable of employment in either role. The most prolific of the Classes was the Isles Class of which, including the 16 built in Canada, 145 came off the slipways.

The appearance of the magnetic mine early in the war caused a tremendous upheaval in minesweeping circles as it was quickly recognised that the sweepers were powerless against them. However, when one was recovered in the Thames estuary in November 1939 and surrendered its secrets to the gentle, if nervous, persuasions of the bomb and mine disposal boffins at HMS VERNON degaussing countermeasures were quickly put into operation, but not before a number of warships and merchantmen fell foul of their destructive powers. Degaussing was achieved by fitting a coil of wire lengthways around a ship's hull and passing a current through to demagnetise the it. Degaussing production however, could not hope to keep up with the prolific "seeding" of magnetic mines carried out around the UK coasts and at one stage it seemed that the Thames might have to be closed to shipping altogether.

VERNON came up with a make-shift idea to combat the immediate problem which comprised an iron bar towed over the stern of a wooden trawler. It was a very basic idea and such was the difficulty in trying to control the device it was quickly christened "The Bosun's Nightmare". To tow this Heath Robinson affair required the services of a vessel with a wooden hull. The metal hulled trawlers would defeat the object and set off a magnetic mine long before it could tow the bar over it. Unfortunately there were not too many wooden hulls in the navy and so an urgent appeal went out via the BBC for wooden-hulled trawlers together with the crews to man them. The response was immediate. Offices in some of the fishing ports were open all night and were packed out with volunteers.

Such was the urgency of the situation, that the volunteers had no opportunity of being properly inducted into the Navy. Most, if not all, would have been unacceptable in the normal course of events due to age, medical standards and various other reasons but these events were far from normal. Of uniforms, there were none. They went into their war wearing their own working-clothes with the addition of only an arm brassard. It is difficult at this distance in time to understand how they managed to identify between a deck-hand and a Skipper from more than a few feet away.

The Silver Badge

Interestingly, it was this emergency situation with its lack of uniform that was the initiator of the badge that came to denote the Patrol Service. The Powers-That-Be were not a little worried that in the unhappy event that any of these emergency "call-up" personnel were captured by the enemy, lack of uniform might bring their bona-fides into question and it was thought quite possible that it could result in them being executed as spies. The worry was sufficiently serious for it to be taken to the very top and it was The Prime Minister, Mr Churchill, who ordered the situation remedied. This resulted in the little silver badge which was eventually issued to all members of the Patrol Service after 6 months service at sea. However the war-time demands on all production lines meant that by the time the badge was ready for issue the problem of the non-uniformed volunteers had gone away. Never-the-less, the badge was set in place and was worn with distinction and pride by the men of the Patrol Service henceforth. This was a rare privilege which was not to be bestowed anywhere in the Service until, in the 1960's, the submarine Service was awarded the "dolphin" badge.

Refitting

The guidelines laid down in Admiralty Orders decreed that trawlers should be taken in hand for minor refitting, boiler cleaning and general maintenance when they had been steaming for one thousand hours, by which time they were in need of such attention.

However, precationary routines set out on paper at the outset rarely take into account the demands of the hurly-burly of war. In emergency conditions such nicities have to be abandoned and every ounce of work has to be induced from both men and machines. So it was with the trawlers. Refitting became a luxury which could be afforded only when there was no alternative. Often the little vessels were pushed over the edge of mechanical fatigue before they were reluctantly withdrawn from operations to limp with wheezing and complaining machinery into the dockyard for revival. There is a story told of the Isles Class trawler EDAY which had been driven relentlessly for over 10,000 miles before being released into dockyard hands. With her propellor worn down to the thinness of paper and trailing strange and exotic marine growths from every inch of her underwater hull she was a sight to behold. Frenzied activity on the part of the dockyard workers had her back at sea in almost no time at all. She was typical of this type of vessel. During her service she steamed over 70,000 miles engaging in operations in the Mediterranean as well as home waters undertaking minesweeping, A/S patrols, convoy escorts, rescue, and ferrying operations with stoicism.

As slowly, agonisingly, the tide of war began to change, the shipyards were able to turn out an increasing flow of precious warships and the hard-pressed trawlers found their burdens being eased by shiny new escort vessels and Minesweepers. But not entirely. Many trawlers continued to fight their way over the oceans to the bitter end of the war whilst others were withdrawn from one job to be reconverted for other tasks.

Dan Layers

With the advent of the long-awaited assault on Europe, which was to take shape in the June 1944 D-Day landings, there was an increasing need for D/Ls and so a number of the M/S trawlers were reconverted for this task and attached to the Minesweeping Flotillas which operated clearing pathways for the great armada to cross the Channel. Dan Layers operated with M/Ss, following in their wakes laying marker-buoys (dans) to indicate the swept channel to approaching vessels. Others were despatched to the Far East as D/Ls and joined the M/S Flotillas of the East Indies Fleet and the British Pacific Fleet.

Fuel Carriers

Also for the D-Day landings (Operation Neptune) there was a need for fuel carriers (Essos) to ferry the essential fuel to support the thousands of tanks, trucks etc. of the invasion force, so yet again numbers of trawlers turned their hand to a task far removed from their original concept. Placed in the hands of various yards they were converted to fuel carriers and ploughed to and from France with their precious cargoes. It appears from the records that this was usually the end of their fighting careers as when the Pipeline Under The Ocean (PLUTO) was established in November 1944, together with other more efficient sources of fuel supply, the trawlers which had been employed on this service were returned to their owners to resume their rightful and proper occupation of fishing.

Supply Vessels

A number of trawlers were converted to supply vessels. Their large and accommodating fish hold was particularly conducive to this task and when so employed they operated with a much reduced crew so that less room was required for accommodation. During 1943 there was a group of trawlers in the Mediterranean employed in running supplies to the various beach-heads in support of the invading forces. They became known colloquially as Walt Disney's Navy and comprised, amongst others, TRANSVAAL, LAPAGERIA and QUERCIA.

Wreck Dispersal

Such had been the havoc wreaked by the bitter conflict around the shores of the UK that the waters were littered with wrecks, a large number of which were hazardous to navigation. Accordingly, a number of the Admiralty built trawlers were converted to Wreck Location and Wreck Dispersal Vessels tasked with finding and clearing those wrecks. For this purpose the ships were stripped of their armament and specialist equipment was installed. Wreck Dispersal was a hazardous game, but then, the trawlers were no strangers to that sort of existence.

Buttoning and Unbuttoning

The convoy system was the country's lifeline and the shipyards had been turning out escort vessels, corvettes and frigates, as a matter of priority. As more and more of these purpose-built ships came into commission so the burden eased on the escort trawlers. Eventually there was a sufficiency of these ships for the Admiralty to decree that trawlers were no longer suitable for escorting ocean convoys and, in the main, they were withdrawn from the task. Instead they were employed on what was known as "buttoning and unbuttoning" whereby they met the ocean convoys when they reached their main destinations and took small groups of merchantmen from the main convoys to intermediate ports around the coasts for unloading. This was "unbuttoning". "Buttoning" was the reverse of this procedure. They would gather individual ships from smaller ports into groups and escort them to the rendezvous where an ocean convoy was being assembled. This work was no less demanding and dangerous and a number of trawlers were lost or damaged whilst carrying out this task.

Miscellaneous Vessels

Whilst the majority of requisitioned trawlers were converted to either A/S or M/Ss there was always the urgent need for vessels to fulfil the many tasks which were vital to support the fighting fleets. Some of those roles were as follows:

Armed Boarding Vessels

A small number of Trawlers were fitted out as Armed Boarding Vessels (ABVs). These vessels operated in coastal waters intercepting neutral and suspected enemy merchant vessels and examining their papers and cargoes. Referred to also as "Contraband Control" and "Examination Service" this was, not surprisingly, a very hazardous occupation. However, after the fall of Europe in 1940 the need for this duty dwindled to the extent that most vessels were re-employed on other duties.

Barrage Balloon Vessels

Some of the less seaworthy trawlers were converted to Barrage Balloon Vessels (BBVs). They were fitted with powerful wiches and barrage balloons which which they flew when there was danger of air attack. They were based in harbours and seldom, if ever, went to sea in this role.

Boom Gate Vessels

Trawlers converted for employment as Boom Gate Vessels (BGVs) were also in the class of the less seaworthy. Their duties comprised being attached to an anti-submarine net at the entrance to a harbour where the only excitement in the normal day's work was to tow the gate portion of the net open to permit the entry or exit of a ship. This was probably one of the most soul-destroying jobs in the Patrol Service.

Controlled Minelayers

Eleven trawlers, 4 Isles Class, 2 Fish Class and 5 requisitioned vessels were converted to Controlled Minelayers (CMs). Their role was the operation of small minefields laid at harbour entrances which could be activated or made safe from the CM.

Harbour Service

Even those vessels certified unseaworthy had their uses to help satisfy the voracious appetite of the fleet. In the confines of harbours they fulfilled a never-ending demand for their services. Ferrying passengers and libertymen to and from the ships moored at buoys or at anchor was a common task as was the carrying of mail, stores, fuel, and ammunition to them in the sheltered waters. They usually spent the whole of their war service in the same harbour. Others joined the band of hard-pressed degaussing vessels performing the essential task of checking and correcting the de-magnetising protection ships needed from the dreaded magnetic mine.

The end of WWII

The cessation of hostilities made life easier (but not much so) for the Minesweeping Flotillas both at home and abroad. As in 1918 the seas around the UK and in the other theatres of the sea war, teemed with unexploded mines of all descriptions, both "friendly" and "enemy". So the hazardous task of minesweeping continued, and still the mines exploded and lives and ships were lost. However, for the trawlers, relief came quite quickly. The production of purpose built minesweepers during hostilities meant that there were then a sufficient number of these vessels to take over from the requisitioned ships - so the trawlers were released back to their owners and the fishing grounds. Once again the fish quays around the British Isles witnessed the scenes of rejoicing and mourning that had been played out in the homecomings of 1919. It was thought then that they would never be repeated but, alas, the terrible events of 1939 changed that again and 1945/6 saw the repeat of the war-weary returning home and the empty chairs by the hearth.

Famous Personnel

A number of personnel serving in trawlers in WWII were to become famous post-war. It is doubtful if anyone aboard CAPE ARGONA relentlessly ploughing her way to and from Iceland on convoy duties could see in the young Ordinary Seaman Callaghan a future Prime Minister. Certainly they had some idea that he was destined for greater things when he left them to go to Portsmouth for Officer training, but surely not all the way to the House of Lords. Equally, did the ship's company have any idea of what was in store for the bespectacled and dapper Eric Barker who was to make his name in some of the truly classic comedy films to come out of the British film studios in the 1950s? Could there have been a more unlikely trawlerman? Was the football enthusiast Ordinary Seaman Fagin foreseen as a future manager of one of England's top football clubs (Liverpool) and did Robert Newton ever look out to the horizon from the foredeck of his trawler and imagine himself as Long John Silver in a ship of a very different type? These, and many others, survived the dreadful privations of sea warfare in trawlers to carve out a distinguished life in the subsequent peace.

The Future?

The 1970s saw the beginning of a huge downturn in the affairs of the British fishing industry. The mainstay of the business had been carried out in Icelandic waters but this came to an end when that country declared a 200 mile exclusion zone around their coast. There was some dissent by the British at the outset and the trawler men refused to acknowledge the zone which led to the "Cod Wars". This involved ships of the Royal Navy protecting trawlers engaged in those fishing grounds from interference by the Icelandic gunboats which were trying to enforce the restriction. However, before very long the Icelanders' declaration was upheld internationally and so fishing grounds that had been the hunting ground for British fishermen for centuries were denied to them.

These events dealt a bitter blow to the trawlers but they may well have survived reasonably by fishing the UK waters and the Atlantic, but worse was to follow. The introduction by the European Community of the "quota" system hammered the nails into the coffin of the industry with the result that the fishing fleet was soon decimated. A benevolent Government went so far as to offer cash incentives to fishermen to take their vessels out of fishing altogether. The numbers of large trawlers dwindled to a mere handful. Many were sold abroad whilst others made their way, prematurely, to the breakers yards. Those that are left struggle to make a go of the quota system. All that remains of this once thriving industry is barely noticable in the basins of the great fishing ports which once were crammed to capacity with trawlers. The glories, disasters and records of this once great occupation are now only seen as exhibits in the brilliant National Fishing Heritage Centre at Grimsby.

So where does this leave the Navy and the Nation? Entering the 21st Century the financial restrictions imposed by successive governments has ensured that the Royal Navy is perilously short of ships and manpower. What if there should come another 1914 or 1939? Of course, we know very well that that cannot possibly happen. Those very same successive governments ably backed up by all manner of knowledgeable pundits have told us so repeatedly. Except that they said that in 1918 and echoed it with excessive zeal right up until the latter part of the 1930s, which left us in a pretty sorry state by 1939. Thank God that in 1914 and 1939 the Navy had the trawlers to pull them back from the brink of a national disaster. But what of now or the future?

Supposing, just supposing, the whole tragic business started again. The Royal Navy has an extremely efficient Minewarfare Department - the modern name for minesweeping. It is reckoned to be one of, if not the, most efficient organisations in the world. However, although the number of operational minehunter/sweepers probably couldn't be counted on the fingers of two hands, the removal of shoes and socks may well find a couple of digits left over once they are counted up. In the event of a conflict of anything like sizable proportions, there will be literally hundreds and hundreds required, as indeed there were on the previous occasions. Even in the comparatively minor conflict of the Falklands in 1982, the Navy found it necessary to hire a number of trawlers to assist them. Next time, though, there will be no trawlers to call up, or at least only a handful, and certainly not enough to make even a small dent in the requirement for sweepers -

let alone any of the other tasks which a beleaguered navy will face. They may well have the technology, but as the Americans found in 1942, technology is not anywhere near enough. Equally, with the run-down in vessels came the loss of experienced men. They have left fishing in their droves and with them has gone all the expertise and experience which will be required and, just as serious, there are very few young people taking up where the old hands left off.

So from where will the minesweepers and their crews come? Let us all pray fervently that that question will never have to be faced for there appears to be no acceptable answer.

The Gem Group trawler RUBY. (Steve Bush Collection)

ARMENTIERS CLASS

In 1917, as part of its trawler building programme, the Admiralty placed orders with three Canadian yards for 12 trawlers to be known as the Armentiers Class. They were to be used for patrol work off the Atlantic seaboard. Six were built by the Polson Ironworks Company, five by Canadian Vickers and the odd one by Kingston SB of Ontario. The six vessels built by Polson were of iron and the manager of the Canadian Steamship Line under the general direction of the Navy Department, was responsible for supervising their building. The remainder were built of steel. By November 1917 they were all in service and remained with, and were manned by, the RCN. Post-war only four left the Service. These four, MESSINES, ST. ELOI, ST. JULIEN and VIMY, were transferred to the Canadian Department of Marine and Fisheries and converted to Lightships. One of them, ST. ELOI, was transferred back to the RCN in WWII and converted to a BGV. Two were lost. The first, THIEPVAL, was wrecked in 1930, and the other, YPRES, was lost in a collision with the battleship REVENGE at Halifax N.S. in 1940.

Displacement:	Iron Built: 440T 320TG
	Steel Built: 440T 357TG
Dimensions:	Iron Built: 135ft oa 130ft pp x 23ft 6in x 13ft 6in (Deep Hold)
	Steel Built: 135ft oa 130ft pp x 25ft x 13ft (Deep Hold)
Engines:	1-shaft reciprocating (VTE). 480 IHP = 10.5 kts
Armament:	Nominally 1 x 3-inch but vessels were armed individually usually with 1 x 12-pdr.
Complement:	18

Vessels in the Class:

ARLIEUX, ARMENTIERS, ARRAS, FESTUBERT, GIVENCHY, LOOS, MESSINES, ST. ELOI, ST. JULIEN, THIEPVAL, VIMY and YPRES

ARMENTIERS CLASS - NOTES

ARLIEUX   1918/46 RCN

1917: Ordered in January. 1918: L. Built at Montreal by Canadian Vickers. Commissioned on 5 June. 1941: Converted to a BGV. 1946: Sold to mercantile and retained the same name. 1949: Mercantile Loss. Sunk by internal explosion on 26 August.

ARMENTIERS   1918/47 RCN   Armament: 1 x 12-pdr
                                             P.No: WWII: J 29

1917: Ordered in January. 1918: L. Built at Montreal by Canadian Vickers.Commissioned on 17 June. 1946: Sold to Mercantile and renamed ARCTIC ROVER.

ARRAS   1918/57 RCN   Armament: 1 x 12-pdr

1917: Ordered in January. 1918: L. Built at Montreal by Canadian Vickers. 1957: Sold to BU.

GIVENCHY	1918/52	Armament:	1 x 12-pdr

1917: Ordered in January. 1918: L. Built in Canada by Canadian Vickers. Commissioned on 22 June. 1952: Sold on 22 November and BU in the USA.

LOOS	1918/20 1942/44	Armament:	1 x 12-pdr

1917: Ordered in January from Vickers, Canada and then transferred to Kingston SB of Ontario. 1918: L. Commissioned on 1 August. 1920: Transferred to the Canadian Government. 1941: Transferred to the RCN. 1942: Converted to a BGV. 1949: BU.

THIEPVAL	1918/30 RCN	Armament:	1 x 12-pdr

1917: Ordered in January. 1918: L. Built at Ontario, Canada by Kingston SB. Commissioned on 24 July. 1930: LOST. Wrecked in Barclay Sound, Vancouver, on 27 February.

FESTUBERT	1917/47 RCN	Armament: P.No:	1 x 12-pdr WWII: J 46

1917: Ordered in January. L. 2 August. Built in Canada by the Polson Iron Works. 1946: Sold to mercantile and renamed *Inverleigh*.

MESSINES	1917/20 RCN	Armament:	1 x 12-pdr

1917: Ordered in January. L. 6 June. Built in Canada by the Polson Iron Works. 1920: Transferred to the Canadian Dept of Marine and Fisheries and converted to a Lightship. Renamed Lightship No.3.

ST. ELOI	1917/20 1941/44	Armament:	1 x 12-pdr

1917: Ordered in January. L. 2 August. Built in Canada by Polson Ironworks. 1920: Transferred to the Canadian Dept.of Marine & Fisheries and converted to a Lightship. Renamed Lightship No.20. 1941: Transferred to the RCN and converted to a BGV. 1944: Returned to the Canadian Dept of Marine & Fisheries.

ST. JULIEN	1917/21 RCN	Armament:	1 x 12-pdr

1917: L. 16 June. Built in Canada by Polson Ironworks. 1920: Transferred to the Canadian Dept. of Marine & Fisheries, converted to a Lightship and renamed Lightship No. 22.

VIMY	1917/20 RCN	Armament:	1 x 12-pdr

1917: Ordered in January. 1918: L. 6 January. Built in Canada by the Polson Ironworks. 1920: Transferred to the Canadian Dept of Marine & Fisheries. Converted to Lightship No.5.

YPRES	1917/40 RCN	Armament: P.No:	1 x 12-pdr WWII: J 70

1917: Ordered in January . L. 6 June. Built by the Polson Ironworks, Canada. 1939: Converted to a BDV in September. 1940: LOST. Rammed and sunk by HMS REVENGE at Halifax, NS, on 12 April.

AXE CLASS

This unusual class comprised 17 Russian vessels which were reportedly seized in the White Sea in August 1918. This was the period when The Royal Navy was involved in northern operations against the Bolsheviks. It would appear, however, that the term "seized" also covers 8 of them which were "handed over" by White Russian Authorities and one, T20 (WOODAXE) was captured on 5 August by the French Admiral Aube. IRONAXE and WOODAXE probably had French crews from August 1918 although listed as RN ships.

They were all British built for the Russian Navy and were numbered with the prefix T. Six vessels, the most modern, came from the T13 - 24 Group, which had been built by Smiths Dock during 1916. Another, POLEAXE, was the last of the Class, built in 1917 by Cochrane and 10 older vessels, built between 1899 and 1910, were part of a number purchased into the Russian service. Vessels of the T30 - T40 Group, again all British built were formerly owned by Argentina before being purchased into the Russian Navy.

The 1916 vessels from Smith's Dock were designed especially for operating in ice-prone waters which resulted in them having specially strengthened bows which were sharply cut away below the water. Perhaps it was this group of vessels with their ice-cutting capability which gave rise to the Class being renamed using the suffix "axe".

Four of their number, BATTLEAXE, GOLDAXE, ICEAXE and STONEAXE, survived to serve in the Second World War and were renamed DEE, GARRY, KENNET and LIFFEY respectively. They all survived the conflict to be sold off to the mercantile in 1946/7.

Displacement:	520T 296TG
Measurements:	139ft oa 130ft pp x 23.6ft x 12ft
Engines	1-shaft Reciprocating (VTE). 525 IHP
Speed	10.5 kts
Armament:	Nominally 1 x 3-inch but vessels were armed individually.

BATTLEAXE (as DEE) De-armed between the wars but showing an array of wireless aerials between her masts. **(MPL)**

Vessels in the Class:

BATTLEAXE, BONEAXE, BRONZEAXE, COALAXE, DREADAXE, FIRMAXE, FROSTAXE, GOLDAXE, GREATAXE, ICEAXE, POLEAXE, SILVERAXE, STEAMAXE, STONEAXE, SUREAXE, WOODAXE

AXE CLASS - NOTES

BATTLEAXE	1916/46	Armament: Admty No:	1 x 75mm 4333

1916: L. 19 June. Built by Smith's Dock for Russian owners. 1918: Seized in the White Sea on 3 August. Commissioned into the RN. 1920: Renamed DEE in September. 1946: Sold to Mercantile and renamed *Safir*.

BONEAXE		Admty No:	4343

1918: Seized from the Russians in the White Sea on 3 August. Taken into the RN on 11 September. 1920: Sold to mercantile.

BRONZEAXE	1918/20	Admty No:	4339

1918: Seized from the Russians in the White Sea on 3 August. Added to the Navy List on 11 September. 1920: Sold to mercantile.

COALAXE	1910/21	Displacement: Admty No:	263TG 4346

1910: L. Built at Aberdeen by Hall Russell for the Russian Navy. 1918: Seized in the White Sea on 3 August. Added to the Navy List. 1920: Sold to mercantile on 11 May. 1921: Renamed *Calicut*.

DREADAXE	1918/20	Admty No: 4341

1918: Russian T-Class seized in the White Sea on 3 August. Added to the Navy List on 11 September. 1920: Sold to mercantile.

FIRMAXE	1918/20	Ex-Russian T-34 Admty No:	ex-*Cuatro* 4345

1908 L. Built at Aberdeen by Hall Russell. 1918: Seized from the Russians in the White Sea on 3 August. Added to the Navy List on 11 November. 1920: Sold to mercantile on 11 May. 1921: Renamed *Cannanore*.

FROSTAXE	1899/1919	Admty No:	4347

1899: L. Built at North Shields by Edwards as *Atlas*. 1918: Siezed from the Russians in the White Sea on 3 August. 1919: LOST. Sunk in a collision with SS *Epiros* off Newhaven.

GOLDAXE	1916/46	Armament: Admty No:	1 x 75mm 4331

1916: L. Built by Smith's Dock for Russian owners. 1918: Seized in the White Sea on 3 August. Converted to a M/S and added to the Navy List in September. 1920: Renamed GARRY in September. 1946: Sold to Norwegian owners and retained the name *Garry*.

STONEAXE (as LIFFEY) - With her 12-pdr retained in peacetime. (Steve Bush Collection)

GREATAXE   1918/20   Ex-T6, ex-*Wostock*, ex-*Alcyon*,
                  ex-*Windsor*
                  Admty No: 4340

1899: L. Built at Glasgow by Aitken & Scott. 1918: Russian owned T-6 seized in the White Sea on 3 August. Added to the Navy List in Sept. 1920: Sold to mercantile and retained the same name. 1925: Acquired by William Masson of Aberdeen. Renamed *Roslin*. PR: A 371.

ICEAXE   1918/46   Ex-Russian T-17
                  Armament: 1 x 75mm
                  Admty No: 4334

1916: L. 17 July. Built at Southport-on-Tees by Smiths Dock for the Russian Govt. 1918: Seized in the White Sea on 3 August. Added to the Navy List. 1920: Renamed KENNET in September. 1940: Based at Grimsby. 1945: Converted to a Fire-float. 1946: Sold to BU.

POLEAXE   1918/21   Ex-T-19
                  Displacement: 540T 304TG
                  Armament: 1 x 12-pdr
                  Admty No: 4335

1917: L. in August. Built at Selby by Cochrane for Russia. 1918: Russian trawler seized in the White Sea on 3 August. Converted to a M/S and Commissioned into the RN. 1921: Sold to mercantile on 22 July and renamed *Dorbie*. Acquired by Kelsall Bros & Beeching of Hull. PR: H 361.

SILVERAXE   1918/20   Ex-T-33 ex-*Tres*
                  Displacement: 272TG
                  Admty No: 4338

1908: L. Built at Aberdeen by Hall Russell. Russian owned fishing vessel. 1918: Seized in the White Sea on 3 August and added to the Navy List on 11 November having been converted to a M/S. 1920: Sold to mercantile and retained the same name. 1925: Renamed *Finmark*.

STEAMAXE	1918/21	Ex-T12, ex-*Zapad*, ex-*Sapad*, ex-*River Dart*	
		Displacement:	332TG
		Armament:	1 x 12-pdr
		Admty No:	4342

1908: L. Built at Goole by Goole SB. Russian owned fishing vessel. 1918: Russian Trawler seized in the White Sea on 3 August and added to the Navy List on 11 November. 1919: LOST. Grounded and wrecked near Inchkieth on 1 November. 1921: Wreck salvaged and sold.

STONEAXE	1918/47	Ex-Russian T-14	
		Armament:	1x 75mm
		Admty No:	4332

1916: L. 1 June Built at Southbank-on-Tees by Smith's Dock. Russian Fishing vessel. 1918: Seized in the White Sea on 3 August. Added to the Navy List and converted to a M/S. 1920: Renamed LIFFEY in September. 1940: Based at Grimsby (Ungrouped). 1947: Sold.

SUREAXE	1918/20 1942/45	Ex-Russian T-31, ex-*Una*		
		Displacement:	195TG	85TN
		Engines:	400 IHP	
		Admty No:	4344	
		Port Reg:	WWII: A 161	
		P.No:	WWII: FY 1843	

1907: L Built at Aberdeen by Hall Russell. Russian fishing vessel. 1918: Seized in the White Sea on 3 August. Added to the Navy List on 11 November. 1920: Sold to mercantile and retained the same name. Acquired by Harrow-Baxter SF Co of Aberdeen. 1942: Requisitioned in August and converted for Target-towing. 1945: Returned to owners in November.

WOODAXE	1918/20	Ex-Russian T-20	
		Armament:	1 x 75mm
		Admty No:	4336

1916: L. 3 August. Built at Southbank-on-Tees by Smith's Dock. Russian owned. 1918: Seized in the White Sea on 3 August. Converted to a M/S and renamed. Added to the Navy List in September. Transferred to the French Navy in December. 1920: Finally stricken from the Navy List

BASSET CLASS

BASSET, the name vessel of this Class was launched in 1935. Built to a modified design of her contemporary mercantile sisters, she incorporated a slightly quicker turn of speed, a larger fo'scle area and the bridge superstructure placed nearly amidships. So successful was the design that it quickly became the prototype for all subsequent Naval built trawlers which were built with but little variation.

Only two of the Class were built in the UK (Both by Henry Robb Ltd. of Leith) and of the rest, four were built in Canada for the RCN, with the remainder being ordered from Indian yards, except for four which were to be built at Rangoon, in Burma, two for the Burmese Government and two for the Government of Ceylon. All four vessels were lost whilst building when the Japanese over-ran Burma.

Originally 44 vessels were ordered in India for service with the RIM as M/Ss. However, engining from local sources was not viable and the shipping out of engines from the UK was considered impractical in war-time conditions which resulted in 23 of them being cancelled.

Displacement:	460 tons MASTIFF and RIN Vessels: 545 tons
Measurements:	163ft 6in oa 150ft pp x 27ft 6in x 10ft 6in BASSET: 160ft 6in oa RIN Vessels: 13ft 6in
Engines:	1-shaft Reciprocating (VTE). 850 IHP MASTIFF: 950 IHP
Speed:	12 kts MASTIFF: 13 kts
Armament:	1 x 4-inch; 2 x LG (2 x single)RIN Vessels: 1 x 12-pdr; 1 x 20mm AA
Complement:	33, RIN vessels: 48

Vessels in the Class:

RIN:

AGRA, AHAMEDABAD, AMRISTSAR, BARODA, BERAR, CALCUTTA, COCHIN, CUTTACK, KARACHI, KOLABA, LAHORE, LUCKNOW, MADURA, MULTAN, NASIK, PATNA, PESHAWAR, POONA, RAMPUR, SHILLONG, TRAVENCORE

RN:

BASSET, MASTIFF

BURMA:

BAY INNAUNG, COCHRANE

RCN:

COMOX, FUNDY, GASPE, NOOTKA

CEYLON:

ELARA, GEMUNU

Cancelled Vessels (All RIN):

ALLAHABAD, AMBALA, BANNU, BAREILLY, BARISAL, BENARES, CAWNPORE,

CHITTAGONG, DACCA, DINAPORE, GAYA, JUBBALPORE, KIAMARI, MONGHYR, NAGPUR, PACHMARI, PURI, QUETTA, SHOLAPORE, SIALKOT, SYLHET, TRICHONOPOLY, VIZAGAPATAM

BASSET - showing clearly the DCRs aft.   **(Steve Bush Collection)**

BASSET CLASS - NOTES

| AGRA | 1942/46 RIN | P.No: | T 254 |

1942: L.18 March. Built by Hooghly D. & E Co. and engined by Lobnitz. Completed as a M/S. 1946: Sold to mercantile and renamed *Fritha*.

| AHAMEDABAD | 1943/47 RIN | P.No: | T 264 |

1943: L. 28 October. Built at Calcutta by Burn and engined by Lobnitz. Completed as a M/S. 1947: Sold to mercantile.

| ALLAHABAD | 1944/45 RIN | P.No: | T 317 |

1944: Ordered from Hooghly D & E Co., India. 1945: Cancelled in March.

| AMBALA | 1942/45 RIN | P.No: | T 320 |

1942: Ordered from Alcock Ashdown of Bombay. 1945: Cancelled.

| AMRITSAR | 1941/50 RIN | P.No: | T 261 |

1941: L. 19 December. Built by Garden Reach of Calcutta and engined by W h i t e s . 1950: Sold to Mercantile.

| BANNU | 1944/45 RIN | P.No: | T 331 |

1944: Ordered from Shalimar D & E Co. India. Suspended in October. 1945: Cancelled in March.

35

BAREILLY   1944/45 RIN   P.No: T 319

1944: Ordered from Shalimar D & E Co. India. Suspended in December. 1945: Cancelled in March.

BARISAL   1944/45 RIN   Ex-SHOLAPORE
                                         P.No: T 270

1944: Ordered from Scindia, India. Laid down as SHOLAPORE and then renamed. Suspended in October. 1945: Cancelled in March.

BARODA   1941/47 RIN   P.No: T 249

1941: L. 22 October. Built by Shalimar D & E Co., India. 1947: Transferred to Pakistan at partitioning and renamed BAHAWALPUR. 1959: Sold to mercantile in January.

BASSET   1935/47   Armament: 1 x 12-pdr 2 x 0.5-inch AA (2 x Single) LG 1 x Twin MG
                                         P.No: T 68

1935: L. 28 September. Built at Leith by Henry Robb Ltd. and completed as A/S. 1947: Sold to mercantile and renamed *Radford*. Subsequently purchased by the Chinese Government and served in the Chinese Navy until 1967.

BAY INNAUNG   1941/42

1941: Ordered from the Irrawadi Flotilla Co., Rangoon. Laid down in August. 1942: Destroyed on the stocks in March in the face of the Japanese advance.

BENARES   1944/45 RIN   P.No: T 318

1944: Laid down in India by the Hooghly D & E Co. Work suspended in November. 1945: Cancelled in March.

BERAR   1942/47 RIN   P.No: T 256

1942: L. 31 July. Built in India by the Hooghly D & E Co. and engined by Lobnitz. 1947: Sold to Mercantile.

CALCUTTA   1939/49 RIN   P.No: T 339

1943: L. Built in India by the Hooghly D & E Co. and engined by Holmes. 1949: Sold to mercantile in August.

CAWNPORE   1942/45 RIN   P.No: T 346

1942: Ordered in July from Burn of Calcutta. 1944: Order deferred in October. 1945: Cancelled in March.

CHITTAGONG   1941/45 RIN   P.No: T 265

1941: Ordered from Burn of Calcutta on 23 September. 1944: Order deferred in October 1945: Cancelled in March.

COCHIN   1943/43 RIN

1941: Ordered from Alcock Ashdown of Bombay on 14 November. 1943: Renamed KOLABA. Cancelled.

COCHIN   1943/50 RIN   Ex-MULTAN
                                            P.No: T 315

1943: Laid down as MULTAN. L. 29 December. Built in India by Scindia and engined by Lobnitz. Renamed. 1950: Sold to mercantile.

COCHIN   1944/44   See under MULTAN

COCHRANE   1941/42

1941: Ordered by the Burmese Govt. Laid down in August at Rangoon by the Irrawadi Flotilla Co. 1942: Destroyed on the stocks in March in the face of the Japanese advance

COMOX   1938/47 RCN   Armament: 1 x 4-inch; 2 x Single
                                                         LG
                                            P.No: J 64

1938: L. 9 August. Built in Canada by Burrard of Vancouver. Engined by Marine Industries. 1947: Sold to mercantile. 1950: Renamed *Sung Ming*.

CUTTACK   1943/46 RIN   P.No: T 251

1943: L. in July. Built at Calcutta by Burns and engined by Lobnitz. 1946: Sold to mercantile and renamed *Figura*.

DACCA   1941/45 RIN   P.No: T 252

1941: Ordered from Burn of Calcutta on 23 December. 1944: Building deferred in December. 1945: Cancelled in March.

DINAPORE   1941/45 RIN   P.No: T 326

1941: Ordered from Burns of Calcutta. 1944: Order deferred. 1945: Cancelled in March.

ELARA   1941/42

1941: Ordered for the Ceylon Govt. Laid down in December at Rangoon by the Irrawadi Flot. Co. 1942: Lost on the stocks at the fall of Rangoon in March.

FUNDY   1938/47 RCN   Armament: 1 x 4-inch; 2 x Single
                                                         LG
                                            P.No: J 88

1938: L. 18 June. Built in Canada by Collingwood SY of Ontario. Engined by Marine Industries and completed as a M/S. 1945: Paid off and reduced to the Reserve. Placed on the Sale List. 1947: Sold to mecantile.

GASPE   1938/47 RCN   Armament: 1 x 4-inch; 2 x Single
                                                         LG
                                            P.No: J 94

1938: L. 12 August. Built in Canada by Morton of Quebec and engined by Marine Industries. Completed as a M/S. 1947: Sold to mercantile. 1950: Renamed *Sung Li.*

GAYA   1942/45   P.No: T 325

1942: Ordered. To be built at Calcutta. 1945: Cancelled.

GEMUNU   1941/42

1941: Ordered by the Govt. of Ceylon from the Irrawadi Flotilla Co of Rangoon. Laid Down in August. 1942: LOST. Destroyed on the stocks at the fall of Rangoon in March.

JUBBALPORE   1942/45 RIN   Ex-QUETTA
                                         P.No: T 323

1942: Ordered from Alcock Ashdown, Bombay, in December as QUETTA. 1944: Renamed. Work deferred in October. 1945: Cancelled in December.

KARACHI   1941/46 RIN   P.No: T 262

1941: L. 1 December. Built at Bombay by Alcock Ashdown. 1946: Sold to mercantile and renamed *Fravaria*.

KIAMARI   1942/45 RIN   P.No: T 330

1942: Ordered from Scindia SN Co in December. 1944: Work deferred. 1945: Cancelled.

KOLABA   1942/42 RIN   See under COCHIN

LAHORE   1941/46 RIN   P.No: T 253

1941: L. 20 December. Built in India by Shalimar D&E Co. 1946: Sold to mercantile.

LAHORE   1948/58   See under RAMPUR

LUCKNOW   1942/59   P.No: T 267

1942: L. 3 April. Built by Shalimar D&E Co. 1946: Renamed BARODA. 1948: Renamed BAHAWALPAR in August. 1959: Sold to mercantile on 22 January.

MASTIFF   **(MPL)**

MADURA   1942/47 RIN   P.No: T 268

1942: L. 22 December. Built at Calcutta by Garden Reach and engined by Whites ME. 1947: Sold to mercantile.

MASTIFF   1938/39   Armament: 1 x 4-inch
                                          P.No: T 10

1937: Ordered on 27 January. 1938: L. 17 February. Built at Leith by Henry Robb and completed as a M/S. 1939: LOST. Mined in the Thames Estuary on 20 November. Notes: Although of the Basset Class she differed in a number of details from the standard.

MONGHYR   1942/44 RIN   P.No: T 327

1942: Ordered from Alcock & Brown of Bombay in December. 1944: Cancelled in December.

MULTAN   1944/45 RIN   Ex-KOLABRA, ex-COCHIN
                                          P.No: T 322

1944: Ordered in India from the Scindia SN Co as KOLABRA. Laid down. Renamed COCHIN. Renamed MULTAN. 1945: Cancelled and BU.

NAGPUR   1943/43 RIN   Ex-RAMPUR, ex-BARISAL

1942: Ordered as BARISAL and then renamed RAMPUR. 1943: Renamed NAGPUR. L. in August. Built at Calcutta by Burn. Completion suspended. 1945: Cancelled in March.

NANOOSE   1944/47   See under NOOTKA

NASIK   1944/50 RIN   P.No: T 258

1944: L. 24 May. Built in India by the Shalimar D&E Co. 1950: Sold to mercantile.

NOOTKA   1938/44   Armament: 1 x 4-inch; 2 x Single
                                                    LG
                                          P.No: J 35

1938: L. 26 September. Built in Canada by Yarrow of Esquimault. 1944: Renamed NANOOSE. 1947: Sold to mercantile. 1950: Renamed *Sung Ling*.

PACHMARI   1942/45 RIN   P.No: T 324

1942: Ordered in December to be built at Calcutta. 1945: Cancelled in February.

PATNA   1942/46 RIN   P.No: T 255

1942: L. 1 September. Built at Calcutta by the Hooghly D & E Co and engined by Holmes. 1946: Sold to mercantile.

PESHAWAR   1942/54 RIN   P.No: T 263

1942: L. 2 May. Built at Bombay by Alcock Ashdown. 1944: Work abandoned. 1954: Uncompleted hull sold.

POONA   1942/46 RIN P.No: T 260

1942: L. 2 April. Built at Calcutta by Garden Reach. 1946: Sold to mercantile and renamed *Firishta.*

PURI   1942/45 RIN P.No: T 328

1942: Ordered in December from Alcock Ashdown of Bombay. 1944: Work deferred. 1945: Cancelled in January.

QUETTA   1942/45 RIN P.No: T 332

1942: Ordered in July from Scindia SN Co of Bombay as JUBBALPORE. Renamed. 1945: Cancelled in March.

RAMPUR   1943/58 RIN Ex-NAGPUR
                  P.No: T 269

1943: Ordered as NAGPUR and then renamed RAMPUR. 1944: L. 11 March. Built at Calcutta by Burn. 1948: Renamed LAHORE in August. 1958: Sold out of Service in January.

SHILLONG   1942/47   P.No: T 250

1942: L. 22 September. Built at Calcutta by Burn and engined by Lobnitz. 1947: Sold to mercantile and renamed *Fatima.*

SHOLAPORE   1942/42 RIN See under BARISAL

SIALKOT   1942/45 RIN P.No: T 321

1942: Ordered July from Alcock Ashdown of Bombay. 1944: Laid down in February but work deferred. 1945: Cancelled in March.

SYLPHET   1942/45 RIN Ex-SHOLAPORE
                  P.No: T 329

1942: Ordered in December from Scindia SN Co of Bombay. 1945: Cancelled in February.

TRAVENCORE   1941/47 RIN P.No: T 312

1941: Launched 7 July. Built at Calcutta by Garden Reach. 1947: Placed on the Disposal List in January. Sold to mercantile and renamed *Forma.*

TRICHONOPOLY 1942/45 RIN P.No: T 314

1942: Ordered from Burn of Calcutta in July. 1945: Cancelled.

VIZGAPATAM   1942/45 RIN P.No: T 313

1942: Ordered from Burn of Calcutta in July. 1945: Cancelled in January.

BIRD CLASS

In 1943 a number of Isles Class and Fish Class trawlers were building in the yards of CWG and Cochrane. The Admiralty had a requirement for mine-laying trawlers and five of the building vessels were selected for completion as such. Designated the Bird Class, they were renamed accordingly.

Details: See under ISLES Class.

Vessels in the Class:

BLACKBIRD, CORNCRAKE, DABCHICK, REDSHANK, STONECHAT

BLACKBIRD   **(IWM Neg: A18179)**

BIRD CLASS - NOTES

BLACKBIRD	1942/53	Ex-SHEPPEY	
		Displacement:	442TG 149TN
		Engines:	850 HP = 12 kts
		Armament:	3 x Single 20mm AA
		P.No:	M 15

1942: Ordered on 29 May as Isles Class SHEPPEY. Renamed and reclassified in November. 1943: L. 20 February. Built at Beverley by CWG and completed as a Controlled M/L. 1949: Sold to mercantile and renamed *Goodmar*. Acquired by Gwent Co of Aberdeen. PR: A 639. 1951: Acquired by Mary A.Johannesson AO of Aberdeen. 1953: Acquired by Greek mercantile and renamed *Iason*. Mercantile Loss on 13 March. Sank in heavy weather near Cape Spartivento.

CORNCRAKE   1942/43   Fish Class. See under MACKEREL

DABCHICK	1943/54	Isles Class. See under THORNEY

REDSHANK	1942/57	Ex-TURBOT	
		Armament:	1 x 4-inch 3 x Single 20mm AA
		P.No:	M 31

1941: Ordered on 17 December as Fish Class TURBOT. 1942: L. 28 August. Built at Selby by Cochrane and engined by Amos & Smith. Completed as a M/L. Renamed in November. 1946: Employed on Mine Clearance at Trincomalee, Ceylon. 1957: Sold to Messrs Young and arrived at Sunderland on 9 July to BU.

STONECHAT		Displacement:	443TG 580T (M/L) 151TN
		Engines:	850 HP = 12 kts
		Armament:	3 x Single 20mm AA
		P.No:	M 25

1943: Laid Down as an Isles Class. Redesigned as a Controlled M/L of the Blackbird Group whilst building. 1944 L. 28 August Built at Beverley by CWG and engined by Holmes. Commissioned on 5 November at Prince's Dock, Hull. 1945: Employed as a convoy escort but carried out one escort only for a convoy northwards from Hull. Left the convoy at Hartlepool and Paid Off there. Entered the Hartlepool Reserve. 1967: Sold and BU at Troon.

STONECHAT (MPL)

BRAZILIAN CLASS

In their desperation for ship-building availability the Admiralty turned to Brazil for assistance in 1941 and ordered from them 6 trawlers to be known as the Brazilian Class. However, before they could be handed over to the RN, Brazil entered into the war on the side of the Allies, and the vessels were transferred to the Brazilian Navy for patrol duties off their Atlantic coast.

Displacement:	680 tons
Measurements:	176ft 6in oa 160ft pp x 28ft x 14ft
Engines:	1 shaft Reciprocating (VTE). 1,000 IHP
Speed:	12.5 kts
Armament:	1 x 12-pdr DP 4 x Single 20mm AA
Complement:	40

Vessels in the Class:

PAMPONA, PAPATERA, PARATI, PARGO, PARU, PELEGRIME

BRAZILIAN CLASS - NOTES

PAMPONA   1942/42   P.No: T 152

1940: Ordered in July. 1942: Transferred to the Brazilian Navy before launching. L. 4 October. Built at Rio de Janiero by Ilha Viana and completed as a M/S. Renamed MATIAS de ALBUQUERQUE.

PAPATERA   1942/42   P.No: T 156

1940: Ordered in July. 1942: L. in July. Built at Rio de Janeiro by Ilha Viana. Transferred to the Brazilian Navy in August and renamed FELIPE CAMARO. Completed as a M/S.

PARATI   1942/42   T 148

1940: Ordered in July. 1942: Transferred to the Brazilian Navy in August and renamed FERNANDES VIERA. L. 10 October. Built at Rio de Janeiro by Ilha Viana and completed as a M/S.

PARGO   1942/42   P.No: T 141

1940: Ordered in July. 1942: L. 26 August. Built at Rio de Janeiro by Ilha Viana. Transferred to the Brazillian Navy in August and renamed HENRIQUE DIAS. Completed as a M/S.

PARU   1942/42   P.No: T 183

1940: Ordered in July. 1942: Transferred to the Brazillian Navy in August and renamed BARETO de MENEZES. 1944: L. in February. Built at Rio de Janeiro by Ilha Viana and completed as a M/S.

PELEGRIME   1942/42   P.No: T 184

1940: Ordered from Brazil in July: 1942: L. 12 December. Built at Rio De Janeiro by Ilha Viana. Transferred to the Brazilian Navy in August and renamed VIDAL de NEGREIROS. Completed as a M/S.

CASTLE CLASS WWI

There were 217 vessels envisaged for this Class but by the end of WWI only 197 had been built and 20 cancelled. However, in addition to the 197 built in UK yards a further 9 were built in India and 60 more (TR 1 - TR 60) in Canada. A number of those built in the closing stages of, or after, the war were completed as fishing vessels and sold immediately into mercantile service. Several of these, together with others sold to the mercantile, were requisitioned in WWII. The names for this Class, together with the "Mersey" and "Strath" Classes were taken from the muster rolls of the VICTORY and ROYAL SOVEREIGN at the Battle of Trafalgar, a splendid tribute to the ordinary sailors of that most famous of battles.

At the time that the orders for these vessels were placed there were a number of trawlers already on the stocks in various yards being built for fishing companies. The Admiralty purchased these hulls, had them completed to their own specifications and alloted them to the classes closest to their dimensions. Thus there were 10 Non-Standard vessels included in the Castle Class. 1917 saw the premature cancellation of 16 orders which had been placed with Smiths Dock, due to the even more urgent requirement for gunboats. This enabled Smiths Dock to clear their stocks for this more urgent building programme.

Displacement:	360T 547T Deep 275TG
Dimensions	134ft oa 125ft 6in pp x 23ft 6in x 12ft 9in (Depth of hold).
Engines:	1 shaft Reciprocating (VTE) 480 IHP
Speed:	10.5 kts
Armament:	Nominally 1 x 3-inch but vessels were armed individually with what was available.
Complement:	Nominally 18 but varied according to role.

Vessels in the Class:

ALEXANDER PALMER, ALEXANDER SCOTT, ANDREW ANDERSON, ANDREW APSLEY, ANDREW SACK, ARTHUR CAVANAGH, ARTHUR LESSIMORE, BENJAMIN COOK, BENJAMIN STEVENSON, CHARLES ANTRAM, CHARLES BOYES, CHARLES CHAPPEL, CHARLES DONNELLY, CHARLES LEGG, DANIEL CLOWDON, DANIEL DICK, DANIEL LEARY, DAVID DILLON, DAVID OGILVIE, DENIS CASEY, DOMINICK ADDISON, DOMINICK DUBINE, DOMQUE GENTILE, EDWARD CATTELLY, EDWARD COLLINGWOOD, EDWARD GALLAGHER, EGILIAS AKERMAN, EMANUEL CAMILAIRE, FRANCIS CONLIN, FREDERICK BUSH, GEORGE ADGELL, GEORGE AIKEN, GEORGE CLARKE, GEORGE COCHRANE, GEORGE CORTEN, GEORGE COUSINS, GEORGE DARBY, GEORGE GREAVES, GEORGE GREENFIELD, GEORGE HARRIS, GIOVANNU GUINTI, GRIFFITH GRIFFITH, HENRY CHEVALLIER, HENRY CORY, ISAAC HEATH, ISAAC ARTHAN, JAMES BURGES, JAMES CEPELL, JAMES CHAPMAN, JAMES CHRISTOPHER, JAMES CONNOR, JAMES COSGROVE, JAMES DINTON, JAMES GILL, JAMES GREEN, JAMES HUNNIFORD, JAMES LAVENNY, JAMES LAY, JAMES PEAKE, JAMES POND, JAMES ROBERTSON, JAMES SECKAR, JAMES SIBBALD, JOHN AIKENHEAD, JOHN ANDERSON, JOHN ASHLEY, JOHN BAPTISH, JOHN BATEMAN, JOHN BENSON, JOHN BOMKWORTH, JOHN BRITTON, JOHN BULLOCK, JOHN CAMPBELL, JOHN CASEWELL, JOHN CATLING, JOHN CHIVERS, JOHN CHURCH, JOHN CLAVELL, JOHN COLLINS, JOHN COOPER, JOHN DAVIES, JOHN DORMOND, JOHN GAUNTLETT, JOHN GEOGHAN, JOHN GRAHAM, JOHN GREGORY, JOHN

GULIPSTER, JOHN KIDD, JOHN LEWIS, JOHN LYONS, JOHN POLLARD, JOHN THORLING, JOSEPH BARRATT, JOSEPH BUTTON, JOSEPH CONNELL, JOSEPH GIDDICE, JOSEPH GORDON, JOSEPH HODGKINS, JOSHUA ARABIN, MATTHEW CASSADY, MATTHEW FLYNN, MICHAEL GING, MICHAEL GRIFFITH, MICHAEL MALONEY, MORGAN JONES, NATHANIEL COLE, NEIL SMITH, OLIVER PICKIN, PATRICK BOWE, PATRICK CULLEN, PATRICK DONOVAN, PETER BLUMBERRY, PETER CAREY, PETER HALL, PETER KILLEN, PETER LOVETT, PHILLIP GODBY, PHINEAS BEARD, RICHARD BACON, RICHARD BAGLEY, RICHARD CROFTS, RICHARD CUNDY, RICHARD ROBERTS, ROBERT BETSON, ROBERT BOWEN, ROBERT CLOUGHTON, ROBERT DAVIDSON, SAMUEL DAWSON, SAMUEL DRAKE, SAMUEL GREEN, SAMUEL SPENCER, SIAM DUFFY, THOMAS ADNEY, THOMAS ALEXANDER, THOMAS ALLEN, THOMAS ALTOFT, THOMAS BARTLETT, THOMAS BOOTH, THOMAS BOUDIGE. THOMAS CHAMBERS, THOMAS CONNOLLY, THOMAS CROFTON, THOMAS DANIELS, THOMAS DOWDING, THOMAS GOBLE, THOMAS GREEN, THOMAS HANKINS, THOMAS LAUNDRY, THOMAS LAWRIE, THOMAS LEEDS, THOMAS ROBINS, THOMAS TWINEY, TIMOTHY CRAWLEY, VANENTINE BOWER, WALTER BURKE, WILLIAM BEATTY, WILLIAM BEETON, WILLIAM BELL, WILLIAM BODY, WILLIAM BROWIS, WILLIAM BUNCE, WILLIAM CALDWELL, WILIAM CALE, WILLIAM CARBERRY, WILLIAM CARR, WILLIAM CARRICK, WILLIAM CHASEMAN, WILLIAM COBURNE, WILLIAM COWLING, WILLIAM CUMMINS, WILLIAM DARNOLD, WILLIAM DOWNES, WILLIAM DRAKE, WILLIAM FLEMING, WILLIAM GRIFFITHS, WILLIAM HANNHAM, WILLIAM HUMPHRIES, WILLIAM KNIGHT, WILLIAM LAMBKIN, WILLIAM LEEK, WILLIAM LOFT, WILLIAM MANNELL, WILLIAM SPENCER, WILLIAM SYMONS, WILLIAM WILLMOT.

Non-Standard Vessels

DANIEL HARRINGTON, DANIEL HENLEY, FESTING GRINDALL, GEORGE AUNGER, HUGH BLACK, JAMES JOHNSON, JOHN ANDERSON, JOHN BRENNAN, JOHN BRICE, JOHN BROOKER, JOHN BURLINGHAM, JOHN GILLMAN, ROBERT BETSON, THOMAS BLACKTHORN, THOMAS BUCKLEY

Cancelled Vessels:

ALEXANDER COLVILLE, ALEXANDER DUNBAR, COLIN CRAIG, EPHRIAM BRIGHT, JAMES BAIRD, JAMES BOYLE, JAMES COILE, JOHN CHATWAY, JOHN COOMBE, JOHN CREIGHTON, JOSEPH CROWELL, JOSEPH DOE, MATTHEW BERRYMAN, RICHARD BANE, WALTER CAVE, WILLIAM BENNETT, WILLIAM BURTE, WILLIAM CABLE, and WILLIAM CORAN.

Indian Built Vessels:

Displacement:	265TG 588T (Deep)
Measurements:	134ft oa 125ft pp x 23ft 6in x 12ft
Engines:	1 shaft Reciprocating (VTE) 480 IHP
Speed:	10.5 kts
Armament:	See individual vessels
Complement:	18

For some time the threat from mines had been apparent around the Indian sub-continent, so, in 1917, along with all the other trawler orders issued by the Admiralty, there was despatched to India an order for nine Castle Class with the intention that they should be employed in those waters. The vessels were to be of composite build, teak planking over steel frames, and the engines were to be shipped out from the UK. Three were to be built by Burns & Co of Calcutta and the remaining six by the Bombay Dockyard. Progress was, however, slow and construction was reported as "still in progress", as late as February 1919 long after the requirement for Minesweepers had ceased, but work was allowed to proceed. Whether they were actually armed on completion is doubtful but with the exception of JUBBLEPORE, which was cancelled, they all appear to have served up until 1932. MADRAS was the only one to have survived beyond this date until she was lost in 1942. SALSETTE became a LV in 1928 and the remainder were probably sold to the Indian mercantile from 1932.

BOMBAY, CALCUTTA, COLOMBO, JUBBLEPORE, KENNERY, KIDDERPORE, MADRAS, SALSETTE, SEALDAH.

Canadian Built Vessels:

Details: As UK built Castle Class.

Notes:

In January 1917 36 vessels were ordered from Canadian yards as Admiralty Trawlers of the Castle Class and an additional 24 were ordered the following July. When completed they were manned by the RCN, or in the case of 9 vessels, by the USN who used them for post-war mine clearance. they were not named, but numbered TR 1 - TR 60. Their main task was that of patrolling the Canadian Atlantic seaboard but it is known that Nos 1 - 10 were completed as M/Ss and others may have been converted for sweeping at a later stage.

JOHN DAVIES showing her bluff bow and distinctive stern   **(Author's Collection)**

ALEXANDER COLVILLE   1918/19   Admty No: 4455

1918: Ordered from George Brown. 1919: Cancelled.

ALEXANDER DUNBAR   1918/19   Admty No: 4493

1918: Ordered from Hepple. 1919: Cancelled

ALEXANDER PALMER	1917/22	Armament:	1 x 12-pdr
		Admty No:	3517

1917: L. 21 May. Built by Smith's Dock. Completed as a M/S. 1920: Renamed NESS in September. Subsequently sold to the Spanish Navy and renamed UAD LUCAS.

ALEXANDER SCOTT	1917/20 1939/45	Displacement:	107TN
		Engines:	61HP
		Armament:	1 x 12-pdr
		Admty No:	3530
		Port Reg:	WWII: LO 361
		P. No:	WWII: FY 515

1917: L. 3 August. Built at Southbank-on-Tees by Smith's Dock. 1920: Sold to Mercantile on 4 May and retained the same name. Acquired by Jenkerson & Jones of Milford Haven. 1939: Requisitioned in August and converted to a M/S. 1945: Returned to owners.

ANDREW ANDERSON   1919/22   Admty No: 4405

1919: L. 15 August. Built at Beverley by CWG and completed as a fishing vessel. 1922: Sold to mercantile on 13 February and renamed *Normanby*. Acquired by the Boston DSF & Ice Co of Boston, Lincs. PR: BN.179. 1929: Acquired by Spanish mercantile. 1949: Spanish mercantile loss. Wrecked near Castillo San Sebation Lighthouse on 2 April.

ANDREW APSLEY	1919/19 1939/41	Displacement:	290TG 127TN
		Engines:	86HP = 10.5 kts
		Admty No:	4298
		Port Reg:	WWII: M 68

1919: L. 2 June. Built at Beverley by CWG and completed as a fishing vessel. Sold to mercantile on 13 October and renamed *Callancroft*. Acquired by HE Rees of Swansea. PR: SA.32. 1930: Acquired by McRae STC of Milford Haven and renamed *Duncan McRae*. 1936: Acquired by Milford STC of Milford Haven and renamed *Milford Earl*. 1939: Requisitioned in August as MILFORD EARL and converted to a M/S. 1941: LOST. Sunk by enemy a/c off Lunan Bay on the East Coast of Scotland on 6 December with the loss of 5 lives and 5 rescued.

ANDREW SACK	1917/19 1940/46	Displacement:	107TN
		Engines:	87HP
		Armament:	1 x 12-pdr
		Port Reg:	WWII: H 11
		P.No:	WWII: 4100

1917: L. 5 July. Built at Middlesborough by Smith's Dock. 1919: Sold to mercantile and renamed *Alexandrite*. Acquired by The Kingston STC of Hull. PR: H 11. Acquired by

Trident SFC of Hull and renamed *North Ness*. Same PR. 1940: Requisitioned in May as NORTH NESS and converted to an APV. 1946: Returned to owners in July.

ARTHUR CAVANAGH	1918/20	1940/45	Displacement:	122TN
			Engines:	61HP
			Armament:	1 x 12-pdr; 1 x 3.5-inch Bomb Thrower (A/S Howitzer)
			Admty No:	3677
			Port Reg:	WWII: M 184

1918: L. Built at Paisley by Bow McLachlan. Delivered on 28 May. 1920: Sold to mercantile and retained the same name. Acquired by Ritchie & Davies of Milford Haven. 1939: Requisitioned in August and converted to a M/S. Subsequently purchased into the RN. 1940: Deployed to the Med. Joined the 91st M/S Group employed off Tobruk, Port Said and in the Suez Canal. TPI Operation Countenance, the cutting out of the German and Italian merchant ships at Bandar Shahpur, Persian Gulf, on 25 August. CO awarded the MBE. 1946: Sold to Mercantile in January and retained the same name. Acquired by Milford Fisheries of Milford Haven. PR: M 161.

ARTHUR LESSIMORE	1917/19	1940/42	Displacement:	107TN
			Engines:	87HP
			Armament:	1 x 12-pdr
			Admty No:	3510
			Port Reg:	WWII: FD 181
			P.No:	WWII: FY 663

1917: L. Built at Southbank-on-Tees by Smith's Dock. Completed as an Escort. 1919: Sold to mercantile and renamed *Avanturina*. Acquired by Marr of Fleetwood and renamed *Irvana*. 1940: Requisitioned in February as IRVANA and converted to an APV 1942: LOST. Sunk by enemy a/c off Great Yarmouth on 16 January.

BENJAMIN COOKE	1917/20	1940/46	Armament:	WWI: 1 x 12-pdr.
				WWII: 1 x 12-pdr; 2 x MG
			Admty No:	3667
			Port Reg:	WWII: Dutch
			P.No:	WWII: 4 104

1917: L. Built at Paisley by Bow McLachlan. Delivered on 1 November. 1920: Sold to mercantile and renamed *Emiel Vandervelde*. 1940: Hired from Dutch owners in May as NAMUR. Converted to an APV. 1940: Converted to a BDV. 1943: Purchased into the RN in November. 1944: Renamed PALISADE. 1946: Paid Off in July and Laid Up. Placed on the Disposal List.

BENJAMIN STEVENSON	1917/17	Armament:	1 x 12-pdr
		Admty No:	3522

1917: L. 19 June. Built by Smith's Dock. LOST. Sunk by gunfire from a German S/M 40 miles east of Fetlar, Shetlands on 18 August.

BOMBAY	1918/32	RIM	Armament:	1 x 12-pdr

1919: L. 21 September. Built at the Bombay Dyd. 1932: Listed until April.

CALCUTTA	1918/33	RIM	Armament:	1 x 12-pdr

1919: L. Built at Calcutta, India, by Burns & Co. 1932: Listed until April.

CHARLES ANTRAM	1919/20 1939/45	Displacement:	290TG 130TN
		Engines:	86HP = 10.5 kts
		Armament:	WWII:
		Admty No:	4401
		Port Reg:	WWII: GY 10
		P.No:	WWII: FY 600

1919: L.18 June. Built at Beverley by CWG and completed as a fishing vessel. 1922: Sold to Belgian mercantile and renamed *Edmund Van Beveren*. 1938: Acquired by the Rhondda SFC of Grimsby and renamed *Flanders*. 1939: Requisitioned in August as FLANDERS and converted to a M/S. 1945: Returned to owners in December. 1959: BU at Troon.

CHARLES BOYES	1918/19 1939/40	Displacement:	290TG 126TN
		Engines:	480HP = 10.5 kts
		Armament:	1 x 12-pdr; 1 x 3.5-inch Bomb thrower (A/S Howitzer)
		Admty No:	3593
		Port Reg:	WWII: H 526

1918: L. 4 February. Built at Beverley by CWG. Fitted with Listening Hydrophones. 1919: Sold to mercantile and retained the same name. Acquired by Lady Beardmore of Glasgow. 1938: Acquired by St Andrews SFC of Hull. 1939: Requisitioned in September and converted to a M/S. Joined the 40th M/S Grp based at Gt.Yarmouth. 1940: LOST. Mined off the E.Coast on 25 May with the loss of 19 of her 22 crew.

CHARLES CHAPPELL	1917/19	Armament:	1 x 12-pdr
		Admty No:	3662

1917: L.19 June. Built at Paisley by Bow McLachlan. Fitted with Listening Hydrophones. 1919: Sold to mercantile and renamed *S.Nicola*.

CHARLES DONELLY	1918/20 1940/45	Displacement:	122TN
		Engines:	61HP
		Admty No:	3679
		Port Reg:	WWII: GN 55
		P.No:	4 103

1918: L. Built at Paisley by Bow McLachlan. Delivered on 12 July. 1920: Sold to mercantile and renamed *Calyclavia*. Acquired by D.Pettit of Milford Haven. PR: M 110. Acquired by L.Carnie AO of Glasgow and renamed *Pelagos*. 1940: Requisitioned in May as PELAGOS and converted to an APV. 1941: Converted to a M/S in June. 1945: Returned to owners in June.

CHARLES LEGG	1918/19 1939/46	Admty No:	4213
		Port Reg:	WWII: M 52
		P.No:	WWII: FY 564

1919: L. Built at S.Shields by J.P.Rennoldson and Sons. 1919: Sold to mercantile and renamed *Roderigo*. Acquired by the Hull Northern FC of Hull. PR: H 862. Acquired by the Milford STC of Milford Haven and renamed *Milford Countess*. 1939: Requisitioned in August as MILFORD COUNTESS. Converted to a M/S. 1940: Transferred to the MF. Joined the 91st M/S Group for sweeping off Tobruk, Port Said and Suez . 1946: Returned to owners in April.

COLIN CRAIG	1918/19	Admty No:	4451

1918: Ordered from George Brown. 1919: Cancelled.

COLOMBO   1919/32   RIM

1919: L. Built at Calcutta by Burn & Co. 1932: Listed until April.

DANIEL CLOWDEN	1919/19 1939/45	Displacement:	113TN
		Engines:	83HP
		Admty No:	4446
		Port Reg:	WWII: LO 129
		P.No:	WWII: FY 531

1919: L. Built at Greenock by George Brown. Sold to mercantile on 8 August whilst building. Completed as a fishing vessel and renamed *Hannah Woodbridge*. Delivered on 13 November. Acquired by Victory STC of Fleetwood. PR: FD 355. Acquired by Iago STC of Milford Haven and renamed *Daniel Clowden*. 1939: Requisitioned in August as DANIEL CLOWDEN. Converted to a M/S 1945: Returned to owners in October.

DANIEL DICK	1919/21 1939/45	Displacement:	107TN
		Engines:	69HP
		Admty No:	4488
		P.No:	FY1596

1919: L. Built at S.Shields by J.P.Rennoldson. 1920: Completed as a fishing vessel and delivered on 25 August. 1921: Sold to mercantile and renamed *Agate*. Acquired by Kingston STC of Hull. PR: H.338. 1939: Requisitioned in August as CLYTHNESS. Converted to a M/S and based at Dover for sweeping in the Channel. 1940: TPI Operation Dynamo, the evacuation of Dunkirk in May/June. 1943: Paid Off. TIH at Aberdeen for conversion to a Water Carrier. Commissioned at Aberdeen and deployed to the Moray Firth and employed in supplying water to the assembling Landing Craft. 1944: TPI Operation Neptune, the D-Day Landings ferrying oil fuel and petrol from Poole to the invasion beaches.. Tanks cleaned to resume water carrying and returned to France supplying water to Allied ships in Brest. 1945: Returned to owners in July.

DANIEL HARRINGTON	1917/20	Displacement:	276TG
		Armament:	1 x 12-pdr
		Admty No:	3505
		P.No:	WWII: FY 894

1917: L. 18 February. Built by Smith's Dock and completed as a M/S. 1920: Sold to mercantile and renamed *Start Point*. 1940: French owned *Lucienne-Jeanne* seized on 3 July in Operation Grab and converted to a M/S. Commissioned in August as LUCIENNE-JEAN with a Free-French crew. 1941: RN Manned. LOST. Stranded near Sheerness on 24 October.

DANIEL HENLEY	1917/20	Displacement:	276TG	107TN
		Engines:	61HP	
		Armament:	1 x 12-pdr	
		Admty No:	3503	

1917: L. 24 January. Built at Southbank-on-Tees by Smith's Dock. 1920: Sold to mercantile and renamed *Kilgerran Castle*. Acquired by Consolidated Fisheries of Grimsby. PR: SA 78.

| DANIEL LEARY | 1920/23 | Admty No: | 4221 |

1920: L. Built at S.Shields by Charles Rennoldson & Co.. Completed as a fishing vessel and delivered on 9 July. 1923: Sold to mercantile and renamed *Strato*.

DAVID DILLON	1919/19 1939/46	Displacement:	120TN
		Engines:	63HP
		Armament:	WWII: 1 x 12-pdr
		Admty No:	4484
		Port Reg:	WWII: FD 412
		P.No:	WWII: FY 624

1919: L. Built at S.Shields by J.P.Rennoldson. Completed as a fishing vessel and delivered on 28 July. Sold on delivery date to mercantile and renamed *Edouard Nierinck*. Acquired by Scarisbrick ST of Fleetwood and renamed *Edward Walmsley*. 1939: Requisitioned in August as EDWARD WALMSLEY and converted to a M/S. 1946: Returned to owners.

DAVID OGILVIE	1917/20 1939/46	Displacement:	107TN
		Engines:	61HP
		Admty No:	3514
		Port Reg:	WWII: LO 363
		P.No:	WWII: FY 147

1917: L. 7 May. Built at Southbank-on-Tees by Smith's Dock. 1920: Sold to mercantile and retained the same name. Acquired by T. Jenkerson & DG Jones of Milford Haven. PR: LO 363. 1939: Requisitioned in September and converted to a M/S. 1946: Returned to owners in September.

| DENIS CASEY | 1918/20 | Armament: | 1 x 12-pdr |
| | | Admty No: | 3711 |

1918: L. Built at Ayr by Ailsa SB and completed as a M/S. 1920: Sold to mercantile and renamed *Cardigan Castle*. Acquired by Consolidated Fisheries of Grimsby. PR: SA 49.

DOMINICK ADDISON	1919/20 1939/45	Displacement:	290TG 126TN
		Engines:	86HP = 10.5 kts
		Admty No:	4296
		Port Reg:	WWII: M 24
		P.No:	FY 517

1919: L. 2 April. Built at Beverley by CWG and completed as a fishing vessel. 1920: Sold to mercantile and renamed *Tenedos*. Acquired by Tucker Tippett of Cardiff. PR: CF 64. 1939: Requisitioned in August, renamed GADFLY and converted to a M/S. 1945: Returned to owners and reverted to original name. 1952: Acquired by Japan FCL of Grimsby and renamed *Hondo*. PR: GY 159. 1960: BU at Boom, Belguim.

| DOMINICK DUBINE | 1918/19 | Armament: | 1 x 12-pdr; 1 x 3.5-inch Bomb Thrower (A/S Howitzer) |

1918: L. Built at S.Shields by J.P.Rennoldson and delivered on 15 May. 1919: Sold to mercantile and retained the same name. Acquired by Casewell SFC of Fleetwood. PR: FD 402. Subsequently renamed *Emildor*. 1939: Served in WWII as the French AD.52 FRUCTIDOR.

| DOMQUE GENTILE | 1918/21 | Armament: | 1 x 12-pdr |
| | | Admty No: | 3793 |

1918: L. 5 August. Built at Ayr by Ailsa SB. 1921: Sold to mercantile. Subsequently renamed *Santiago Rusinol*.

| EDWARD CATTELLY | 1919/19 1939/40 | Displacement: | 121TN |
| | | Engines: | 83HP |

			Admty No:	4459
			Port Reg:	WWII: A 41

1919: L 17 March. Built at Troon by Ailsa SB and completed as a fishing vessel. Sold to mercantile and renamed *Sir John Hotham*. Acquired by M.Smith Ltd of Aberdeen and renamed *Loch Naver*. 1939: Requisitioned in August as LOCH NAVER. Converted to a M/S. 1940: LOST. Sunk in a collision off Hartlepool on 6 May.

EDWARD COLLINGWOOD 1918/21 1939/45
Displacement:	109TN
Engines:	61HP
Armament:	1 x 12-pdr
Admty No:	3675
Port Reg:	WWII: LO 210
P.No:	WWII: FY 532

1918: L. Built at Paisley by Bow McLachlan. Delivered on 26 April. 1921: Sold to mercantile and renamed *Mumby*. Acquired by the Boston DSF & Ice Co of Boston. PR: BN 174. Acquired by the Iago SFC of Fleetwood and renamed *T.R. Ferens*. 1939: Requisitioned in August as T.R. FERRANS and converted to a M/S. 1945: Returned to owners in April.

EDWARD GALLAGHER 1919/19 1939/46
Displacement:	113TN
Engines:	87HP
Admty No:	4216
Port Reg:	WWII: SA 90
P.No:	WWII: FY 512

1919: L.14 February. Built at S.Shields by C. Rennoldson and completed as a fishing vessel. Sold to mercantile and renamed *Ebor Downs*. Acquired by Harley & Miller Ltd of Liverpool. PR: MH 54. Acquired by the Consolidated Fisheries of Grimsby and renamed *Cardiff Castle*. 1939: Requisitioned in August as CARDIFF CASTLE and converted to a M/S 1946: Returned to owners in January.

EGILIAS AKERMAN 1919/19 1939/45
Displacement:	290TG 126TN
Engines:	86HP = 10.5 kts
Admty No:	4294
Port Reg:	WWII: GN 42
P.No:	WWII: FY 635

1919: L. 18 March. Built at Beverley by CWG and completed as a fishing vessel. Sold to mercantile and renamed *Kesteven*. Acquired by Boston DSF & Ice Co of Boston, Lincs. PR: BN 146. 1926: Acquired by French owners and renamed *Imprevu*. 1930: Reacquired by Boston DSF & Ice Co and renamed *Daily Mirror*. PR: FD 71. 1935: Acquired by T.L.Devlin of Leith and renamed *Computator*. 1939: Requisitioned as COMPUTATOR and converted to a M/S. 1945: LOST. Sunk in a collision with the destroyer VANOC in Seine Bay, Normandy on 21 January.

EMMANUEL CAMELAIRE 1918/21 1939/45
Displacement:	106TN
Engines:	61HP
Armament:	1 x 12-pdr
Admty No:	3717
Port Reg:	WWII: GY 544
P.No:	WWII: FY 586

1918: L. 25 April. Built at Troon by Ailsa and completed as a M/S. 1921: Sold to Mercantile and renamed *President Francqui*. Acquired by the Rhondda FCL of Grimsby and renamed *Brabant*. 1939: Requisitioned in August as BRABANT and converted to a M/S. 1945: Returned to owners.

EPHRIAM BRIGHT   1918/19   Admty No: 4407

1918: Ordered from CWG. 1919: Cancelled. 1920: Completed by the builders as a fishing vessel. Acquired by Fiskeriselskabet of Reykjavik, Iceland and renamed *Mai*. 1926: Acquired by Samvinnufelaginu of Iceland. 1955: BU in Denmark.

FESTING GRINDALL   1917/20   Armament: 1 x 12-pdr
                                  Admty No: 3501

1917: L. 9 January. Built by Smith's Dock and completed as a M/S. 1919: Renamed PEKIN. 1920: Sold to mercantile on 11 May and renamed *Festing Grindall*.

FRANCIS CONLIN   1919/19   Admty No: 4458

1919: L. 21 January. Built at Troon by Ailsa and completed as a fishing vessel. Sold to mercantile and renamed *Inverythan*. Acquired by A.Hardie of Aberdeen.

FREDERICK BUSH   1918/20   Armament: 1 x 12-pdr
                               Admty No: 3594

1918: L.14 March. Built at Beverley by CWG. Fitted with Listening Hydrophones. 1920: Sold to mercantile and renamed *Cawdor*. Acquired by D.Petitt of Milford Haven. PR: M 249.

GEORGE ADGELL   1919/19 1940/46   Displacement: 127TN
                                      Engines: 86HP
                                      Admty No: 4402
                                      Port Reg: FD 368
                                      P.No: WWII: FY 1926

1919: L. Built at Beverley by CWG and completed as a fishing vessel. 1919: Sold to mercantile and retained the same name. 1940: Requisitioned in June and converted to an APV . 1941: Converted to a M/S. 1946: Returned to owners in Janaury.

GEORGE AIKEN   1919/19   Admty No: 4291

1918: Renamed CECIL COOPER in November. L. 19 December. Built at Beverley by CWG and completed as a fishing vessel. 1920: Sold to mercantile and renamed *Highbridge*.

GEORGE AUNGER   1917/22   Armament: 1 x 12-pdr
                              Admty No: 3611

1917: L. 20 September. Built at Beverley by CWG. 1922: Sold to mercantile and retained the same name.

GEORGE CLARK   1917/22 1939/41   Displacement: 109TN
                                     Engines: 513HP
                                     Armament: 1 x 12-pdr
                                     Admty No: 3714
                                     Port Reg: WWII: M 196
                                     P.No: WWII: 4 233

1917: L. 2 October. Built at S.Shields by JP Rennoldson and completed as a M/S. 1919: Temporary Loan to the USN. 1922: Sold to mercantile and renamed *Tranio*. Acquired by H.E.Rees of Milford Haven and B.L. Koppenhagen of Roehampton. 1940: Requisitioned on 12 June as TRANIO and converted to an APV. 1941: LOST. Sunk by enemy a/c whilst in tow in the North Sea on 26 June.

| GEORGE COCHRANE | 1918/20 | Armament: | 1 x 12-pdr |
| | | Admty No: | 3721 |

1918: L. 28 June. Built at Beverley by CWG. 1919: Temporary Loan to the USN. 1920: Sold to mercantile and retained the same name.

GEORGE CORTON	1918/21 1939/44	Displacement:	107TN
		Engines:	87HP
		Admty No:	3697
		Port Reg:	H 329
		P.No:	FY 548

1918: L. Built at Falmouth by Cox and delivered on 16 February. 1921: Sold to mercantile and renamed *Zencon*. Subsequently renamed *Zircon*. 1939: Owned by J.Marr & Son Ltd of Fleetwood. Requisitioned in August as NORTHCOATES and converted to a M/S. 1944: LOST. Sank in heavy weather whilst in tow in the Channel on 2 December.

GEORGE COUSINS	1919/19 1939/45	Displacement:	122TN
		Engines:	61HP
		Admty No:	4461
		Port Reg:	LO 66
		P.No:	WWII: FY 627

1919: L. 13 June. Built at Ayr by Ailsa and completed as a fishing vessel. Sold to mercantile and retained the same name. Acquired by the Iago ST Co. Ltd. of Fleetwood. 1939: Requisitoned in August and converted to a M/S. 1945: Returned to owners.

| GEORGE DARBY | 1918/22 | Armament: | 1 x 12-pdr |
| | | Admty No: | 3681 |

1918: L. Built at Paisley by Bow McLachlan and delivered on 21 October. 1922: Sold to Mercantile and renamed *Bulby*.

| GEORGE GREENFIELD | 1918/22 | Armament: | 1 x 12-pdr |
| | | Admty No: | 3787 |

1918: L. Built at Greenock by George Brown and completed as an Escort. Delivered on 15 October. 1922: Sold to mercantile. 1922: Renamed *Rio Mesa*.

GEORGE GREEVES	1919/19 1939/47	Displacement:	113TN
		Engines:	83HP
		Admty No:	3790
		Port Reg:	WWII: SA 6
		P.No:	WWII: FY 631

1919: L. Built at Greenock by George Brown and completed as a fishing vessel. Delivered on 12 May. Sold to mercantile and renamed *Raglan Castle*. Acquired by Consolidated Fisheries of Grimsby. 1939: Requisitioned in August as RAGLAN CASTLE and converted to a M/S. 1940: Transferred to the MF. Joined the 91st M/S Group sweeping off Tobruk, Port Said and Suez. 1947: Sold to the Ceylon Govt. in September.

| GEORGE HARRIS | 1918/19 1939/46 | Armament: | 1 x 6-pdr |
| | | Admty No: | 3854 |

1918: L. Built at S.Shields by Hepple and delivered on 12 December. 1919: Sold to mercantile and renamed *Karachi*. 1921: Renamed *Laxmi*. 1939: Hired into the RIN as LAXMI and converted to an APV. 1946: Returned to owners in June.

| GIOVANNI GUINTI | 1918/20 | Armament:
Admty No: | 1 x 4-inch
3792 |

1918: L. 31 May. Built at Ayr by Ailsa and completed as an escort. 1919: Renamed IDAHO in January. 1920: Sold to mercantile and renamed *Cymrea*.

| GRIFFITH GRIFFITH | 1918/20 | Admty No: | 3780 |

1918: L. 27 August. Built at Beverley by CWG. 1920: Sold to mercantile. 1921: Renamed *Kilindini*.

| HENRY CHEVALLIER | 1918/22 1940/45 | Displacement:
Engines:
Armament:
Admty No:
Port Reg:
P.No: | 107TN
61HP
1 x 12-pdr
3673
WWII: GY 60
WWII: FY 1765 |

1918: L. Built at Paisley by Bow McLachlan and delivered on 3 April. 1922: Sold to mercantile and renamed *Albert*. 1938: Owned by Walbro Fishing Co. of Aberdeen. Acquired by the Rhondda FCL of Grimsby and renamed *Ligny*. 1940: Requisitioned in September as LIGNY and converted to a M/S. 1945: Returned to owners.

| HENRY CORY | 1919/19 1939/46 | Displacement:
Engines:
Admty No:
Port Reg:
P.No: | 123TN
88HP
3698
H 76
WWII: Z 131 |

1919: L. Built at Falmouth by Cox & Co and completed as a fishing vessel. Delivered on 28 May and placed on the Disposal List. Sold to mercantile and renamed *Caliban*. Acquired by Brand & Curzon of Milford Haven. 1939: Requisitioned as CALIBAN in December and converted to a BDV. Subsequently purchased into the RN. Based at Grimsby. 1946: Sold to mercantile in December.

| HUGH BLACK | 1917/22 1940/44 | Displacement:
Engines:
Armament:
Admty No:
Port Reg:
P.No: | 107TN
62HP
1 x 12-pdr
3602
GY 69
WWII: FY 803 |

1917: L. 10 May. Built at Beverley by CWG and completed as a M/S. 1923: Sold to mercantile. Acquired by a Hull Company and renamed *Macbeth*. 1929: Acquired by the Diamond SF Co. Ltd. of Grimsby and renamed *Ogano*. 1940: Requisitioned in May as OGANO and converted to a M/S. 1944: Returned to owners in July. 1950: Mercantile Loss. Took the ground off Iceland and abandoned.

| ISAAC ARTHAN | 1919/21 1939/46 | Displacement:
Engines:
Admty No:
Port Reg:
P.No: | 110TN
86HP
4297
WWII: A 401
WWII: FY 688 |

1919: L. 1 May. Built at Beverley by CWG and completed as a fishing vessel. 1921: Sold to mercantile and renamed *Amber*. Acquired by Kingston STC of Hull. PR: H 359. 1934: Acquired by Ocean SFC of Hull and renamed *Ocean Harrier*. 1936: Acquired by M. Smith of Aberdeen and renamed *Loch Buie*. 1938: Owned by the Bon Accord SFC of Aberdeen. 1939: Requisitioned in August as LOCH BUIE and converted to a M/S. 1946: Returned to owners on 11 March. 1959: Arrived at Boom, Belguim, to BU.

ISAAC HEATH	1918/19 1939/45	Displacement:	109TN
		Engines:	61HP
		Armament:	1 x 12-pdr
		Admty No:	3829
		Port Reg:	WWII: FD 17
		P.No:	WWII: FY 527

1918: L. Built at S.Shields by Rennoldson and delivered on 21 August. 1919: Sold to mercantile and retained same name. Subsequently renamed *Rylston*. Acquired by Marr of Fleetwood and renamed *Teroma*. 1939: Requisitioned in August as TEROMA and converted to a M/S. 1943: 41st M/S Grp based at Grimsby. 1945: 40th M/S Grp based at Grimsby. Returned to owners in March.

JAMES BAIRD	1918/18 1939/46	Displacement:	110TN
		Engines:	85HP = 9 kts
		Admty No:	4414
		Port Reg:	WWII: M 39
		P.No:	WWII: FY 612

1918: Ordered. Laid Down and then cancelled. 1920: Completed by builders, CWG, as a fishing vessel and renamed *Ijuin*. Acquired by Neale & West of Cardiff. 1929: Acquired by Pettit & Youd of Milford Haven. Retained the same name. 1939: Requisitioned on 30 August as IJUIN and converted to a M/S. Commissioned on 16 November and deployed to Portland. 1940: TIH at Cowes by Whites for repair and degaussing. 1942: TIH at Southampton in January for refitting and fitting with SA gear. Completed refitting in July and returned to Portland. 1943: TIH at Southampton for refitting and rearming. Completed refitting in May and returned to Portland. 1944: Converted to a D/L and joined the 9th M/S Flot. TPI Operation Neptune, the D-Day Landings in June, as a D/L with the 9th M/S Flot operating off Juno Beach. 1945: TIH by Thornycroft, Southampton for refitting. Completed in February and employed on Channel Sweeping. Transferred to Ardrossan in May for sweeping in the Clyde. Transferred to Swansea for sweeping in the Bristol Channel. Paid Off in August and reduced to the Reserve. 1946: Returned to owners on 15 January. 1952: Renamed *Woodburn*. 1959: BU in Belgium in November.

| JAMES BOYLE | 1918/18 | Admty No: | 4414 |

1918: Ordered from CWG and subsquently cancelled.

JAMES BURGESS	1917/19 1940/45	Displacement:	113TN
		Engines:	61HP
		Admty No:	3653
		Port Reg:	WWII: SA 51
		P.No:	WWII: FY 993

1917: L. 31 August. Built at S.Shields by C.Rennoldson. Commissioned as an Escort vessel. 1919: Sold to mercantile and renamed *Beaumaris Castle*. Acquired by Consolidated Fisheries of Grimsby. 1940: Requisitioned in February as BEAUMARIS CASTLE. Converted to a M/S. 1945: Returned to owners in November.

JAMES CEPELL	1918/22 1940/45	Armament:	1 x 12-pdr
		Admty No:	3718
		Port Reg:	WWII: French
		P.No;	WWII: FY 1746

1918: L. 29 March. Built at Greenock by Geo. Brown. 1922: Sold to mercantile and renamed *Clixby*. 1940: Hired from French owners in July as ANTIOCH II and converted to a M/S. 1945: Returned to owners.

JAMES CHAPMAN 1917/22 Armament: 1 x 12-pdr
             Admty No: 3649

1917: L. 8 September. Built at Greenock by Geo.Brown. 1922: Sold to mercantile and renamed *Dunsby*.

JAMES CHRISTOPHER 1918/19 1939/40 Displacement: 109TN
                 Engines: 61HP
                 Armament: 1 x 12-pdr
                 Admty No: 3715
                 Port Reg: WWII: FD 21
                 P.No: WWII: FY 714

1918: L. Built at S. Shields by J.P. Rennoldson and delivered on 27 March. 1919: Sold to mercantile and retained the same name. Acquired by Skomer SSC of Cardiff. PR: LO 248. Subsequently renamed *Marsona*. Acquired by J.Marr & Son of Fleetwood. 1939: Requisitioned in October as MARSONA and converted to a M/S. 1940: LOST. Sunk by a mine off Cromarty on 4 August.

JAMES COILE 1918/18 Admty No: 4454

1918: Ordered from Geo.Brown and subsequently cancelled.

JAMES CONNER 1917/22 Armament: 1 x 12-pdr
            Admty No: 3700

1917: L. 19 July. Built at Middlesborough by Harkess. 1920: Renamed WAVENEY in September. 1922: Sold to Spanish Navy and renamed UAD MULUYA.

JAMES COSGROVE 1918/19 1939/46 Armament: 1 x 12-pdr
                 Admty No: 3716

1918: L. 5 March. Built at Ayr by Ailsa. 1919: Sold to mercantile and retained the same name. 1939: Requisitioned in October for the RNZN and converted to a M/S. 1944: Converted to a BGV in April. 1946: Returned to owners.

JAMES DINTON 1918/22 1939/45 Armament: 1 x 12-pdr
               Admty No: 3675
               Port Reg: WWII: M 19

1918: L. Built at Paisley by Bow McLachlan and delivered on 29 May. Fitted with Listening Hydrophones. 1922: Sold to mercantile and renamed *Scawby*. Acquired by Boston DSF & Ice Co of Boston. PR: BN 187. Acquired by Milford STC of Milford Haven and renamed *Milford Duke*. 1939: Requisitioned in August as MILFORD DUKE and converted to a BDV. 1945: Returned to owners in November.

JAMES GILL 1919/19 1939/44 Displacement: 120TN
               Engines: 89HP
               Admty No: 4217
               Port Reg: WWII: M 17
               P.No: WWII: FY 613

1919: L. 17 February. Built at S.Shields by C.Rennoldson and completed as a fishing vessel. Sold to mercantile and renamed *Pierre Francios Deswarte*. Subsequently acquired by the Milford ST Co.Ltd of Milford Haven and renamed *Milford Duchess*. 1939: Requisitioned in August as MILFORD DUCHESS and converted to a M/S. 1944: Returned to owners in December.

JAMES GREEN	1917/21	1940/46	Displacement:	107TN
			Engines:	87 HP
			Armament:	1 x 12-pdr
			Admty No:	3537
			Port Reg:	WWII: M 252
			P.No:	WWII: Z 240

1917: L. 3 October. Built at Southbank-on-Tees by Smiths Dock and completed as a M/S. 1921: Sold to mercantile and retained the same name. Subsequently acquired by Elizabeth Owens of Milford Haven and renamed E & F. 1940: Requisitioned in May as E & F and converted to a BDV. 1943: Purchased into the RN in November and renamed LAVEROCK. 1946: Sold to mercantile.

JAMES HUNNIFORD	1917/19	1939/40	Armament:	1 x 12-pdr
			Admty No:	3504
			Port Reg:	FD 363

1917: L. 24 January. Built at Southbank-on-Tees by Smiths Dock. 1919: Sold to mercantile and renamed *Cremlyn*. Subsequently acquired by The New Docks ST Co. of Fleetwood and renamed *Ethel Taylor*. 1939: Requisitioned as ETHEL TAYLOR and converted to an APV. 1940: LOST. Mined off the Tyne on 22 November.

JAMES JOHNSON	1917/21		Displacement:	107TN
			Engines:	61HP
			Armament:	1 x 12-pdr
			Admty No:	3506

1917: L 18 February. Built at Southbank-on-Tees by Smiths Dock. Completed as a M/S. 1919: Renamed THOMAS DEAS in December. 1921: Sold to mercantile and retained the same name. Acquired by Elizabeth A.H. Petit of Milford Haven. PR: M 253.

JAMES LAVENNY	1919/22		Admty No:	4215

1919: L. Built at Lowestoft by Chambers and delivered on 30 October. 1922: Sold to mercantile and renamed *Kelby*. 1939: Served as French AD 186 LA BLANCHE II in WWII.

JAMES LAY	1918/19	1939/44	Displacement:	121TN
			Engines:	61HP
			Armament:	1 x 12-pdr
			Admty No:	4222
			Port Reg:	WWII: LO 333
			P.No:	WWII: FY 667

1918: L. Built at Limehouse by Fletcher & Fearnall and delivered on 4 February. 1919: Sold to mercantile and retained the same name. Acquired by Sir William Beardmore of Glasgow. 1939: Requisitioned in September and converted to a M/S. 1940: TPI Operation Quentin/Quidnunc/Quixote on 18/19 May, the cutting of the N. Sea telephone cable between Germany and the UK. 1944: TPI Operation Neptune, the D-Day Landings in June, as a D/L attached to the 15th M/S Flot. in Force S. Returned to owners in October.

JAMES PEAKE	1917/22		Armament:	1 x 12-pdr
			Admty No:	3540

1917: L. 17 October. Built at Southbank-on-Tees by Smiths Dock. Fitted with Listening Hydrophones. 1922: Sold to mercantile and renamed *Aragonite*.

JAMES POND   1917/18   Admty No: 3515

1917: L. 21 May. Built at Southbank-on-Tees by Smiths Dock. 1918: LOST. Sunk by German Destroyers in the Dover Straits on 15 February.

JAMES ROBERTSON   1917/21 1940/45 Armament: 1 x 12-pdr
                                         Admty No: 3159
                                         Port Reg: WWII: M 243
                                         P.No: WWII: 4 174

1917: L. 6 June. Built at Southbank-on-Tees by Smiths Dock. Fitted with Listening Hydrophones. 1921: Sold to mercantile and renamed *Capstone*. Acquired by The Boston Deep Sea Fishing & Ice Co of Fleetwood. 1940: Requisitioned in June as CAPSTONE and converted to a M/S. 1945: Returned to owners in October.

JAMES SECKAR   1917/17   Admty No: 3526

1917: L. 20 July. Built at Southbank-on-Tees by Smith's Dock. LOST. Foundered in the Atlantic on 25 September. Last seen in position 46.30N 12.00W.

JAMES SIBBALD   1917/19 1939/46 Admty No: 3525
                                         Port Reg: LO 76
                                         P.No: FY 1566

1917: L. 20 July. Built at Southbank -on-Tees by Smiths Dock. Employed as an Escort vessel. 1919: Sold to mercantile and renamed *Kirkland*. Subsequently acquired by Thomas Jenkerson AO of Milford Haven and renamed *Our Bairns*. 1939: Requisitioned in December as OUR BAIRNS and converted to a M/S. 1944: Converted to an Esso in January. 1945: Employed on Target Towing. 1946: Returned to owners in July.

JOHN AIKENHEAD   1918/19 1939/40 Displacement: 290TG   127TN
                                         Engines: 86HP = 10.5 kts
                                         Admty No: 4292
                                         Port Reg: WWII: H 322

1918: L. 19 December. Built at Beverley by CWG and completed as a fishing vessel. 1919: Sold to mercantile. Acquired by J.Johnson of Scarborough and renamed *Polly Johnson*. PR: SH 171. 1922: Acquired by Massey of Hull. PR: H 322. 1939: Requisitioned in August as POLLY JOHNSON and converted to a M/S. 1940: TPI Operation Dynamo, the evacuation of Dunkirk in May. LOST. Sunk by air attack off Dunkirk on 29 May.

JOHN ANDERSON   1918/22 1940/45 Displacement: 260TG   112TN
                                         Engines: 62HP = 10.5 kts
                                         Armament: 1 x 12-pdr
                                         Admty No: 3610
                                         Port Reg: WWII: A 460
                                         P.No;   WWII: FY 597

1917: Purchased whilst on the stocks. 1918: L. 20 September. Built at Beverley by CWG. 1919: Renamed CHARLES DORAN in December. 1922: Sold to mercantile and retained the same name. Acquired by the St. Andrew's SF Co. of Hull. PR: H 760. 1937: Acquired by AM.Morrice of Aberdeen. 1940: Re-acquired by the St.Andrews SFC of Aberdeen. Requisitioned in February as CHARLES DORAN and converted to a M/S. Based at Gt. Yarmouth for sweeping in the N.Sea between Cromer and Sheringham. 1945: Returned to owners in November. 1957: BU at Barrow by Messrs TW.Ward.

JOHN ASHLEY   1919/19   Admty No: 4293

1919: L. 18 March. Built at Beverley by CWG and completed as a fishing vessel. Sold to mercantile and renamed *Limeslade*. Acquired by Rhondda SF Co of Swansea. PR: SA 10. 1952: BU.

JOHN BAPTISH	1918/19 1939/40	Displacement:	290TG 127TN
		Engines:	61HP = 10.5 kts
		Armament:	1 x 12-pdr
		Admty No:	3596
		Port Reg:	WWII: M 275

1918: L. 29 April. Built at Beverley by CWG. 1920: Sold to mercantile. Acquired by Skomer Steam Shipping Co of London. PR: LO 234. 1921: Acquired by Brand & Curzon Ltd of London. 1938: Acquired by Milford Fishing of Milford Haven. PR: M 275. 1939: Requisitioned on 28th August and designated as a M/S but not converted. Returned to owners on 11 October. 1940: Mercantile Loss. Presumed mined S. of the Coningbeg LV in September. Lost with all hands.

JOHN BATEMAN	1918/22	Displacement:	290TG 126TN
		Engines:	480HP = 10.5 kts
		Armament:	1 x 12-pdr
		Admty No:	3599

1918: L. 29 April. Built at Beverley by CWG. 1922: Sold to mercantile and renamed *Anderby*. Acquired by Boston DSFC of Boston. PR: BN 176. 1926: Sold to Spanish Mercantile. 1936: Served in the Spanish Nationalist Navy as CANTABRICO. 1939: Returned to owners. 1964: BU.

JOHN BENSON   1918/18   Admty No: 4409

1918: Ordered from CWG and Laid Down. Subsequently cancelled. Completed by the builders as a fishing vessel. Sold to mercantile and named *Kari Solmundarson*. Acquired by Utvegsbanki Islands HF of Reykjavik, Iceland. PR: GK 153. 1932: Renamed *Kari*. 1946: Acquired by Faroe Islands mercantile and renamed *Barmur*. 1955: BU in Denmark.

JOHN BOMKWORTH	1918/22	Displacement:	290TG 126TN
		Engiunes:	480HP = 10.5 kts
		Armament:	1 x 6-pdr 1 x 7.5-inch
			Bomb Thrower (A/S
			Howitzer)
		Admty No:	3597

1918: L. 29 May. Built at Beverley by CWG. 1920: Renamed WEAR in September. 1922: Sold to Spanish Navy and renamed UAD RAS. 1933: Reported as Lost.

JOHN BRENNAN	1917/22 1940/45	Armament:	1 x 12-pdr
		Admty No:	3609
		Port Reg:	GY 100
		P.No: WWII:	FY 580

1917: Purchased on the stocks. L. 4 September. Built at Beverley by CWG and completed as a M/S. 1922: Sold to mercantile and renamed *Iolite*. Acquired by Kingston STC of Hull. PR: H 576. 1934: Acquired by Diamonds SF Co of Grimsby and renamed *Osako*. PR: GY100. 1940: Requisitioned in February as OSAKO and converted to a M/S. 1945: Returned to owners in December. 1956: Mercantile Loss. Sank on 21 April off the Faroes after springing a leak in the fish room.

JOHN BRICE	1917/23 1940/46	Displacement:	260TG 112TN
		Engines:	480IHP = 10.5 kts
		Armament:	1 x 12-pdr
		Admty No:	3608
		Port Reg:	WWII: French
		P.No:	WWII: Z.247

1917: Purchased into the RN whilst on the stocks. L. 22 August. Built at Beverley by CWG. 1920: Renamed DERWENT in September. 1923: Sold to Belgian mercantile and renamed *Beauline Vernueil*. Acquired by R. Maubaillarca & Cie. 1939: Acquired by FE Menu of La Rochelle, France. Requisitioned by the French Navy as M/S No.AD 100. 1940: Seized at Plymouth in Operation Grab on 3 July and coverted to a BGV. 1946: Returned to France on 30 March. 1952: BU at Grays by TW. Ward.

| JOHN BRITTON | 1919/19 | Admty No: | 4427 |

1919: L. 2 May. Built at Aberdeen by Hall Russell and completed as a fishing vessel. Sold to mercantile and renamed *Elsie Jessop*. Acquired by R.W.Crawford of Scarborough. PR: SH 98.

JOHN BROOKER	1917/21 1940/46	Displacement:	249TG 102TN
		Engines:	480IHP = 10.5 kts
		Armament:	1 x 12-pdr
		Admty No:	3605
		Port Reg:	WWII: H 219
		P.No:	WWII: FY 1835

1916: Ordered by Kingston STC of Hull. 1917: Purchased into the RN whilst on the stocks. L. 9 June. Built at Beverley by CWG. 1921: Sold to mercantile and renamed *Obsidian*. Acquired by the original owners. PR: H 333. 1934: Acquired by Ocean SFC of Hull. 1935: Acquired by Lander & Paterson of Aberdeen. PR: A 301. 1939: Acquired by Loch FCL of Hull and renamed *Loch Park*. PR: H 219. 1940: Requisitioned in June as LOCH PARK and converted to an APV. 1941: Converted to a M/S. 1945: Returned to owners in April. 1946: Acquired by Anglo SFC of Grimsby. PR: GY 259. 1962: BU at Copenhagen, Denmark.

JOHN BULLOCK	1917/21 1940/41	Displacement:	106TN
		Engines:	87HP
		Armament:	1 x 12-pdr
		Admty No:	3651
		Port Reg:	WWII: H 60

1917: L. 9 July. Built at S.Shields by C.Rennoldson. 1921: Sold to mercantile and retained the same name. Subsequently renamed *Filiep Coenen*. Acquired by St.Andrews SFC of Hull and renamed *Flying Admiral*. PR: H 60. 1940: Requisitoned on 30 May as FLYING ADMIRAL and converted to an APV. 1941: Returned to owners on 31 December.

JOHN BURLINGHAM	1917/20 1940/45	Displacement:	105TN
		Engines:	80NHP = 10.5 kts
		Armament:	1 x 12-pdr; 1 x 7.5-inch Bomb Thrower (A/S Howitzer)
		Admty No:	3600
		Port Reg:	WWII: GY 829
		P.No:	WWII: FY 1794

1916: Ordered by Sleight of Grimsby as *Reheara*. 1917: Purchased into the RN whilst on the stocks. L. 21 April. Built at Beverley by CWG and completed as a M/S. 1920: Sold to mercantile and renamed *Rehearo*. Acquired by the original owners. PR: GY 829. 1940: Requisitioned in September as REHEARO and converted to a M/S. 1945: Returned to owners in December. 1961: BU in Holland.

JOHN CAMPBELL	1917/21	Armament:	1 x 12-pdr
		Admty No:	3695

1917: L. 1 November. Built at Greenock by George Brown. 1919: Renamed GEORGE DIXON in December. 1921: Sold to mercantile and renamed *Lushby*.

JOHN CASEWELL	1917/20	Armament:	1 x 12-pdr 1 x 3.5-inch Bomb Thrower (A/S Howitzer)
		Admty No:	3713

1917: L. 3 October. Built at Troon by Ailsa SB and completed as a M/S. 1920: Sold to mercantile and retained the same name. 1921: Mercantile Loss.

JOHN CATTLING	1918/20 1939/45	Displacement:	113TN
		Engines:	61HP
		Armament:	1 x 12-pdr 1 x 3.5-inch Bomb Thrower (A/S Howitzer)
		Admty No:	3676
		Port Reg:	WWII: LO 364
		P.No:	WWII: FY 536

1918: L. Built at Paisley by Bow McLaughlan and delivered on 29 April. Fitted with Listening Hydrophones. 1920: Sold to mercantile and retained the same name. Acquired by Iago ST Co of Milford Haven. 1939: Requisitioned in August and converted to a M/S. 1943: 51st M/S Grp based at Grimsby. 1945: Returned to owners in July.

JOHN CHATWAY	1918/22	Admty No:	4447

1918: Ordered from George Brown and subsquently cancelled.

JOHN CHIVERS	1917/20	Armament:	1 x 12-pdr
		Admty No:	3671

1917: L. 17 December. Built at Paisley by Bow McLachlan and completed as a M/S. 1920: Renamed ERNE in September. 1922: Sold to Spanish Navy and renamed UAD MARTIN.

JOHN CHURCH	1917/20	Admty No:	3658

1917: L. 16 October. Built at Paisley by Bow McLachlan. Employed as an Escort. 1920: Sold to mercantile and retained the same name. Subsequently renamed *Antares*.

JOHN CLAVELL	1920/22	Admty No:	4480

1920: L. Built at S.Shields by Hepple and completed as a fishing vessel. Delivered on 18 October. 1922: Sold to mercantile and renamed *Denis*.

JOHN COLLINS	1917/20	Armament:	1 x 12-pdr
		Admty No:	3712

1917: L. 19 November. Built at Troon by Ailsa SB. 1919: Temporary Loan to USN. Returned to RN. 1920: Sold to mercantile and renamed *Janera*.

| JOHN COOMBE | 1918/18 | Admty No: | 4453 |

1918: Ordered from George Brown and subsequently cancelled.

| JOHN COOPER | 1917/22 | Armament:
Admty No: | 1 x 12-pdr
3699 |

1917: L. 5 July. Built at Middlesborough by Harkess. 1922: Sold to mercantile and renamed *Penfret*.

| JOHN CREIGHTON | 1918/18 | Admty No: | 4449 |

1918: Ordered from George Brown and subsquently cancelled.

| JOHN DAVIES | 1918/21 | Armament:
Admty No: | 1 x 12-pdr
3682 |

1918: L. Built at Paisley by Bow McLachlan and delivered on 22 October. 1922: Sold to mercantile and renamed *Cesar de Paepe*.

| JOHN DORMOND | 1919/22 | Admty No: | 4485 |

1919: L. Built at S.Shields by JP Rennoldson and completed as a fishing vessel. Delivered on 15 October. 1922: Sold to mercantile and retained the same name. Subsequently renamed *Amethyst*.

| JOHN EVANS | 1919/20 | See under JOHN LEWIS |

| JOHN GAUNTLET | 1918/20 | Admty No: | 3779 |

1918: L. 12 July. Built at Beverley by CWG. 1920: Sold to mercantile and retained the same name. 1922: Mercantile Loss.

| JOHN GEOGHAN | 1918/22 1940/46 | Armament:
Admty No:
Port Reg:
P.No: | 1 x 12-pdr
3749
WWII: French
WWII: FY 1919 |

1918: L. 19 October. Built at Troon by Ailsa SB. 1922: Sold to mercantile and retained the same name. Subsequently acquired by French owners and renamed *Congre*. 1940: Hired from French owners as CONGRE and converted to a M/S. 1946: Returned to owners in January.

| JOHN GILLMAN | 1917/20 | Displacement:
Engines:
Armament:

Admty No: | 106TN
78HP
1 x 12-pdr; 1 x 7.5-inch Bomb Thrower (A/S Howitzer)
3502 |

1917: L. 9 January. Built at Southbank-on-Tees by Smith's Dock. 1920: Sold to mercantile and retained the same name. Acquired by N.E.Fisheries Ltd of Aberdeen. Port Reg: A 230.

| JOHN GRAHAM | 1918/21 1939/45 | Displacement:
Engines:
Admty No:
Port Reg:
P.No: | 290TG   108TN
480IHP = 10.5 kts
3778
WWII: H 393
WWII: FY 1771 |

1918: L. 27 July. Built at Beverley by CWG. 1919: Temporary Loan to the USN from May. Returned to the RN in August. 1921: Sold to mercantile and renamed *Ruby*. Acquired by Kingston STC of Hull. PR: H 393. 1935: Acquired by City SFC of Hull. Renamed *Eastcoates* in November. 1939: Requisitioned in August as EASTCOATES and converted to a M/S. Returned to owners in October. 1940: Re-requisitioned in August. Converted to a M/S. Same P.No. 1945: Returned to owners in April. 1955: BU at Troon.

JOHN GREGORY	1919/19	Admty No:	3789

1919: L. Built at Greenock by George Brown and completed as a fishing vessel. Sold to mercantile and renamed *Inverdee*. Acquired by Onward STL of Fleetwood. PR: A 176. 1939: French AD 57 NADINE in WWII.

JOHN GULIPSTER	1918/19 1939/45	Displacement:	290TG 127TN
		Engines:	480IHP = 10.5 kts
		Admty No:	3782
		Port Reg:	GN 39
		P.No:	FY 633

1918: L. 29 September. Built at Beverley by CWG and completed as a fishing vessel. 1919: Sold to mercantile and renamed *Betty Johnson*. Acquired by J.Johnson of Scarborough. PR: SH 50. 1922: Acquired by Prince Fletcher Trs of Fleetwood. PR: FD 168. 1928: Acquired by Melling Trs of Fleetwood and renamed *Annie Melling*. 1932: Acquired by Farrows SFC of Hull and renamed *Andrew Marvel*. PR: H 399. 1933: Acquired by Hudson Bros of Hull. 1935: Acquired by Thomas Devlin of Leith and renamed *Comitatus*. PR: GN 39. 1939: Requisitioned in October as COMITATUS and converted to a M/S. 1945: Returned to owners in October. 1956: BU at Ghent, Belgium.

JOHN KIDD	1917/20 1940/46	Displacement:	129TN
		Engines:	87HP
		Armament:	1 x 12-pdr
		Admty No:	3508

JOHN KIDD   **(MPL)**

			Port Reg:	WWII: SA 39
			P.No:	WWII: FY 1822

1917: L. 20 February. Built at Southbank-on-Tees by Smith's Dock and completed as a M/S. 1920: Sold to mercantile on 11 May and renamed *Rotherslade*. Acquired by the Rhondda Fishing Co of Swansea. 1940: Requisitioned in June as ROTHERSLADE and converted to a M/S. 1945: 113th M/S Grp based at Grimsby. 1946: Returned to owners in May.

JOHN LEWIS	1919/21	1939/45	Displacement:	113TN
			Engines:	87HP
			Admty No:	4219
			Port Reg:	WWII: LO 55
			P.No:	WWII: FY 538

1919: L. Built at S.Shields by C.Rennoldson and completed as a fishing vessel. Renamed JOHN EVANS in January and delivered on 30 March. 1921: Sold to mercantile and renamed *Harry Melling*. Acquired by The Iago ST Co.Ltd of Fleetwood. 1939: Requisitioned in August as HARRY MELLING and converted to a M/S. 1945: Returned to owners in July.

JOHN LYONS	1917/22		Armament:	1 x 12-pdr 1 x 3.5-inch Bomb Thrower (A/S Howitzer)
			Admty No:	3511

1917: L. 23 March. Built at Southbank-on-Tees by Smith's Dock. Fitted with Listening Hydrophones. 1922: Sold to French mercantile and renamed *Les Illates*.

JOHN POLLARD	1917/20	1940/46	Displacement:	107TN
			Engines:	61 HP
			Armament:	1 x 12-pdr 1 x 7.5-inch Bomb Thrower (A/S Howitzer)
			Admty No:	3516
			Port Reg:	WWII: SA 77
			P.No:	WWII: FY 671

1917: L. 21 May. Built at Southbank-on-Tees by Smith's Dock. 1920: Sold to mercantile on 4 May and renamed *Grosmont Castle*. Acquired by Consolidated Fisheries of Grimsby. 1940: Requisitioned in February as GROSMONT CASTLE and converted to a M/S. 1946: Returned to owners in February.

JOHN THORLING	1917/21	1939/46	Displacement:	107TN
			Engines:	61HP
			Armament:	1 x 12-pdr
			Admty No;	3527
			Port Reg:	WWII: GN 8
			P.No:	WWII: FY 637

1917: L. Built at Southbank-on-Tees by Smith's Dock and completed as a M/S. 1921: Sold to mercantile and renamed *River Kent*. Acquired by T.L. Davies of Leith and renamed *Concertator*. 1939: Requisitioned in August as CONCERTATOR and converted to a M/S. 1946: Returned to owners in January.

JOSEPH BARRETT	1917/19	1939/40	Displacement:	290TG 119TN
			Engines:	480IHP = 10.5K
			Armament:	1 x 12-pdr

1917: L. 2 November. Built at Beverley by CWG. 1919: Sold to mercantile and renamed *Loch Morar*. Acquired by Skomer SS Co. Acquired respectively by Brand & Curzon of London, AS.Bowlby of London, Vanessa FCL of London. Same name. 1933: Acquired by P.Fischeaux of Bordeaux and renamed *St.Barnaby*. 1934: Acquired by Boston DSFC of Fleetwood and renamed *Harry Hawke*. 1935: Acquired by Caledonian FCL of Hull and renamed *Loch Kinnord*. PR: H 204. 1939: Acquired by Trident SFC of Hull and renamed *Tilbury Ness*. 1939: Requisitioned in September as TILBURYNESS and converted to a M/S. 1940: LOST. Sunk by enemy a/c in the Thames Estuary on 1 November.

JOSEPH BUTTON	1917/19 1939/40	Displacement:	119TN
		Engines:	61HP
		Armament:	1 x 12-pdr
		Admty No:	3584
		Port Reg:	WWII: M 272

1917: L. 17 December. Built at Beverley by CWG. 1919: Sold to mercantile and retained the same name. Acquired by Brand & Curzon of Milford Haven. PR: L 241. Acquired by J.Marr & Sons of Fleetwood. 1939: Requisitioned in August and converted to a M/S. 1940: LOST. Mined off Aldeburgh, Suffolk, on 22 October.

JOSEPH CONNELL	1917/22	Armament:	1 x 12-pdr
		Admty No:	3696

1917: L. 20 December. Built at Greenock by George Brown. 1922: Sold to mercantile and renamed *Hourtin*.

JOSEPH CROWELL	1919/19	Admty No:	4448

1919: Ordered from George Brown and subsequently cancelled.

JOSEPH DOE	1918/18	Admty No:	4494

1918: Ordered from Hepple and subsequently cancelled

JOSEPH GIDDICE	1918/22	Armament:	1 x 12-pdr
		Admty No:	3786

1918: L. Built at Greenock by George Brown and delivered on 12 December. 1922: Sold to mercantile and renamed *Oseby*.

JOSEPH GORDON	1918/22	Armament:	1 x 12-pdr 1 x 3-inch Bomb Thrower (A/S Howitzer)
		Admty No:	3785

1918: L. 29 June. Built at Greenock by George Brown. Fitted with Listening Hydrophones. 1922: Sold to French mercantile and renamed *Grouin du Cou*. 1939: French GROUIN DU COU in WWII.

JOSEPH HODGKINS	1919/19	Admty No:	3855

1919: L. Built at S.Shields by Hepple and completed as a fishing vessel. Delivered on 20 June. Sold to mercantile and retained the same name. Acquired by FR Samson of London. PR: A 186. 1921: Mercantile Loss.

JOSHUA ARABIN 1919/19 1940/45 Displacement: 290TG 127TN
Engines: 86NHP = 10.5 kts
Armament: 1 x 12-pdr
Admty No: 4299
Port Reg: WWII: H 234
P.Nos: WWII: 4 129 (APV)
FY 558 (M/S)

1919: L. 1 May. Built at Beverley by CWG and completed as a fishing vessel. 1919: Sold to mercantile and renamed *River Forth*. Acquired by the Montrose FCL. PR: ME 67. 1923: Acquired by Melling Trs of Fleetwood and renamed *Lena Melling*. PR: FD 417. 1932: Acquired by Farrows SFC of Hull and renamed *De La Pole*. PR: H 395. 1933: Acquired by Hudson SFC of Hull. 1935: Acquired by H.E.Rees of Milford Haven. PR: M 195. 1939: Acquired by Henrikson & Co of Hull. PR: H 234. 1940: Requisitioned in May as DE LA POLE and converted to an APV. 1941: Converted to a M/S. 1945: Returned to owners in December. 1957: BU by TW Ward at Milford Haven.

JUBBALPORE 1919/19 RIM

1919: Ordered from Bombay Dyd and subsequently cancelled.

KENNERY 1919/19 RIM

1919: Ordered from Bombay Dyd and subsequently cancelled. Notes: Also reported to have been launched in 1919 and listed to 1932. NFI

KIDDERPORE 1918/32 RIM
Armament: 1 x 12-pdr

1919: L. Built by Bombay DY. 1932: Listed until April.

MADRAS 1919/42 RIN
P.No: T 33

1919: L. Built at Calcutta by Burn. 1941: Renamed TANJORE. 1942: LOST. Stranded off the N.W.Coast of India on 25 May.

NATHANIEL COLE (MPL)

MATTHEW BERRYMAN 1919/19 1939/45 Displacement: 122TN
                                  Engines: 91HP
                                  Admty No: 4412
                                  Port Reg: WWII: GY 1267
                                  P.No: WWII: FY 604

1918: Ordered from CWG. 1919: Cancelled. 1920: Completed at Beverley by builders as a fishing vessel. Sold to mercantile and named *Righto*. Accquired by Sleight of Grimsby. 1939: Requisitioned in September as RIGHTO and converted to a M/S. 1944: TPI Operation Neptune, the D-Day Landings as a D/L attached to the 4th M/S Flot. in Force O. Returned to owners in November. 1962: BU in Belguim.

MATTHEW CASSADY 1918/19   Admty No: 4457

1918: L. 18 December. Built at Troon by Ailsa and completed as a fishing vessel. 1919: Sold to mercantile and renamed *Inverdon*. Acquired by A.Hardie of Aberdeen. PR: A 166

MATTHEW FLYNN   1918/21 1939/45 Displacement: 108TN
                                  Engines: 61HP
                                  Armament: 1 x 12-pdr
                                  Admty No: 3745
                                  Port Reg: WWII GN 34
                                  P.No: WWII: FY 636

1918: L. 23 February. Built at S.Shields by Hepple. 1921: Sold to mercantile and renamed *Admiral Marquer*. Acquired by T.L. Devlin of Leith and renamed *Commiles*. 1939: Requisitioned in August as COMMILES and converted to a M/S. 1945: Returned to owners.

MICHAEL GING   1918/22   Armament: 1 x 12-pdr
                                  Admty No: 3784

1918: L. 11 May. Built at Greenock by George Brown. 1922: Sold to mercantile and retained the same name.

MICHAEL GRIFFITHS 1918/21 1939/45 Displacement: 127TN
                                  Engines: 480IHP = 10.5 kts
                                  Admty No: 3781
                                  Port Reg: LO 529
                                  P.No: FY 567

1918: L. 5 September. Built at Beverely by CWG. 1921: Sold to mercantile and retained the same name. Acquired by H.Leetham & Sons of Hull. PR.LO 529. 1930: Acquired by Ritchie & Davies of London. 1939: Requisitioned in August and converted to a M/S. 1944: Converted to a BDV in January. 1945: Returned to owners in January. Acquired by Clifton STL of Fleetwood. PR: FD 249. 1953: Mercantile Loss. Wrecked S of Barra Head with the loss of all 13 hands.

MICHAEL MALONEY 1917/20   Armament: 1 x 12-pdr
                                  Admty No: 3513

1917: L. 7 May. Built at Southbank-on-Tees by Smith's Dock. 1920: LOST. Stranded at Egersund, Norway, on 19 February.

MORGAN JONES   1918/19 1940/45 Displacement: 116TN
                                  Engines: 61HP
                                  Armament: 1 x 12-pdr
                                  Admty No: 3845

		Port Reg:	LO 116
		P.No:	WWII: 4.114

1918: L. Built at Limehouse by Fletcher & Fearnall. 1919: Sold to mercantile and retained the same name. Acquired by Mills SS Co of London. 1940: Requisitioned in June and converted to an APV. 1945: Returned to owners in April.

NATHANIEL COLE	1917/18	Admty No:	3507

1917: L. 20 February. Built at Stockton-on-Tees by Smith's Dock. 1918: LOST. Foundered off Buncrana, Lough Swilly.

NEIL SMITH	1917/21 1939/44	Displacement:	107TN
		Engines:	87HP
		Admty No:	3524
		Port Reg:	WWII: LO 328
		P.No:	WWII: FY.529

1917: L. 5 July. Built at Southbank-on-Tees by Smith's Dock. 1921: Sold to mercantile and retained the same name. Acquired by Pater ST Co of Milford Haven. 1939: Requisitoned in August and converted to a M/S. 1944: TPI Operation Neptune, the D-Day Landings in June, as a D/L attached to the 4th M/S Flot in Force O. Returned to owners in November.

OLIVER PICKIN	1917/22 1939/46	Displacement:	107TN
		Engines:	61HP
		Armament:	1 x 12-pdr
		Admty No:	3518
		Port Reg:	WWII: LO 81
		P.No:	WWII: FY 521 (M/S)
			Y7.9 (Esso)

1917: L. 21 May. Built at Southbank-on-Tees by Smith's Dock. 1922: Sold to mercantile and renamed *Fermo*. Acquired by WJ.Allen of Grimsby & W.Lambert of Cleethorpes. Acquired by T.Jenkerson of Milford Haven AO and renamed *Damito*. 1939: Requisitioned as DAMITO in August and converted to a M/S. 1943: Converted to an Esso. 1946: Returned to owners in January.

PATRICK BOWE	1918/22	Displacement:	119TN
		Engines:	480IHP = 10.5 kts
		Armament:	1 x 12-pdr
		Admty No:	3591

1918: L 17 January. Built at Beverley by CWG. Fitted with Listening Hydrophones. 1920: Renamed TEST in September. 1922: Sold to Spanish navy and renamed UAD TARGA. 1931: Spanish Navy Loss. Wrecked in Arosa Bay in September.

PATRICK CULLEN	1919/19	Admty No:	4460

1919: L. 31 March. Built at Troon by Ailsa SB and completed as a fishing vessel. Sold to mercantile and renamed *Briarlyn*. Acquired by Brooklyn FCL of Fleetwood. PR: FD 220.

PATRICK DONOVAN	1920/20	Admty No:	4248

1920: L. 16 April. Built at Selby by Cochrane and completed as a fishing vessel. Sold to mercantile and renamed *Kelvin*. Acquired by F & T Ross of Hull. PR: H 85.

PETER BLUMBERRY   1917/21   Displacement: 290TG   119TN
                                        Engines: 480IHP = 10.5 kts
                                        Admty No: 3583

1917: L. 18 October. Built at Beverley by CWG and completed as a M/S. Employed as an escort. 1921: Sold to French mercantile and renamed *Ingouville*. 1926: Renamed *St.Pierre-St.Paul*. 1930: Acquired by JH.Dove of Milford Haven and renamed *Stanfrel*. 1933: Mercantile Loss. Foundered after being abandoned off Dingle in May.

PETER CAREY   1919/20 1939/45 Displacement: 113TN
                                  Engines: 83HP
                                  Admty No: 4445
                                  Port Reg: LO 126
                                  P.No: WWII: FY 537

1919: L. 25 June. Built at Greenock by George Brown and completed as a fishing vessel. 1920: Sold to mercantile and renamed *Cicely Blanche*. Acquired by Victory STC of Fleetwood. PR: FD 350. Acquired by Iago ST Co of Milford Haven and reverted to original name. 1939: Requisitioned in August and converted to a M/S. 1945: Returned to owners in September.

PETER HALL   1918/21 1940/45 Armament: 1 x 12-pdr
                                  Admty No: 3795
                                  Port Reg: WWII: Belgian
                                  P.No: WWII: 4.118

1918: L. 6 November. Built at Troon by Ailsa SB. 1921: Sold to mercantile and renamed *Transport Union*. Acquired by Belgian owners and renamed *Alvis*. 1940: Hired from Belgian owners in June as ALVIS and converted to a M/S. 1945: Returned to Belgium in March.

PETER KILLIN   1919/19 1939/45 Displacement: 109TN
                                  Engines: 87HP
                                  Admty No: 4207
                                  Port Reg: WWII: H 509
                                  P.No: WWII: FY 622

1919: L. Built at Aberdeen by Duthie and completed as a fishing vessel. Delivered on 3 March. Sold to mercantile and retained the same name. Acquired by A. Hardie of Aberdeen. PR: A 149. Subsequently renamed *Craonne Beauriex*. Acquired by Hudson SF Co of Hull and renamed *Sir John Lister*. 1939: Requisitioned in September as SIR JOHN LISTER and converted to a M/S. 1945: Returned to owners in August.

PETER LOVITT   1917/21   Displacement: 107TN
                                     Engines: 61HP
                                     Armament: 1 x 12-pdr
                                     Admty No: 3509

1917: L. 9 March. Built at Southbank-on-Tees by Smith's Dock. 1921: Sold to mercantile and renamed *Lowdock*. Acquired by The Shields Eng. & DD Co of N.Shields. PR: SN 14.

PHILLIP GODBY   1918/19   Displacement: 290TG   126TN
                                     Engines: 480IHP = 10.5 kts
                                     Admty No: 3783

1918: L. 24 September. Built at Beverley by CWG and completed as a fishing vessel. 1919: Sold to mercantile and retained the same name. Acquired by H.Smethurst of Grimsby. PR: GY 309. 1923: Acquired by Godby SFC of Fleetwood. PR: FD 407. 1924:

Renamed *Cisnell*. 1926: Renamed *Togimo*. PR: LO 122. 1940: Mercantile Loss. Captured by U-37 and sunk by gunfire off West Coast of Ireland on 11 February.

PHINEAS BEARD	1917/19 1939/41	Displacement:	290TG 114TN
		Engines:	61HP = 10.5 kts
		Armament:	1 x 12-pdr
		Port Reg:	WWII: M 271

1917: L. 17 November. Built at Beverley by CWG. 1919: Sold to mercantile and retained the same name. Acquired by Brand & Curzon Ltd. of Milford Haven. PR: LO 283. 1938: Acquired by Milford Fishing Ltd of Milford Haven. 1939: Requisitioned in August and converted to a M/S. 1941: LOST. Sunk in an a/c attack off the E.Coast of Scotland on 8 December.

RICHARD BACON	1917/21 1939/45	Displacement:	281TG 109TN
		Engines:	480IHP = 10.5 kts
		Armament:	1 x 12-pdr
		Admty No:	3587
		Port Reg:	WWII: GN 6
		P.No:	WWII: FY 634

1917: L. Built at Beverely by CWG. 1921: Sold to mercantile and renamed *Hagnaby*. Acquired by Boston DSFC of Fleetwood. PR: BN 179. 1926: Acquired by French owners and renamed *Proffesseur Bergonie*. 1930: Re-acquired by Boston DSFC of Fleetwood and renamed *Daily Chronicle*. PR: FD 69. 1934: Acquired by Devlin of Granton and renamed *Commodator*. 1939: Requisitioned as COMMODATOR and converted to a M/S. 1943: Acquired by Mrs.Breen of Granton. 1945: Returned to owner. Acquired by Grimsby Merchants Amalg. FCL. PR: GY 57. 1948: Renamed *Lynandi*. 1954: BU at Milford Haven.

RICHARD BAGLEY	1917/22 1939/45	Displacement:	249TG 109TN
		Engines:	62HP = 10.5K
		Armament:	1 x 12-pdr
		Admty No:	3604
		Port Reg:	WWII: GY 342
		P.No:	WWII: FY 796

1917: Originally ordered by Kingston STL and purchased into the RN whilst on the stocks. L. 9 June. Built at Beverely by CWG. 1922: Sold to mercantile and renamed *Malcolite*. Acquired by Kingston STC of Hull. PR: H 574. 1931: Acquired by W.Beeley of Grimsby. PR: GY 342. Acquired by Princess SFC of Grimsby. 1939: Requisitioned in August as MALCOLITE and converted to a M/S. 1945: Returned to owners in September. 1950: Renamed *Strathallen*. PR: A 650. 1954: BU at Ghent, Belgium

| RICHARD BAIVE | 1919/19 | See under RICHARD BANE |

RICHARD BANE	1919/19 1939/46	Displacement:	110TN
		Engines:	85HP
		Admty No:	3649
		P.No:	WWII: FY 528

1918: Ordered from CWG and Laid Down. 1919: Cancelled. Completed by the builders as a fishing vessel. Sold to mercantile and renamed *Kyoto*. Acquired by Hakin TCL of Milford Haven. PR: M 5. 1938: Acquired by Westward Trs of Milford Haven and renamed *Rudilais*. 1939: Requisitioned in September as RUDILAIS and converted to a M/S. 1946: Returned to owners in January. 1948: Renamed *Wyre Corsair*. PR: FD 287. 1956: BU at Antwerp. Note: Sometimes listed as RICHARD BAIVE.

RICHARD CROFTS   1918/20 1939/45 Displacement: 290TG   127TN
                                    Engines: 480IHP = 10.5 kts
                                    Armament: 1 x 12-pdr
                                    Admty No: 3720
                                    Port Reg: LO 365
                                    P.No: WWII: FY 530

1918: L. 13 June. Built at Beverley by CWG. 1920: Sold to mercantile and retained the
same name. Acquired by the Iago ST Co of Milford Haven. 1939: Requisitioned in August
and converted to a M/S. 1940: Returned to owners. 1941: Re-requisitioned in July and
converted to a M/S. 1945: Returned to owners in August. 1953: Mercantile Loss.
Foundered off Coll in the Inner Hebrides on 20 February. Skipper and seven men lost.

RICHARD CUNDY   1919/20 1939/40 Displacement: 122TN
                                    Engines: 61HP
                                    Admty No: 4462
                                    Port Reg: FD 418

1919: L 12 August. Built at Ayr by Ailsa SB and completed as a fishing vessel. 1920: Sold
to mercantile and renamed *River Clyde*. Acquired by River SF Co of Fleetwood. 1939:
Requisitioned in August as RIVER CLYDE and converted to a M/S. 1940: LOST. Mined
off Aldeburgh, Suffolk, on 5 August.

RICHARD ROBERTS   1917/20   Armament: 1 x 12-pdr
                                       Admty No: 3520

1917: L. 6 June. Built at Southbank-on-Tees by Smith's Dock and completed as a M/S
Employed on Escort Duties. 1920: Sold to mercantile on 11 May and retained the same
name. 1922: Mercantile Loss.

ROBERT BETSON   1917/19 1940/41 Displacement: 266TG   105TN
                                    Engines: 80HP = 10.5 kts
                                    Armament: WWII: 1 x 3-pdr
                                    Port Reg: WWII: GY 852

1917: Originally ordered by Sleight of Grimsby as *Remillo* and purchased into the RN
whilst on the stocks. L. 21 April. Built at Beverley by CWG. 1919: Sold to mercantile and
renamed *Remillo* - the original name. Acquired by Sleight of Grimsby. PR: GY 852. 1940:
Requisitioned in April as REMILLO and converted to a D/L. Converted to an APV in
September. Based at Grimsby. 1941: LOST. Mined off the Humber on 27 February.

ROBERT BOWEN   1918/19 1939/40 Displacement: 290TG   127TN
                                    Engines: 480IHP = 10.5 kts
                                    Port Reg: WWII: LO 254

1918: L 14 March. Built at Beverley by CWG. 1919: Sold to mercantile and retained the
same name. Acquired by Britannic TCL of London. PR: LO 254. 1939: Acquired by
J.Marr of Fleetwood. Requisitioned in August and converted to a M/S. M/S Group Leader
ICW FORT ROYAL, OHM and THOMAS ALTOFT, based at Aberdeen for sweeping
duties off the East Scottish coast. 1940: LOST. The Group was sweeping approx. 20
miles N.E. of Aberdeen on 9 February when they were attacked by two Heinkel He111s.
On the first pass she was struck amidships by a bomb intended for the FORT ROYAL
and disintegrated with the loss of all hands.

ROBERT CLOUGHTON   1917/46   Armament: WWII: 1 x 3-inch
                                       P. No: WWII: Z 30

1917: L. Built at Paisley by Bow McLachlan. 1919: Employed on ferry service. 1922:
Paid Off and Reduced to the Reserve. 1933: Brought forward and converted to a BDV.

Renamed CORONET. 1946: Sold to mercantile in April. 1953: BU at Northam.

ROBERT DAVIDSON   1917/19

1917: L. 30 November. Built at South Shields by C.Rennoldson. 1919: Sold to mercantile and renamed *Augustine Isabelle*.

SALSETTE   1918/21   RIM

1919: L. Built at Bombay by the Bombay Dyd. Composite Built. 1921: Transferred to the Canadian Dept of Marine & Fisheries and converted to a Lightship.

SAMUEL DAWSON   1919/21   Admty No: 4486

1919: L. Built at South Shields by J.P.Rennoldson. 1921: Completed as a fishing vessel and delivered on 5 February. Sold to mercantile and retained the same name. Acquired by MW.Howell of Milford Haven. PR: M 255. Subsequently renamed *San Juan*.

SAMUEL DRAKE	1918/22 1940/45	Displacement:	108TN
		Engines:	61
		Armament:	1 x 12-pdr
		Admty No:	3683
		Port Reg:	WWII: H 5
		P.No:	WWII: 4 140

1918: L. Built at Paisley by Bow McLachlan. 1922: Sold to mercantile and renamed *Rhodolite*. Acquired by Marr of Fleetwood and renamed *Southcoates*. 1940: Requisitioned in June as SOUTHCOATES and converted to an APV. 1945: Returned to owners in November.

SAMUEL GREEN	1919/19 1939/45	Displacement:	383T (WWII TRV)
		Admty No:	3791
		P.No:	WWII: 4 64

1919: L. 30 April. Built at Greenock by George Brown and completed as a fishing vessel. Sold to a private owner, converted to a Yacht and renamed *Ocean Rover*. 1939: Purchased into the RN in November as Yt. OCEAN ROVER and converted to a TRV. 1943: Converted to a Calibrating Yt. 1945: Paid Off in August and Laid Up. Placed on the Sale List.

SAMUEL SPENCER	1917/21	Armament:	1 x 12-pdr 1 x 7.5-inch Bomb Thrower (A/S Howitzer)
		Admty No:	3535

1917: L. 17 September. Built at Southbank-on-Tees by Smith's Dock. 1921: Sold to mercantile and renamed *Flash*.

SEALDAH	1919/32	RIM	
		Armament:	1 x 12-pdr

1919: L. Built in India by Bombay Dyd. 1932: Stricken in April.

SIAM DUFFY	1918/21 1940/40	Armament:	1 x 12-pdr
		Admty No:	3684
		Port Reg:	WWII:
		P.No:	WWII:

1918: L. Built at Paisley by Bow McLachlan and delivered on 27 November. 1919: Temporary Loan to the USN. 1921: Returned to the RN and placed on the Disposal List. Sold to mercantile and renamed *Edouard Anseele*. 1940: Hired in February as FONTENOY. LOST. Sunk by enemy a/c off Lowestoft on 19 November.

THOMAS ADNEY	1919/19	Admty No:	4295

1919: L. on 2 April. Built at Beverley by CWG and completed on 6 November. Sold to mercantile and renamed *Lindsay*. Acquired by the Boston DSFC of Boston, Lincs. PR: BN.150. 1920: Mercantile Loss. Sailed from Boston on 3 September and not seen or heard from again. Posted missing with all hands on 8 September.

THOMAS ALEXANDER	1919/20 1939/46	Admty No:	4404
		Port Reg:	WWII: A 416
		P.No:	WWII: FY 690

1919: L. on 18 July. Built at Beverley by CWG. 1920: Completed as a fishing vessel on 4 June. Sold to mercantile. Acquired by Remy & Huret of Boulogne and renamed *Etoile Polaire III*. 1930: Acquired by Boston DSFC and renamed *Daily Express*. Port Reg: FD.68. 1933: Acquired by Hellyer Bros. of Hull and renamed *Turcoman*. Port Reg: H.523. 1939: Requisitioned in August as BEN DEARG and converted to a M/S. 1942: Acquired by Marr of Fleetwood. Port Reg: FD.286. 1946: Returned to owners in June. 1949: Acquired by Ango Australian FC of Port Albany, Australia. 1953: Acquired by the RAN and expended as a target.

THOMAS ALLEN	1919/20 1939/45	Admty No:	4403
		Port Reg:	WWII: M 224
		P.No:	WWII: FY 614

1919: Launched. Built at Beverley by CWG. 1920: Completed as a fishing vessel on 17 March. Sold to mercantile and acquired by Soc. Anon Armement Ostendais of Ostend and renamed *Theophile Massart*. 1933: Acquired by Hellyer Bros. of Hull and renamed *Bengali*. PR: H.533. 1936: Acquired by Milford ST Co of Milford Haven and renamed *Milford Prince*. 1939: Requisitioned in August as MILFORD PRINCE and converted to a M/S. 1944: Converted to a D/L in April and TPI Operation Neptune, the D-Day Landings in June as a D/L attached to the 6th M/S Flot. 1945: Returned to owners in December. 1951: Renamed *Philippian*, Port Reg: GY.164. 1960: BU at Gateshead.

THOMAS ALTOFT	1919/20 1939/46	Admty No:	4300
		Port Reg:	WWII: H 132
		P.No:	WWII: FY 552

1919: L. on 2 June. Built at Beverley by CWG. 1920: Completed as a fishing vessel on 1 July. Sold to mercantile, acquired by Iago STL of London and retained the same name. Port Reg: H.132. 1922: Acquired by Albion SFC of Hull. 1939: Acquired by Mills Steam Ship Co. of Hull. Requisitioned in August and converted to a M/S. ICW FORT ROYAL, OHM, and ROBERT BOWEN, formed the 41st M/S Flot. based at Aberdeen for sweeping off NE Scotland. 1940: Sweeping 20 miles NE of Aberdeen on 9 February when they were attacked by 2 x Heinkel IIIs. She escaped serious damage but two of the Group were sunk. 1942: Acquired by Marr & Sons of Fleetwood. 1946: Returned to owners in April. 1947: Mercantile Loss. Wrecked on rocks off Glas Island, Harris, on 8 November. No loss of life.

THOMAS BARTLETT	1918/20 1939/40	Armament:	1 x 6-pdr
		Admty No:	3598
		Port Reg:	WWII: LO 373
		P.No:	WWII: FY 553

1918: L. on 29 May. Built at Beverley by CWG and completed in August. 1920: Sold to mercantile and retained the same name. Acquired by Brand & Curzon of London and based at Milford Haven. Port Reg: LO 373. 1938: Acquired by Milford Fishing Ltd., and renamed *Hordern*. 1939: Requisitioned in November as THOMAS BARTLETT and converted to a M/S. 1940: LOST. Sunk by a "friendly" British mine off Calais on 28 May.

THOMAS BOOTH	1918/20 1939/39	Armament:	WWI: 1 x 12-pdr
			WWII: None
		Admty No:	3592
		Port Reg:	WWII: M 274

1918: L. on 15 August. Built at Beverley by CWG. Completed as a M/S on 6 June. Fitted with Listening Hydrophones. 1920: Sold to mercantile, acquired by Skomer Steam Shipping of London. Port Reg: LO 277. 1923: Acquired by Brand & Curzon of Milford Haven. 1938: Acquired by Milford Fishing of Milford Haven. Port Reg: M 274. 1939: Requisitioned in August and designated as a M/S. Returned to owners in October. 1955: BU at Milford Haven.

THOMAS BOUDIGE	1919/21 1939/45	Admty No:	4406
		Port Reg:	WWII: H 340
		P.No:	WWII: FY 542

1919: L. on 15 August. Built at Beverley by CWG. Completed on 17 August as a fishing vessel. 1921: Sold to mercantile, acquired by Kingston STC of Hull and renamed *Jade*. Port Reg: H 340. 1934: Acquired by the Trident SFC of Hull and renamed *Darnett Ness*. 1939: Requisitioned in August as DARNETT NESS and converted to a M/S. 1944: Acquired by Marr of Fleetwood. 1945: Returned to owners in September. 1956: BU at Dublin.

THOMAS CHAMBERS	1917/22 1940/46	Armament:	WWI: 1 x 12-pdr, 1 x 3.5-inch Bomb Thrower (A/S Howitzer)
			WWII: 1 x 12-pdr, 1 x MG.
		Admty No:	3670
		Port Reg:	WWII: M 79
		P.No:	WWII: 4 170

1917: L. on 1 December. Built at Paisley by Bow McLachlan and completed as a M/S. 1922: Sold to mercantile and renamed *Prosper*. Acquired by Yolland Bros. of Milford Haven and renamed *Lorraine*. 1940: Requisitioned in June as LORRAINE and converted to an APV. 1941: Converted to a M/S in February. 1946: Returned to owners in January.

THOMAS CONNOLLY	1917/19 1939/40	Armament:	1 x 12-pdr
		Admty No:	3589
		Port Reg:	WWII: M 270

1917: L. on 29 November. Built at Beverley by CWG. 1918: Completed as a M/S on 10 April. 1919: Sold to mercantile, acquired by Brand & Curzon of Milford Haven and retained the same name. 1938: Acquired by Milford Fishing Co of Milford Haven. Port Reg: M 270. 1939: Requisiitoned in November and converted to a BDV. Based at Sheerness. 1940: LOST. Mined off Sheerness on 17 December.

THOMAS CROFTON	1917/20 1939/46	Armament:	1 x 12-pdr
		Admty No:	3661
		Port Reg:	WWII: M 28
		P.No:	WWII: Z 135

1917: L. on 18 June. Built at Paisley by Bow McLachlan. Fitted with Listening Hydrophones. 1920: Sold to mercantile and retained the same name. Acquired by W.W. Howell of Milford Haven and renamed *Gwmaho*. 1939: Requisitioned in November as GWMAHO and converted to a BDV. 1946: Returned to owners in January.

| THOMAS DANIELS | 1918/21 | Armament: | 1 x 12-pdr, 1 x 3.5-inch Bomb Thrower (A/S Howitzer) |
| | | Admty No: | 3680 |

1918: Launched. Built at Paisley by Bow McLachlan. Fitted with Listening Hydrophones. 1921: Sold to mercantile and renamed *Jan Volders*.

THOMAS DOWDING	1917/22 1939/45	Armament:	1 x 12-pdr
		Admty No:	3742
		Port Reg:	WWII: A 422
		P.No:	WWII: FY 1681

1917: L. on 16 November. Built at South Shields by C. Rennoldson. 1922: Sold to mercantile and renamed *Lenato*. Acquired by Pegasus TC of Fleetwood and renamed *Ben Bheula*. 1939: Requisitioned as BEN BHEULA in August and converted to a M/S. 1945: Returned to owners in October.

THOMAS GOBLE	1917/21 1940/45	Armament:	1 x 12-pdr
		Admty No:	3539
		Port Reg:	WWII: M 244
		P.No:	WWII: FY 550

1917: Launched on 17 October. Built at Middlesborough by Smiths Dock. 1921: Sold to mercantile, acquired by the Boston DSF & Ice Co. of Fleetwood and renamed *Cotsmuir*. 1940: Requisitioned in February as COTSMUIR and converted to a M/S. 1945: Returned to owners in November.

| THOMAS GREEN | 1919/20 1939/41 | Admty No: | 4218 |
| | | Port Reg: | WWII: SA 92 |

1919: L. on 28 May. Built at South Shields by C. Rennoldson and completed as a fishing vessel. 1920: Sold to mercantile, acquired by Harley & Miller of Liverpol and renamed *Ebor Elect*. Port Reg: MH 112. Acquired by Consolidated Fisheries of Grimsby and renamed *Caerphilly Castle*. 1939: Requisitioned in August as CAERPHILLY CASTLE and converted to a M/S. Purchased into the RN. 1940: Sold to mercantile in January to return to the fishing grounds. Retained the same name. 1941: Mercantile Loss. Sunk by enemy a/c on 27 January in position 52.35°N 12°W.

| THOMAS HANKINS | 1918/19 | Armament: | 1 x 12-pdr |
| | | Admty No: | 3828. |

1918: Launched. Built at S. Shields by J.P. Rennoldson and completed as a M/S. Delivered on 19 June. 1919: Sold to mercantile, acquired by Dove of Milford Haven and retained the same name. Port Reg: LO 372.

| THOMAS LAUNDRY | 1918/20 | Admty No: | 4212 |

1918: Launched. Built at S. Shields by J.P. Rennoldson and delivered on 27 November. 1919: Temporary loan to the USN for M/S operations in the N.Sea and returned to the RN in October. 1920: Sold to mercantile on 11 May and renamed *Tees Bay*.

THOMAS LAWRIE 1919/22 Admty No: 4214

1919: Launched. Built at Oulton Broad by Chambers, completed as a fishing vessel and delivered on 1 October. 1922: Sold to mercantile and renamed *Somersby*.

THOMAS LEEDS 1919/19 1939/45 Admty No: 4210
  Port Reg: WWII: M 70
  P.No: WWII: FY 520

1919: Launched. Built at Aberdeen by Duthie and completed as a fishing vessel. Delivered on 12 September. Sold to mercantile, acquired by H. Westenborg of Milford Haven and retained the same name. 1939: Requisitioned in August and converted to a M/S. 1945: Returned to owners in November.

THOMAS ROBINS 1917/20 Armament: 1 x 12-pdr
  Admty No: 3531

1917: Launched on 3rd September. Built at Southbank-on-Tees by Smiths Dock. 1920: Sold to mercantile, acquired by the Boston DSF & Ice Co of Fleetwood and renamed *Cheriton*. Port Reg: M 118.

THOMAS TWINEY 1917/21 Armament: 1 x 12-pdr
  Admty No: 3528

1917: Launched on 10 July. Built at Middlesborough by Smiths Dock and completed as a M/S. 1921: Sold to mercantile, acquired by D. Pettit of Milford Haven and renamed *Clyro*. Port Reg: M 245.

TR 1 1917/20 1926/47 RCN/RNZN
  Armament: 1 x 12-pdr
  P.No: WWII: T 00

1917: L. Built in Ontario by Port Arthur SB and completed as a M/S in August. Commissioned into the RCN. 1919: Paid Off in August. 1920: Sold to Captain Munro ICW TRs 10,11,13,14,18 and 53. Converted for mercantile. 1926: Purchased into the RNZN and renamed WAKAKURA. Converted to a M/S. Commissioned into the RNZN on 9 April and employed as a M/S Training ship for reservists. 1944: Converted to a D/L. 1947: Sold to mercantile and retained the same name. Acquired by the Tasman SS Co.

TR 2 1917/20 RCN

1917: Built in Ontario by Port Arthur SB and completed in November as a M/S. 1919: Paid Off in August. 1920: Sold to mercantile.

TR 3 1917/20 RCN

1918: Built in Ontario by Port Arthur SB and completed as a M/S in May. 1919: Paid Off in August. 1920: Sold to mercantile.

TR 4 1918/20 RCN

1918: L. Built in Ontario by Port Arthur SB and completed as a M/S in May. 1919: Paid Off. 1920: Sold to mercantile. 1926: Renamed *Cartegena*.

TR 5 1917/19 RCN

1917: Built in Ontario by Port Arthur SB and completed as a M/S in May. 1919: Paid Off. Sold to the Brazillian Navy and renamed COMMANDANTE LORETTI.

TR 6   1918/20   RCN

1918: L. Built in Ontario by Port Arthur SB and completed in May as M/S. 1919: Paid Off in August. 1920: Sold to mercantile.

TR 7   1918/20 1939/46 RCN/RAN
                                                    P.No: WWII: FY 75

1918: L. Built in Ontario by Collingwood SB and completed in May as a M/S. 1919: Paid Off on 31 January. 1920: Sold to mercantile (See under TR.1). 1926: Renamed *Santander*. 1939: Requisitioned in October as GOOLGWAI and converted to a M/S. Commissioned into the RAN. 1946: Returned to owners in June.

TR 8   1918/20   RCN

1918: Built in Ontario by Collingwood SB and completed in June as a M/S. 1919: Paid off in February. 1920: Sold to mercantile.

TR 9   1918/20   RCN

1918: Built in Ontario by Collingwood SB and completed in May as a M/S. 1919: Paid Off in February. 1920: Sold to mercantile.

TR 10   1918/20   RCN

1918: L. Built in Ontario by Collingwood SB and completed in May as a M/S. 1920: Sold to mercantile (See under TR.1).

TR 11   1918/20   RCN

1918: L. Built in Ontario by Collingwood SB and completed in June as a M/S. 1919: Paid off in August. 1920: Sold to mercantile (See under TR1).

TR8   **(D. Brindle Collection)**

TR 12	1918/20	RCN

1918: Built in Ontario by Collingwood SB and completed in August. 1919: Paid Off in February. 1920: Sold to mercantile.

TR 13	1918/20	RCN

1918: L. Built at Toronto by Thor Iron Works and completed in June. 1919: Paid Off in August. 1920: Sold to mercantile (See under TR.1). 1926: Renamed *Malaga*.

TR 14	1918/20	RCN

1918: Built at Toronto by Thor Iron Works and completed in June. 1919: Paid Off on 7 January. 1920: Sold to mercantile (See under TR.1). 1926: Renamed *Pasages*.

TR 15	1918/20	RCN

1918: Built in Canada by Polson Ironworks and completed in June. 1919: Paid off on 31 January. 1920: Sold to mercantile and renamed *Jacqueline*.

TR 16	1918/20	RCN

1918: Built in Canada by Polson Iron Works and completed in June. 1919: Paid off on 14 January. 1920: Sold to Mercantile.

TR 17	1918/20	RCN

1918: Built in Canada by Polson Iron Works and completed in July. 1919: Paid Off on 21 January. 1920: Sold to mercantile and renamed *Jeanne*.

TR 18	1918/19 1940/46 RCN	
	P.No:	WWII: Z 238

1918: Built in Canada by Polson Iron Works and completed on 1 August. 1919: Paid Off on 31 January. Taken over by Captain Munro and subsequently sold to Belgian mercantile. 1940: Hired into the RN from Belgian owners in October as MARIE LOUISE and converted to a BDV. 1946: Returned to owners in January.

TR 19	1918/20 1939/47 RCN/RAN	
	P.No:	WWII: FY 75

1918: L. Built in Ontario by Kingston SB. Completed by Collingwood SB in August. 1919: Paid off on 7 January. 1920: Sold to mercantile. 1926: Renamed *Almeria*. 1939: Requisitioned in October and converted to a M/S. Renamed GOOLGWAI and commissioned into the RAN in October. 1947: Returned to owners in June.

TR 20	1918/20 1940/46 RCN/RAN	
	P.No:	WWII: FY 93

1918: L. Built in Ontario by Kingston SB. Completed by Collingwood SB in August. 1919: Paid Off on 14 January. 1920: Sold to mercantile. 1926: Renamed *Saville*. 1940: Requisitioned into the RAN in July as DURRAWEEN and converted to a M/S. 1946: Returned to owners.

TR 21	1918/20	RCN

1918: Built at Montreal by Canadian Vickers and completed in May. Paid Off on 19 December. 1920: Sold to mercantile and subsequently renamed *Bacip*.

TR 22	1918/20	RCN

1918: L. Built at Montreal by Canadian Vickers and completed in August. Paid off on 19 December. 1920: Sold to Mercantile.

TR 23	1918/20	RCN

1918: L. Built at Montreal by Canadian Vickers and completed on 1 August. 1919: Paid Off on 31 January. 1920: Sold to mercantile. 1926: Renamed *Fontenay.*

TR 24	1918/20	RCN

1918: L. Built at Montreal by Canadian Vickers and completed in November. 1919: Paid Off in January. 1920: Sold to mercantile and renamed *Gosse.* 1939: Served in WWII as French AD 278.

TR 25	1918/20	RCN

1918: L. Built at Montreal by Canadian Vickers and completed in June. 1919: Paid Off on 14 January. 1920: Sold to mercantile and renamed *Yvonne Claude.*

TR 26	1918/20	RCN

1918: Built at Montreal by Canadian Vickers and completed in May. Paid Off on 19 December. 1920: Sold to mercantile.

TR 27	1918/20	RCN

1918: Built at Montreal by Canadian Vickers and completed in May. 1919: Paid off on 22 January. 1920: Sold to mercantile and renamed *Galopin.*

TR 28	1918/20	RCN

1918: Built at Montreal by Canadian Vickers and completed in May. 1919: Paid Off on 31 January. 1920: Sold to mercantile. 1926: Renamed *Wellvale.*

TR 29	1918/20	RCN

1918: Built at Montreal by Canadian Vickers and completed on 30 May. Paid Off on 19 December. 1920: Sold to mercantile and renamed *Fernando De C.*

TR 30	1918/20	RCN

1918: Built at Montreal by Canadian Vickers and completed on 28 May. 1919: Paid Off on 21 January. 1920: Sold to mercantile and renamed *Blanca De C.*

TR 31	1918/19	RCN

1918: Built at Montreal by Canadian Vickers and completed on 20 May. 1919: Paid Off on 10 January. 1920: Sold to mercantile and renamed *Jose Ignacio De C.*

TR 32	1918/20	RCN

1918: Built at Sorel, Quebec by Govt. SY and completed on 16 May. 1919: Paid Off on 22 January. 1920: Sold to mercantile. 1926: Renamed *Authorpe.*

TR 33	1918/20	RCN

1918: Built at Sorel, Quebec by Govt. SY and completed on 4 June. 1920: Sold to mercantile. 1927: Renamed *Windroos.*

TR 34	1918/19	RCN

1918: Built at Sorel, Quebec, by Govt. SY and completed on 28 July. 1919: Paid Off on 4 January. Sold to mercantile and renamed *Valentia.* 1939: Served in WWII as French AD.1, ETOILE Du NORD.

TR 35	1918/19	RCN

1918: Built at Quebec by Davie SB & Rep and completed on 5 June. 1919: Paid Off on 31 January. 1920: Sold to mercantile.

TR 36	1918/20	RCN

1918: Built at Quebec by Davie SB & Rep and completed on 5 June. 1919: Paid Off on 7 January. 1920: Sold to mercantile. 1926: Renamed *Ferrol.*

TR 37	1917/19 1939/45	RCN	
	Port Reg:	WWII: LO 56
	P.No:	WWII: FY 522

1917: Built at Port Arthur, Ontario, by Port Arthur SB and completed on 1 November. 1919: Paid Off on 19 January. Temporary Loan to the USN and renamed CT 37. 1920: Returned to the RCN and placed on the Sale List. Sold to mercantile. 1925: Renamed *Their Merit.* Acquired by T. Jenkinson of Milford Haven and D.J. Jones of Pembroke Dock. 1939: Requisitioned into the RN in August as THEIR MERIT and converted to a M/S. 1945: Returned to owners in November.

TR 38	1918/19	RCN

1918: Built at Port Arthur, Ontario by Port Arthur SB and completed on 20 August. Paid Off on 21 December. 1919: Sold to mercantile and subsequently renamed *Alcatraz.*

TR 39	1918/20 1939/43	RCN/RIN	
	Port Reg:	WWII: Indian

1918: Built at Port Arthur, Ontario, by Port Arthur SB and completed on 1 November. 1919: Paid Off on 15 August. Temporary Loan to the USN and renamed CT 39. 1920: Returned to the RCN and placed on the Sale List. Sold to mercantile. 1930: Renamed *Chandbali.* 1939: Requisitioned into the RIN as CHANDBALI and converted to an APV. 1943: Returned to owners.

TR 40	1918/20	RCN

1918: Built at Port Arthur, Ontario, by Port Arthur SB and completed on 1 November. 1919: Paid Off on 15 August. Temporary Loan to the USN and renamed CT 40. 1920: Returned to the RCN and placed on the Sale List. Sold to mercantile. 1921: Renamed *Marie Yette.*

TR 41	1919/20	RCN

1919: L. Built at Port Arthur, Ontario, by Port Arthur SB and completed on 5 May. Not Commissioned. 1920: Sold to mercantile and renamed *Marie Simone.* 1939: Served in WWII as French AD 110.

TR 42 1919/20 RCN

1919: Built at Port Arthur, Ontario, by Port Arthur SB and completed on 5 May. Not Commissioned. 1920: Sold to mercantile and renamed *Marie Gilbert*. 1939: Served in WWII as French AD 158.

TR 43 1919/20 RCN

1919: Built at Port Arthur, Ontario, by Port Arthur SB and completed on 12 May. Not Commissioned. 1920: Sold to mercantile and renamed *Marie Anne*. 1939: Served in WWII as a French AD.

TR 44 1919/19 RCN

1919: Built at Port Arthur, Ontario, by Port Arthur SB and completed on 12 May. Not Commissioned. Sold to mercantile and retained the same name. Acquired by the Newfoundland Development Co. 1920: Renamed *Florencia*.

TR 45 1919/19 RCN

1919: Built in Quebec by Davie SB & Repair Co and completed on 12 May. Not Commissioned. Sold to mercantile. Acquired by the Gulf of St. Lawrence Shipping & Trading Co. Subsequently acquired by the Dept of Transport and underwent a number of name changes including *Labrador*, *Mardep* and *Bernier*.

TR 46 1919/20 1939/40 RCN/SAN

1919: Built in Quebec by Davie SB & Rep Co and completed on 12 May. Paid Off on 4 October. 1920: Sold to mercantile. 1926: Renamed *Algoa Bay*. 1939: Requisitioned into the SAN in October as ALGOA BAY and converted to a M/S. 1940: Returned to owners in December.

TR 47 1919/19 1939/46 RCN
                                 P.No: WWII: 4204

1919: Built in Quebec by Davie SB & Rep Co and completed on 12 May. Paid Off on 14 October. Sold to mercantile and renamed *Heron*. 1939: Requisitioned as FOAM-CREST and converted to an APV. Subsequently purchased into the RN. 1941: Based at Grimsby. 1946: Sold to mercantile in March.

TR 48 1919/19 RCN

1919: Built in Quebec by Davie SB & Rep. Co. and completed on 12 May. Paid Off on 25 October. Sold to mercantile and renamed *Dragon Vert*. Notes: Reported to have served in WWII as MIQUELON. NFI.

TR 49 1919/19 RCN

1919: L. Built at Quebec by Davie SB & Rep and completed on 12 May. Paid Off on 25 October. Sold to mercantile and renamed *Joselle*.

TR 50 1919/19 RCN

1919: Built in Quebec by Davie SB & Rep Co. and completed on 12 May. Not Commissioned. Sold to mercantile and renamed *Colonel Rockwell*.

TR 51   1918/19   RCN

1918: Built at Sorel, Quebec by Govt. SY and completed on 20 November. 1919: Paid Off on 23 July. Loaned to the USN and renamed CT 51 for the duration of the loan. Returned to the RCN, reverted to original name and placed on the Sale List. Sold to mercantile and renamed *Marie Caroline.*

TR 52   1918/19   RCN

1918: Built at Sorel, Quebec, by Govt. SY and completed in November. 1919: Paid Off on 23 July. Designated for Loan to the USN but not taken up. Sold to mercantile and renamed *Marie Mad.* 1939: Served as the French AD 148 in WWII.

TR 53   1918/20   RCN

1918: Built at Sorel, Quebec, by Govt. SY and completed in November. 1919: Paid Off in September. Placed on the Sale List. 1920: Sold to mercantile (See under TR 1) and subsequently renamed *Marie Therese III.* 1939: Served in WWII as the French AD 149.

TR 54   1918/20   RCN

1918: Built in Ontario by Kingston SB and completed on 30 September. 1919: Paid Off in August and placed on the Sale List. 1920: Sold to mercantile. 1925: Renamed *Table Bay.*

TR 55   1918/20   RCN

1918: Built in Ontario by Kingston SB and completed on 8 November. 1919: Paid Off on 25 July. Loaned to the USN and renamed CT 53. 1920: Returned to the RCN and placed on the Sale List. Sold to mercantile and renamed *Marie Jacqueline.*

TR 56   1918/20   RCN

1918: Built in Ontario by Kingston SB. 1919: Paid Off on 15 August. Loaned to the USN and renamed CT 56. 1920: Returned to the RCN and placed on the Sale List. Sold to mercantile and renamed *Romanita.*

TR 57   1919/20 1940/44 RCN

1919: Built in Ontario by Kingston SB and completed in October. Not Commissioned. 1920: Sold to mercantile and renamed *Colonel Roosevelt.* 1940: American Pilot vessel purchased into the RN as TEXAS and converted to an APV. 1944: LOST. Sunk in a collision off Jamaica on 19 July.

TR 58   1918/20   RCN

1918: Built at Trois Rivieres, Quebec, by Tidewater SB and completed on 21 November. 1919: Paid Off on 23 July. Loaned to the USN and renamed CT 58. 1920: LOST. Wrecked in Barra Sound on 20 November.

TR 59   1918/20   RCN

1918: Built at Trois Rivieres, Quebec, by Tidewater SB and completed on 21 November. 1919: Paid Off on 15 August. Loaned to the USN and renamed CT 59. 1920: Returned to the RCN and placed on the Sale List. Sold to mercantile and renamed *Pilote Gironde*

TR 60   1919/19 1939/46 RCN/SAN

1918: Built at Trois Rivieres, Quebec, by Tidewater SB and completed on 25 November.

1919: Paid Off on 15 August. Loaned to the USN and renamed CT 60. Returned to the RCN and placed on the Sale List. Sold to mercantile and renamed *David Haigh*. 1939: Purchased into the SAN on 19 September as DAVID HAIGH and converted to a M/S. 1943: Converted to a BDV. 1946: Sold to mercantile on 25 June.

VALENTINE BOWER	1917/23 1939/45	Armament:	1 x 12-pdr
		Admty No:	3654
		Port Reg:	WWII: M 226
		P.No:	WWII: FY1573 (M/S)
			Y7 36 (Esso)

1917: L 1 October. Built at S.Shields by C.Rennoldson and completed as a M/S. 1923: Sold to mercantile and renamed *Malvolio*. Acquired by Milford ST.Co of Milford Haven and named *Milford King*. 1939: Requisitioned in December as MILFORD KING and converted to an APV. 1940: Converted to a M/S in April. 1944: Converted to an Esso in March. 1945: Paid Off in July and returned to owners in November.

WALTER BURKE	1917/22	Armament:	1 x 12-pdr
		Admty No:	3532

1917: L. 3 September. Built at Middlesborough by Smith's Dock. Fitted with Listening Hydrophones. 1922: Sold to mercantile and retained the same name. 1924: Renamed *Gonerby*.

WALTER CAVE	1918/19	Admty No:	4456

1918: Ordered from George Brown. 1919: Cancelled.

WILLIAM BEATTY	1917/20	Displacement:	107TN
		Engines:	61HP
		Armament:	1 x 12-pdr 1 x 7.5-inch Bomb Thrower (A/S Howitzer)
		Admty No:	3534

1917: L 17 September. Built at Southbank-on-Tees by Smith's Dock. 1920: Sold to mercantile and renamed *Cresswell*. Acquired by the Boston DSF & Ice Co. PR: M 129.

WILLIAM BEETON	1917/21	Armament:	1 x 12-pdr
		Admty No:	3652

1917: L. 20 July. Built at South Shields by C.Rennoldson. 1921: Transferred to the Maltese Govt. and renamed *Girolamo Cassar*.

WILLIAM BELL	1918/19 1940/46	Displacement:	119TN
		Engines:	61HP
		Armament:	WWI: 1 x 12-pdr.
			WWII: 1 x 6-pdr
		Admty No:	3590
		Port Reg:	WWII: LO 201
		P. No:	WWII: FY 1727

1918: L 17 January. Built at Beverley by CWG. Fitted with Listening Hydrophones. 1919: Sold to mercantile and retained the same name. Acquired by Mills SS Co of London. 1940: Requisitioned in June and converted to an APV. 1941: Converted to a M/S with LL Sweep and Acoustic Hammer. Joined the 110th M/S Group based at Grimsby for sweeping Cromer-Flamborough Head. 1944: Transferred to Portsmouth in June for Channel Sweeping during D-Day operations. Returned to Grimsby in December. 1945: Transferred back to Portsmouth in June for Sweeping in the Channel and barge-towing from Portsmouth to Tilbury. 1946: Returned to owners in February.

WILLIAM BENNETT   1918/19   Admty No: 4408

1918: Ordered from CWG. 1919: Cancelled. Completed by the builder as a fishing vessel. Sold to mercantile and renamed *Njordur*. Acquired by Icelandic owners. PR: RE 36. 1932: Renamed *Haukanes*. 1952: BU in Belgium.

WILLIAM BODY   1917/19 1940/46   Armament: WWI: 1 x 12-pdr
                                                          1 x 7.5-inch Bomb
                                                          Thrower (A/S
                                                          Howitzer).
                                                          WWII: 1 x 12-pdr
                                           Admty No: 3585

1917: L 17 December. Built at Beverley by CWG. 1919: Sold to mercantile and retained the same name. 1940: Requisitioned in June and converted to an APV. 1946: Returned to owners in February.

WILLIAM BROWIS   1917/21 1939/45 Displacement: 118TN
                                             Engines: 86HP
                                             Armament: 1 x 12-pdr
                                             Admty No: 3582
                                             Port Reg: WWII: M 225
                                             P.No: WWII: FY 615

1917: L 18 October. Built at Beverley by CWG. 1922: Sold to mercantile and renamed *Gonerby*. 1923: Renamed *John*. Acquired by Milford ST Co of Milford Haven and renamed *Milford Queen*. 1939: Requisitioned in August as MILFORD QUEEN and converted to a M/S. 1940: TPI Operations Quentin/Quidnunc/Quixote, the cutting of the telephone cable between Germany and the UK in the N.Sea on 18/19 May. 1945: Returned to owners in December

WILLIAM BUNCE   1917/22 1939/39 Displacement: 107TN
                                            Engines: 61HP
                                            Armament: 1 x 12-pdr 1 x 3.5-
                                                            inch Bomb Thrower
                                                            (A/S Howitzer)
                                            Admty No: 3538
                                            Port Reg: WWII: LO 482

1917: L 3 October. Built at Southbank-on-Tees by Smith's Dock. 1922: Sold to mercantile and retained the same name. Acquired by T. Jenkerson & D.G. Jones of Pembroke Dock. 1939: Requisitioned in August and designated as a M/S. Returned to owners.

WILLIAM BURTE   1918/19 1939/45 Displacement: 278TG 122TN
                                            Engines: 91HP = 10.5 kts
                                            Admty No: 4413
                                            Port Reg: WWII: GY 1268
                                            P.No: WWII: FY 602

1918: Ordered from CWG. 1919: Cancelled. 1920: Completed by builders as a fishing vessel and sold to mercantile. Acquired by GF. Sleight of Grimsby and renamed *Reboundo*. 1939: Requisitioned in September as REBOUNDO and converted to a M/S. 1945: Returned to owners in December. 1962: BU in Belgium

WILLIAM CABLE   1918/19   Admty No: 4450

1918: Ordered from George Brown. 1919: Cancelled.

WILLIAM CALDWELL	1918/19 1940/46	Displacement:	127TN
		Engines:	86HP
		Armament:	1 x 12-pdr
		Admty No:	3719
		Port Reg:	WWII: LO 374
		P.No:	WWII: Z 142

1918: L 12 June. Built at Beverley by CWG. 1919: Temporary Loan to the USN. Returned to the RN. Sold to mercantile on 11 May and retained the same name. Acquired by Mrs.G.E. Dove of Milford Haven. 1940: Purchased into the RN in January and converted to a BDV. 1946: Sold to mercantile in December.

WILLIAM CALE	1917/21 1939/45	Displacement:	113TN
		Engines:	61HP
		Armament:	1 x 12-pdr
		Admty No:	2666
		Port Reg:	WWII: LO 79
		P.No:	WWII: FY 535

1917: L. 19 September. Built at Paisley by Bow McLachlan. 1921: Sold to mercantile and retained the same name. Acquired by Iago SF Co of Milford Haven. 1939: Requisitioned in August and converted to a M/S. 1945: Returned to owners in July

| WILLIAM CARBERRY | 1919/19 | Admty No: | 4479 |

1919: L. 13 December. Built at South Shields by Hepple and completed as a fishing vessel. Sold to mercantile and retained the same name. Subsequently renamed *Micaela de C.*

WILLIAM CARR	1918/21 1940/45	Armament:	1 x 12-pdr
		Admty No:	3647
		Port Reg:	WWII: French
		P.No:	WWII: FY 1815

1918: L. 4 April. Built at Paisley by Bow McLachlan. 1921: Sold to mercantile and retained the same name. Subsequently renamed *Jacques*. 1939: Taken up by the French Navy as NAZARETH and converted to an APV. 1940: French APV seized at Plymouth in Operation Grab on 3 July. Converted to a M/S. 1945: Returned to the French in August.

| WILLIAM CARRICK | 1917/19 | Armament: | 1 x 12-pdr |
| | | Admty No: | 3665 |

1917: L 18 September. Built at Paisley by Bow McLachlan. 1919: Sold to the Indian Government and retained the same name.

WILLIAM CHASEMAN	1917/20 1939/47	Displacement:	107TN
		Engines:	61HP
		Armament:	1 x 12-pdr
		Admty No:	3529
		Port Reg:	WWII: SA 56
		P.No:	WWII: FY 511

1917: L. 3 March. Built at Southbank-on-Tees by Smith's Dock. 1920: Sold to mercantile on 4 May and renamed *Radnor Castle*. Acquired by Consolidated Fisheries of Grimsby. 1939: Purchased into the RN in August as RADNOR CASTLE and converted to a M/S. 1947: Sold to Messrs Ward and arrived at Briton Ferry, Swansea, on 17 May to BU.

WILLIAM COBURNE 1917/20 Admty No: 3664

1917: L. 24 July. Built at Paisley by Bow McLachlan and completed as an escort. 1920: Sold to mercantile and renamed *Carnarvon Castle*.

WILLIAM CORAN 1918/19 Admty No: 4452

1918: Ordered from George Brown. 1919: Cancelled.

WILLIAM COWLING 1917/22 Admty No: 3663

1917: L. 23 July. Built at Paisley by Bow McLachlan. 1922: Sold to mercantile and renamed *Asterby*.

WILLIAM CUMMINS 1917/22 1940/45

Displacement:	105TN
Engines:	61HP
Armament:	WWI: 1 x 12-pdr
	WWII: 1 x 6-pdr
Admty No:	3669
Port Reg:	WWII: FD 77

1917: L. 17 November. Built at Paisley by Bow McLachlan and completed as a M/S. 1922: Sold to mercantile and renamed *Ernest Solvay*. Acquired by Wyre ST of Fleetwood and renamed *Niblick*. 1940: Requisitioned in June as NIBLICK and converted to an APV. 1941: Converted to a M/S. 1944: Converted to a D/L. TPI Operation Neptune, the D-Day Landings in June, as a D/L attached to the 15th M/S Flotilla in Force S. 1945: Returned to owners.

WILLIAM DARNOLD 1918/20

Armament:	1 x 12-pdr
Admty No:	3722

1918: L. 11 July. Built at Beverley by CWG and completed as a M/S. 1919: Temporary Loan to the USN for mine clearance operations. Returned to the RN. 1920: Sold to mercantile and renamed *Cape Hatteras*.

WILLIAM DOWNES 1917/21

Displacement:	110TN
Engines:	87HP
Armament:	1 x 12-pdr
Admty No:	3723

1917: L. 5 November. Built at S.Shields by C.Rennoldson. 1921: Sold to mercantile and retained the same name. Acquired by J.Ritchie & W.T. Davies of Milford Haven. PR: LO 530.

WILLIAM DRAKE 1919/19 Admty No: 4483

1919: L. Built at S.Shields by J.P. Rennoldson and completed as a fishing vessel. Delivered on 19 May. Sold to mercantile and renamed *Ebor Court*.

WILLIAM FLEMING 1918/20

Displacement:	109TN
Engines:	61HP
Armament:	1 x 12-pdr 1 x 3.5-inch Bomb Thrower (A/S Howitzer)
Admty No:	3746

1918: L. Built at S.Shields by Hepple and delivered on 18 May. Fitted with Listening Hydrophones. 1920: Sold to mercantile and renamed *Trawler Prince*. Acquired by H.E.Rees of Milford Haven. Also listed as FLEMING in some lists.

WILLIAM GRIFFITHS	1918/19		Armament:	
			Admty No:	3785

1918: L. Built at Greenock by George Brown and completed as a M/S. Delivered on 21 February. 1919: Sold to mercantile and renamed *Inverspey*.

WILLIAM HANNAM	1918/20	1939/40	Displacement:	119TN
			Engines:	61HP
			Admty No:	4206
			Port Reg:	WWII: LO 383
			P.No:	WWII: Z 129

1918: L. Built at Aberdeen by Duthie. 1919: Delivered on 20 February. 1920: Sold to mercantile and retained the same name. Acquired by Pater ST of Pembroke. 1939: Requisitioned in October and converted to a BDV. 1940: Returned to owners in April.

WILLIAM HUMPHREYS	1918/21		Displacement:	119TN
			Engines:	87HP
			Admty No:	4205

1918: L. Built at Aberdeen by Duthie and delivered on 24 December. 1921: Sold to mercantile and retained the same name. Acquired by J. Ritchie & W.T. Davies of Milford Haven. Notes: Also listed as HUMPHRIES in some lists.

WILLIAM KNIGHT	1919/19	1940/41	Armament:	WWII: 1 x 12-pdr
			Admty No:	4208

1919: L. Built at Aberdeen by Duthie and completed as a fishing vessel. Delivered on 19 June. Sold to mercantile and renamed *Henricus*. 1940: Requisitioned as COBBERS and converted to an APV. 1941: LOST. Sunk by enemy a/c in the North Sea on 3 March.

WILLIAM LAMBKIN	1919/19		Admty No:	4209

1919: L. Built at Aberdeen by Duthie and completed as a fishing vessel. Delivered on 16 July. Sold to mercantile and renamed *Nellie Crawford*.

WILLIAM LEEK	1918/19	1939/46	Displacement:	123TN
			Engines:	480HP
			Armament:	1 x 12-pdr
			Admty No:	4211
			Port Reg:	WWII: FD 180
			P.No:	WWII: FY 541

1918: L. Built at South Shields by J.P.Rennoldson and completed as an escort. Delivered on 10 October. 1919: Sold to mercantile on 11 May and renamed *Cavendish*. Acquired by J. Marr of Fleetwood and renamed *Hildina*. 1939: Requisitioned in August as HILDINA and converted to a M/S. 1946: Returned to owners in April.

WILLIAM LOFT	1919/22	1939/46	Displacement:	113TN
			Engines:	87HP
			Admty No:	4220
			Port Reg:	WWII: H 853
			P.No:	WWII: FY 643

1919: L. Built at South Shields by C.Rennoldson and completed as a fishing vessel. 1922: Sold to mercantile and renamed *Tamora*. Acquired by Henderson Tr Co of Hull. 1939: Requisitioned in August as TAMORA and converted to a M/S. 1946: Returned to owners in March.

WILLIAM MANNELL	1917/20 1940/45	Displacement:	107TN
		Engines:	87HP
		Armament:	1 x 12-pdr
		Admty No:	3512
		Port Reg:	WWII: LO 370
		P.No:	WWII: FY 1665

1917: L. Built at Southbank-on-Tees by Smith's Dock and completed as an escort. 1920: Sold to mercantile and retained the same name. Acquired by Boston DSF & Ice Co. 1940: Requisitioned in June and converted to a M/S. 1945: Returned to owners in October.

WILLIAM SPENCER	1917/22 1939/46	Displacement:	107TN
		Engines:	87HP
		Admty No:	3521
		Port Reg:	WWII: GN 48
		P.No:	WWII: Z 130

1917: L. 19 June. Built at Southbank-on-Tees by Smith's Dock. 1922: Sold to mercantile and renamed *Normanby*. Acquired by W.Carnie AO of Glasgow and renamed *Astros*. 1939: Requisitioned in December as ASTROS and converted to a BBV. 1946: Returned to owners.

WILLIAM SYMONS	1917/22 1939/44	Displacement:	107TN
		Engines:	61HP
		Armament:	1 x 12-pdr
		Admty No:	3535
		Port Reg:	WWII: LO 458
		P.No:	WWII: FY 519 (M/S)
			Y7.17 (Esso)

1917: L. 1 October. Built at Southbank-on-Tees by Smith's Dock and completed as a M/S. 1922: Sold to mercantile and renamed *Rayvernol*. Acquired by T. Jenkerson of Milford Haven AO and renamed *Lephreto*. 1939: Requisitioned in August as LEPHRETO and converted to a M/S. 1944: Converted to an Esso. Employed on ferrying fuel to the Normandy beaches. Returned to owners in November.

| WILLIAM WILLMOT | 1917/20 | Armament: | 1 x 12-pdr |
| | | Admty No: | 3536 |

1917: L. 1 October. Built at Southbank-on-Tees by Smith's Dock. 1920: LOST. Sunk in collision with *SS.Meissonier* in the Irish Sea in September. Remained in the Lists until 1921.

CASTLE CLASS RNZN

In 1941 the need for Minesweeper trawlers for the RNZN became apparent. New Zealand had the capability of building her own vessels and also for engining. The design chosen was that of the prolific First World War Mersey Class with appropriate modernising. Accordingly, orders for 16 trawlers were placed with NZ yards and the first ones were launched in 1942. Stevenson & Cook had received orders for nine of the Class and had successfully launched six but the remaining three were cancelled in 1945. Most were of standard build, but three were composite.

All the serving trawlers survived the war to be subsequently sold to the mercantile, the last two, RIMU and WAIPU being sold in 1955.

```
Displacement:    625 tons
Measurements:    134ft oa 125ft pp x 23ft 6in x 12ft
Engines:         1 shaft Reciprocating (VTE)
Speed:           10 kts
Armament:        1 x 12-pdr    4 x LG(2 x twin)
Complement:      32
```

Vessels in the Class:

AROHA, AWATERE, HAUTAPU, HINAU, MAIMAI, MANUKA, PAHAU, RIMU, TAWHAI, WAIHO, WAIKATO, WAIMA, WAIPU, WAKAKURA

Cancelled Vessels:

WAIITI, WAIKAKA and WAIKANAE.

WAKAKURA (MPL)

90

CASTLE CLASS RNZN - NOTES

AROHA 1942/46 P.No: T 396

1942: L. 8 September. Built at Port Chalmers, NZ, by Stevenson & Cook. Engined by A.G.Price. 1946: Sold to Mercantile and renamed *Matong*.

AWATERE 1942/46 P.No: T 397

1942: L. 26 September. Built by Patent Slip Co., Wellington, NZ and engined by A.G.Price. 1946: Sold to mercantile and retained the same name.

HAUTAPU 1942/50 P.No: T 340

1942: L. 18 November. Built in New Zealand by Stevenson & Cook of Port Chalmers. Engined by A.G. Price and completed as a M/S. 1950: Sold to mercantile.

HINAU 1941/55 P.No: T 399

1941: L. 28 August. Built in New Zealand by the Senior Foundry, Aukland. Composite construction, engined by A.G. Price. 1955: Sold as a hulk in January.

MAIMAI 1943/46 P.No: T 338

1943: L. Built at Port Chalmers, NZ, by Stevenson & Cook and engined by Price. 1946: Sold to mercantile and retained the same name.

MANUKA 1941/52 P.No: T 401

1941: L. 23 September. Built in NZ by Mason of Auckland and engined by Price. Composite Built. 1952: LOST. In October.

PAHAU 1943/46 P.No: T 351

1943: L. 3 April. Built at Port Chalmers, NZ, by Stevenson & Cook and engined by New Zealand Railway. 1946: Sold to mercantile in March and retained the same name.

RIMU 1941/55 P. No: T 402

1941: L. 9 September. Built at Auckland, NZ, by Seager and engined by A.G.Price. Composite built. 1955: Sold to BU. 1958: Hull sunk in August as a bombing target off Cuvier Island, NZ.

TAWHAI 1943/46 P.No: T 348

1942: Ordered in May. 1943: Launched. Built at Aukland, NZ, by Seagar Bros and engined by A.G. Price. Composite built. 1946: Not completed and sold to mercantile

WAIAU 1944/46

1944: Ordered from Mason of Aukland and Laid Down. 1946: Cancelled and BU on the stocks.

WAIHO 1944/46 P.No: T 403

1941: Ordered on 19 September for the RN. 1941: L. 19 February. Built at Port Chalmers by Stephenson & Cook and engined by Price. Transferred to the RNZN. 1946: Sold to mercantile and renamed *Moona*.

WAIITI   1941/43

1941: Ordered for the RN from Stevenson & Cook of Port Chalmers on 19 Sept. 1943: Cancelled in October.

WAIKAKA   1941/43

1941: Ordered for the RN from Stevenson & Cook of Port Chalmers on 19 Sept. 1943: Cancelled in October.

WAIKANAE   1941/43

1941: Ordered for the RN from Stevenson & Cook of Port Chalmers on 19 Sept. 1943: Cancelled in October.

WAIKATO   1943/46   P.No: T 343

1942: Ordered in May. 1943: L. 16 October. Built in NZ by Mason and engined by NZ Railways. 1946: Not completed. Sold to mercantile and renamed *Taiaora*.

WAIMA   1943/46   P.No: T 349

1941: Ordered on 19 September. 1943: L. 11 December. Built at Port Chalmers by Stevenson & Cook and engined by A.G.Price. 1946: Sold to mercantile and renamed *Maldonna*.

WAIPU   1943/46   P.No: T 357

1941: Ordered in August as PAPAKURA and then renamed. 1943: L. 31 July. Built at Port Chalmers by Stevenson & Cook and engined by A.G.Price. 1946: Sold to mercantile in October and retained the same name. 1955: Renamed *Mulloka*.

WAKAKURA   1926/47   See under TR 1

DANCE CLASS

This Class of 20 trawlers was ordered on 9 September 1939 under the 1939 Programme. Somewhat smaller than previous classes they were all completed as M/Ss. There was only one war loss, SWORD DANCE, and the remainder were up for disposal after the war. Three were transferred to the Italian Navy, two to the War Department and the remainder were sold to mercantile at home and abroad.

Displacement:	300 tons
Measurements:	160ft 6in oa 150ft pp x 27ft 6in x 10ft 6in
Engines:	1 shaft Reciprocating (VTE) 850 IHP
Speed:	11.5 kts
Armament:	1 x 12-pdr AA 3 x Single 20mm AA
Complement:	35

Vessels in the Class:

COTILLION, COVERLEY, FANDANGO, FOXTROT, GAVOTTE, HORNPIPE, MAZURKA, MINUET, MORRIS DANCE, PIROUETTE, POLKA, QUADRILLE, RUMBA, SARABANDE, SALTERELO, SWORD DANCE, TANGO, TARANTELLA, VALSE, VELETA

TANGO seen with her forward gun "boxed in" with side protection.   (IWM Neg: A6111)

COTILLION	1940/47	Armament:	1 x 4-inch
			3 x Single 20mm AA
		P.No:	T 104

1939: Ordered on 9 September. 1940: L. 26 December. Built at Ardrossan by the Ardrossan DY Co. and engined by Plenty. Completed as a M/S. 1947: Sold to mercantile in March.

COVERLEY	1941/47	Armament:	1 x 4-inch
			3 x Single 20mm AA
		P.No:	T 106

1939: Ordered on 9 September. 1941: L. 27 May. Built at Ardrossan by the Ardrossan DY. Co. and engined by Plenty. Completed as a M/S. 1947: Sold to mercantile on 12 March and renamed *Jannikke*. 1949: Renamed *Ofotfjord*.

FANDANGO	1940/46	Armament:	1 x 4-inch
			3 x Single 20mm AA
		P.No:	T 107

1939: Ordered on 9 September. 1940: L. 26 March. Built at Selby by Cochrane and engined by Amos & Smith. Completed as A/S. 1946: Sold to mercantile and retained the same name.

FOXTROT	1940/46	Armament:	1 x 4-inch
			3 x Single 20mm AA
		P.No:	T 109

1939: Ordered on 9 September. 1940: L. 23 April. Built at Selby by Cochrane, engined by Amos & Smith and completed as A/S. 1943: Transferred to the MF and employed on N.African convoys. 1946: Transferred to the War Dept. in July retaining the same name. 1951: BU at Barrow in September.

GAVOTTE	1940/46	Armament:	1 x 4-inch
			3 x Single 20mm AA
		P.No:	T 115

1939: Ordered on 9 September. 1940: L. 6 May. Built at Beverley by CWG and engined by Holmes. Completed as an A/S. 1946: Transferred to the Italian Navy and renamed RD 312.

HORNPIPE	1940/46	Armament:	1 x 4-inch
			3 x Single 20mm AA
			1 x Twin VMG
			1 x Twin Browning MG
		P.No:	T 120

1939: Ordered on 9 September. 1940: L. 21 May, Built at Beverley by CWG and engined by Holmes. Completed as A/S. Commissioned at S.Shields and worked up at Port Edgar. 1943: Deployed to the MF and joined the 34th A/S Group working off N.Africa. Transferred to Italian waters after the surrender. 1944: Took part in Operation Shingle, the Landings at Anzio in January escorting invasion convoys and then working as a D/L. Group based at Leghorn. 1946: Transferred to the Italian Navy on 16 March.

| MAZURKA | 1940/46 | Armament: | 1 x 4-inch |
| | | | 3 x Single 20mm AA |

1939: Ordered on 9 September. 1940: L. 25 November. Built at Port Glasgow by Ferguson Bros. and completed as A/S. 1946: Sold to mercantile.

MINUET	1941/46	Armament:	1 x 4-inch
			3 x Single 20mm AA
		P.No:	T 131

1939: Ordered on 9 September. 1941: L. 1 March. Built at Port Glasgow by Ferguson Bros. and completed as A/S. 1943: Transferred to the MF as Leader of the 34th M/S Group. Operating off North Africa. 1944: Group based at Leghorn. 1946: Sold to the Italian Navy on February and renamed RD 307.

MORRIS DANCE	1940/46	Armament:	1 x 4-inch
			3 x Single 20mm AA
		P.No:	T 117

1939: Ordered on 9 September. 1940: L. 6 August. Built at Goole by Goole SB and engined by Amos & Smith. Completed as an A/S. 1943: Based at Free town ICW SARA-BANDE. Employed on Freetown-Gibraltar convoys. 1946: Sold to mercantile and renamed *Tottan*. Notes: Reputed to have been haunted by the ghost of a sailor who had committed suicide whilst onboard.

PIROUETTE	1940/46	Armament:	1 x 4-inch
			3 x Single 20mm AA
		P.No:	T 39

1939: Ordered on 9 September. 1940: L. 22 June. Built at Goole by Goole SB and engined by Amos & Smith. Completed as A/S. Based at Belfast for convoy duties W.Coast of UK - Iceland. 1942: Taken in hand for conversion for tropical service. 1943: Based at Gibraltar for sweeping in the Straits and as far as West Africa. Took part in the North Africa Landings. Med. operating off North Africa and Italy. Took part in Operation Avalanche the Salerno Landings in September. 1944: Took part in Operation Shingle the Anzio Landings but played only a minor part and failed to win the Battle Honour. 1946: Sold to mercantile in July and renamed *Tridente*.

POLKA	1941/46	Armament:	1 x 4-inch
			3 x Single 20mm AA
		P.No:	T 139

1940: Ordered on 9 September. 1941: L. 29 January. Built at Aberdeen by Hall Russell and completed as A/S. 1946: Sold to mercantile in April.

| QUADRILLE | 1941/46 | Armament: | 1 x 4-inch, |
| | | | 3 x Single 20mm AA |

1939: Ordered 9 September. 1941: L. 15 March. Built at Aberdeen by Hall Russell. Completed as A/S. 1946: Sold to mercantile 6 June and renamed *Elsa*. 1950: Renamed *Murten*.

RUMBA	1940/46	Armament:	1 x 4-inch
			3 x Single 20mm AA
		P.No:	T 122

1939: Ordered on 9 September. 1940: L. 31 July. Built at Glasgow by A & J.Inglis and engined by Aitchison Blair. Completed as A/S. 1946: Sold to mercantile in March and retained the same name.1953: Renamed *Buk Hae Ho*.

SALTARELO   **(P. Phelps Collection)**

| SARABANDE | 1940/46 | Armament: | 1 x 4-inch
3 x Single 20mm AA
LGs; DCs |
| | | P.No: | T 125 |

1939: Ordered on 9 September. 1940: L. 29 August. Built at Glasgow by Inglis and engined by Aitchison Blair. Completed as A/S. 1943: Employed off the W. Coast of Africa on the Freetown - Gibraltar convoys ICW MORRIS DANCE. Employed LE stokers. 1944: Rescued the survivors from the stranded SOUTHERN PRIDE on 16 June. 1945: Returned to the UK and Paid Off. Reduced to the Reserve and placed on the Disposal List. 1946: Sold to mercantile and renamed *Volen*. 1953: Renamed *Betty*.

| SALTARELO | 1940/46 | Armament: | 1 x 4-inch BL
3 x Single 20mm AA,
2 x 0.5-inch MG (1 x twin), 4 x 0.303
Brownings (2 x twin),
2 x DC Throwers |
| | | P.No: | T 120 |

1939: Ordered on 9 September. 1940: L. 9 August. Built at Leith by Henry Robb and engined by White's ME. Completed as A/S. 1942: Based on the Firth of Forth. Employed on convoy duties from the Forth to Loch Ewe, W.Coast of Scotland. 1943: Taken in hand for refitting at Grangemouth. Bridge superstructure concreted between the plates, fitted with RDF and Echo Sounder, 4 x 0.303 Brownings mounted on Bridge wings, and 2 x 20mm AA mounted either side of wheelhouse. Completed refitting and deployed to the Med. Based at Algiers for convoy duties. 1944: Took part in the landings on the W. Coast of Italy. 1945: Taken in hand at Malta for conversion to a D/L. Joined the M/S Flots off Trieste. 1946: Sold to the Portuguese Navy in August and renamed SALVADOR CORREIA.

| SWORD DANCE | 1940/42 | Armament: | 1 x 4-inch
3 x Single 20mm AA |
| | | P.No: | T 132 |

1939: Ordered on 9 September. 1940: L. 3 September. Built at Leith by Henry Robb and engined by Whites ME. Completed as A/S and employed on coastal convoy work. 1942: Alongside at Hull during an air-raid and lost two men killed. LOST. Rammed and sunk by a merchantman in thick fog in the Moray Firth on 5 July. No loss of life.

| TANGO | 1940/46 | Armament: | 1 x 4-inch,
3 x Single 20mmAA
4 x LMG (1 x twin, 2
x single). |
| | | P.No: | T 146 |

1939: Ordered 9 September. 1940: L. 29 November. Built at Southbank-on-Tees by Smith's Dock and completed as A/S. 1946: Sold to mercantile in July and renamed *Ramskapelle*.

| TARANTELLA | 1941/43 | Armament: | 1 x 4-inch,
3 x Single 20mmAA |
| | | P.No: | T 142 |

1939: Ordered 9 September. 1941: L. 27 January. Built at Middlesborough by Smith's Dock and completed as A/S. 1943: Renamed TWOSTEP in February. Transferred to the MF. Joined the 34th M/S Grp operating off N.Africa. 1944: Group transferred to Leghorn. 1945: Returned to the UK. 1946: Transferred to the Italian Navy in February and renamed RD 308.

| TWOSTEP | 1943/46 | See under TARANTELLA |

| VALSE | 1941/46 | Armament: | 1 x 4-inch
3 x Single 20mm AA |
| | | P.No: | T 15 |

1939: Ordered on 9 September. 1941: L. 12 March. Built at Middlesborough by Smith's Dock and completed as A/S. 1946: Transferred to the War Dept in May and retained the same name. 1951: BU at Port Glasgow in September.

| VELETA | 1941/46 | Armament: | 1 x 4-inch
3 x Single 20mm AA |
| | | P.No: | T 130 |

1939: Ordered on 9 September. 1941: L. 28 March. Built at Middlesborough by Smith's Dock and completed as A/S. 1944: Took part in Operation Neptune, the D-Day Landings in June, as an A/S escort. 1946: Sold to mercantile in March.

VELETA   **(P. Phelps Collection)**

FISH CLASS

This Class of 10 trawlers was built by Cochrane & Sons Ltd., at Selby, Yorkshire and based on their successful design for the commercial *Gulfoss* which they built in 1929. The Class was completed as A/S vessels with the exception of MACKEREL and TURBOT which were completed as Bird Class Controlled M/Ls and renamed. MACKEREL was the only one of the 10 which failed to survive the war, having foundered in the Atlantic in 1943. The remainder were all sold to the mercantile post-war.

Displacement:	670T 358TG
Measurements:	162ft oa 146ft pp x 25ft 3in x 12ft 6in
Engines:	1 shaft Reciprocating (VTE) 700 IHP
Speed:	11kts
Armament:	1 x 4-inch 3 x single 20mm AA
Complement:	35

Vessels in the Class:

BONITO, BREAM, GRAYLING, GRILSE, HERRING, MACKEREL, MULLET, POL-LACK, TURBOT, WHITING

MACKEREL and TURBOT were transferred to the Bird Class whilst building and renamed CORNCRAKE and REDSHANK respectively.

GRAYLING - The 4-inch gun has only a shield with no side protection.

(M. Cocker Collection)

FISH CLASS - NOTES

BONITO   1941/46   P.No: T 231

1941: Ordered on 27 February. L. 8 October. Built at Selby by Cochrane and engined by Holmes. Completed as an A/S. 1946: Sold to mercantile. Acquired by Consolidated Fisheries of Grimsby. Renamed *Blaefell* GY 456. 1956: Sold to S.African owners and renamed *Benjamin Gelcer*. 1967: Mercantile loss.

BREAM   1942/46   P.No: T 306

1942: Ordered on 17 April. L. 10 December. Built at Selby by Cochrane and engined by Amos & Smith. Completed as an A/S. Employed on Russian convoy duties. 1946: Sold to mercantile and renamed *Valafell*. Acquired by Consolidated Fisheries of Grimsby. PR: GY.383.

GRAYLING   1942/46   Displacement: 142TN
                                            Engines: 125HP
                                            P.No: T 243

1941: Ordered on 13 June. 1942: L. 4 March. Built at Selby by Cochrane and engined by Amos & Smith. Completed as an A/S. 1946: Sold to mercantile. Acquired by Consolidated Fisheries of Grimsby. Renamed *Barry Castle* PR: SA 33. 1955: Mercantile Loss. Wrecked in heavy weather off Iceland on 1 November. Notes: The ship's bell was subsequently dredged up in an Icelandic Trawler's nets and eventually returned to the UK where it was placed in the National Fishing Heritage Museum at Grimsby.

GRILSE   1943/46   Displacement: 127TN
                                            Engines: 103HP
                                            P.No: T 368

1942: Ordered on 2 June. 1943: L. 6 April. Built at Beverley by CWG and engined by Amos & Smith. Completed as an A/S. 1946: Sold to mercantile in June and renamed *Cardiff Castle*. Acquired by Consolidated Fisheries of Grimsby. PR: SA 66.

HERRING   1942/43   P.No: T 307

1942: Ordered on 17 April. L. 24 December. Built at Selby by Cochrane and engined by Amos & Smith. Completed as A/S. 1943: LOST. Sunk in a collision in the North Sea on 22 April.

MACKEREL   1942/43   Displacement: 700TG (As M/L)
                                            P.No: M 55

1941: Ordered on 13 June. 1942: L. 6 March. Built at Selby by Cochrane and engined by Amos & Smith. Renamed CORNCRAKE in November. Completed in November as a Controlled M/L. 1943: LOST. Foundered in a gale in the N.Atlantic on 25 January.

MULLETT   1942/46   Displacement: 142TN
                                            Engines: 109HP
                                            P.No: T 311

1941: Ordered on 17 December. 1942: L. 14 August. Built at Selby by Cochrane and engined by Amos & Smith. Completed as A/S. 1946: Sold to mercantile and renamed *Neath Castle*. Acquired by Consolidated Fisheries of Grimsby. PR: SA 49

POLLACK   1943/46   P.No: T 347

1942: Ordered on 2 June. 1943: L. 22 April. Built at Selby by Cochrane and engined by

Amos & Smith. Completed as A/S. 1946: Sold to mercantile in April. Acquired by Consilidated Fisheries of Grimsby and renamed *Swansea Castle* PR: SA 27. 1952: Renamed *Julia Brierley*.

TURBOT	1942/42	See under REDSHANK (Bird Class)
WHITING	1941/46	P.No: T 232

1941: Ordered on 27 February. L 22 October. Built at Selby by Cochrane and engined by Holmes. Completed as A/S. 1946: Sold to mercantile and renamed *Burfell*. Acquired by Consolidated Fisheries of Grimsby. PR: GY 346. 1960: BU at Sunderland in June

MULLET   **(Author's Collection)**

HILLS CLASS

The 8 steam powered vessels of this class were all built at Beverley, Yorkshire by CWG and engined by Holmes, having been ordered in late 1940 or early 1941. They were built to a design by CWG, Holmes, a subsidiary of the builders and was first used for the 1937 commercial trawler *Barnett*. The design was for a large vessel incorporating something akin to warship lines and, by contemporary standards, a large bridge area.

In the main they were employed as A/S convoy escorts over a wide ranging area from the North Atlantic to the coast of Africa. War losses were BIRDLIP, (1941) and BREDON (1943). The survivors of the class were all sold to the mercantile in 1946.

Displacement:	750 tons
Measurements:	181ft 3in oa 166ft 3in pp x 28ft x 12ft
Engines:	1 shaft Reciprocating (VTE). 970 IHP
Speed:	11kts
Armament:	1 x 12-pdrAA 3 x 20mm AA(3 x single)
Complement:	35

Vessels in the Class:

BIRDLIP, BREDON, BUTSER, DUNCTON, DUNKERY, INKPEN, PORTSDOWN, YESTOR.

BUTSER - The large bridge can be clearly seen, as can the 12-pdr AA in a bandstand and DCRs aft.   **(IWM Neg: A21765)**

HILLS CLASS - NOTES

BIRDLIP	1941/44	Displacement:	510TG 160TN
		Engines:	970HP = 11kts
		Armament:	1 x 12-pdrAA
			3 x 20mm AA (single)
			2 x DCT 2 x DCR
		P.No:	T 218

1940: Ordered on 28 November. 1941: L. 9 July. Built at Beverley by CWG and engined by Holmes. Completed as an A/S. 1942: Commissioned at Birkenhead in May. One of the first Trawlers to be fitted with radar. Employed on Convoy duties. Transferred to the Med. TPI Operaton Torch, the N. African Landings in November. 1943: Transferred to the West African Escort Force based a Freetown. Employed on Convoy Escort duties. Transferred to the 2nd A/S Grp based at Freetown. 1944: LOST. ICW Trawlers INKPEN and TUR COMAN escorting the French ST. BASTILE off Lagos, Nigeria on 13 June, she was torpedoed and sunk by the U-547. There were only 15 survivors who managed to reach shore on 2 liferafts. The sole surviving officer, a S/Lt. RNVR, trekked through the jungle to fetch help.

BREDON	1941/43	Displacement:	510TG 160TN
		Engines:	970HP = 11kts
		P.No:	T 223

1941: Ordered on 15 March. L. 20 November. Built at Beverley by CWG and completed as an Escort. 1942: Joined the 2nd A/S Group based at Freetown. 1943: LOST. Sunk by U-521 in the North Atlantic on 8 February.

BUTSER	1941/46	Displacement:	510TG 160TN
		Engines:	970HP = 11 kts
		P.No:	T 219

1940: Ordered on 20 November. 1941: L. 29 July. Built at Beverley by CWG and engined by Holmes. 1942: Completed in January as A/S. Based at Freetown, W.Africa for convoy duties. 1946: Sold to mercantile and renamed *Balthazar*. Acquired by Devon FCL of Hull. PR: H 359. 1952: Acquired by the Loyal SFC of Grimsby and renamed *Royal Marine*. PR: GY 213. 1960: Acquired by Wyre Trs of Fleetwood. PR: FD 63. 1963: Suffered a fire in the stoke-hold whilst fishing in the Mull of Galoway in July. Declared a TCL and Laid Up. BU at Troon in October.

DUNCTON	1941/46	Displacement:	510T G 160TN
		Engines:	970HP = 11kts
		P.No:	T 220

1941: Ordered on 18 January. L.6 September. Built at Beverley by CWG and engined by Holmes. 1942: Completed on 11th February as an A/S. 1943: Based at Freetown for operations on the W.Coast of Africa. 1944: TIH at Capetown in April for refitting. Completed refitting in July. On passage to Lagos after the refit she suffered an engine breakdown. For 2 weeks she was without engines and at one stage constructed sails out of an awning and bunting. The engines were finally repaired and she made Lagos considerably overdue. 1946: Sold to mercantile in April and renamed *Colwyn Bay*. Acquired by Marine SFC of Hull. PR: H 387. 1964: BU in Holland.

DUNKERY	1941/46	Displacement:	510TG 160TN
		Engines:	970HP = 11kts
		P.No:	T 244

1941: Ordered on 15 March. L. 4 December. Built at Beverley by CWG and engined by Holmes. 1942: Completed on 29 May as an A/S. 1946: Sold to mercantile in October and renamed *Spaniard*. Acquired by Hellyer Bros of Hull. PR: H 366. 1949: Mercantile Loss. Wrecked off the Norwegian coast on 22 March. No loss of life.

INKPEN	1941/46		
		Displacement:	510TG 160TN
		Engines:	970IHP = 11 kts
		P.No:	T 225

1941: Ordered on 15 March. Laid Down on 13 August. L. 2 December. Built at Beverley by CWG and Engined by Holmes. 1942: Completed in June as A/S. 1943: W.African Escort Force based at Freetown. 1946: Sold to mercantile in October. Acquired by East Riding Trs Ltd and renamed *Stella Capella*.

PORTSDOWN	1941/46		
		Displacement:	510TG 195TN
		Engines:	970IHP = 11kts
		P.No:	T 221

1941: Ordered on 18 January. L. 24 September. Built at Beverley by CWG and engined by Holmes. Completed as A/S. 1946: Sold to mercantile in April. Acquired by Hull Merchants Amalgamated Trawlers of Hull and renamed *Sollum*. PR: H 369. 1949: Acquired by Crampin of Grimsby and renamed *Hargood* (Cricketer Group). PR: GY 8. 1955: Renamed *Red Sabre*. PR: LO 71. 1965: BU in S. Ireland.

YESTOR	1941/46		
		Displacement:	198TN
		Engines:	157HP
		P.No:	T 232

1941: Ordered on 18 January. L. 21 October. Built at Beverley by CWG and engined by Holmes. Completed as A/S. 1946: Sold to mercantile in April and renamed *Cape Cleveland*. Acquired by Clyde Trawlers Ltd. PR: H 355. 1947: Renamed *Stella Carina*. 1949: Renamed *Cape Finesterre*. 1952: Renamed *Dragoon*.

ISLES CLASS

This was the most prolific Class of the Second World War. A total of 145 were built including the 16 which were built in Canada for the RCN. Building continued from 1940 through to 1944. As the war progressed, requirements changed from the urgent demand for Minesweepers and Anti-Submarine trawlers so that the Admiralty were able to side-track four of them to be completed as Minelayers and 14 others were completed as Dan Layers.

Their war service was ubiquitous - they were here, there, and everywhere. Every theatre of war saw Isles Class trawlers beavering away at convoy escorts, minesweeping and any other task they were called upon to perform. In 1942 three trawlers, KILLEGRAY, SANDA and SARDA, were transferred to the RNZN. Also in 1942 BRORERAY was renamed DWEAL. Unusually for such a large class at the end of the war there were none left uncompleted on the stocks, so there were no cancellations. Thirteen failed to survive the hostilities and after the war the remainder went mainly to the mercantile where a number were converted to cargo vessels. Of those that didn't go to the mercantile 3 were transferred to the War Department, 7 became dockyard tank cleaning vesses, 4 transferred to the Portuguese Navy, 10 the the Italian Navy, 5 to the Norwegian Navy, 1 to the Royal Malaysian Navy and 2 of the RCN vessels went to the West German Navy. Eight RN and 2 RCN trawlers remained in the Service as Wreck Dispersal Vessels but they were all up for disposal in the 1960s.

Displacement:	545T
Measurements:	164ft oa 150ft pp x 27ft 6in x 10ft 6in
Engines:	1 shaft Reciprocating (VTE) 850 IHP
Speed:	12 kts
Armament:	1 x 12-pdr 3 x 20mm AA Danlayers: 3 x 20mm AA
Complement:	40

Vessels in the Class:

AILSA CRAIG, ANNET, ANTICOSTI (RCN), ARRAN, BAFFIN (RCN), BALTA, BARDSEY, BENBECULA, BERN, BIGGAL, BRESSAY, BRORA, BRORERAY, BRURAY, BRYHER, BURRA, BUTE, CAILIFF, CALDY, CALVAY, CAMPOBELLO, CANNA, CAVA, COLL, COLSAY, COPINSAY, CROWLIN, CUMBRAE, DAMSAY, DOCHET, EARRAID, EDAY, EGILSAY, ENSAY, ERISKAY, FARA, FARNE, FETLAR, FIARAY, FILLA, FLATHOLM, FLINT, FLOTTA, FOULA, FOULNESS, FUDAY, GAIRSAY, GANILLY, GATESHEAD, GILLSTONE, GORREGAN, GRAEMSAY, GRAIN, GRASSHOLM, GRUINARD, GULLAND, HANNARY, HARRIS, HASCOSAY, HAYLING, HELLISAY, HERMTRAY, HERSCHELL, HILDASAY, HOXA, HOY, HUNDA, IMERSAY, INCHCOLM, INCHKIETH, INCHMARNOCK, IRONBOUND (RCN), ISLAY, JURA, KERRARA, KILLEGRAY, KINTYRE, KITTERN, LINDISFARNE, LINGAY, LISCOMB (RCN), LONGA, LUNDY, MAGDALEN (RCN), MANITOULIN (RCN), MEWSTONE, MINALTO, MINCARLO, MISCOU (RCN), MOUSA, MULL, NEAVE, ORFASY, ORONSAY, ORSAY, OXNA, PLADDA, PORCHER, PROSPECT, RONALDSAY, RONAY, ROSEVEAN, ROUSAY, RUSKHOLM, RYSA, ST. AGNES, SANDA, SANDRAY, SCALPAY, SCARAVAY, SCARBA, SHAPINSAY, SHEPPEY (i), SHEPPEY (ii), SHIANT, SHILLAY, SKOKHOLM, SKOMER, SKYE, SLUNA, STAFFA, STEEPHOLM, STONECHAT, STROMA, STRONSAY, SURSAY, SWITHA, TAHAY, TEXADA, THORNEY, TIREE, TOCOGAY, TRODDAY, TRONDRA, ULVA, UNST, VACEASY, VALLAY, VATERSAY, WALLASEA, WESTRAY, WHALSAY, WHITETHROAT, WIAY.

RONAY - The ultimate design in Admiralty built trawlers. Note the spacious roofed-in bridge and greatly increased upperworks.

(MPL)

ISLES CLASS - NOTES

AILSA CRAIG　　　　　　　1943/46　　　P.No:　　　　　T 377

1942: Ordered on 13 December. 1943: L.16 October. Built at Beverley by CWG and engined by Holmes. Completed as a M/S-A/S. 1944: Joined the 34th M/S Flot. MF based at Naples. TPI Operation Dragoon, the Landings in Southern France in August. Transferred to Leghorn and employed on sweeping and A/S patrols. 1945: Employed sweeping off the Anzio Beaches after hostilities had ended. Returned to the UK and Paid Off. Reduced to the Reserve and placed on the Disposal List. 1946: Sold to Norwegian mercantile and renamed *Veslemoy*. 1947: Converted to a tanker. 1952: Renamed *Toran*. 1955 Mercantile Loss. Sank in ice off Sandefjiord on 19 February.

ANNET　　　　　　　　　　1945/58　　　Displacement:　　452TG　142TN
　　　　　　　　　　　　　　　　　　　　Engines:　　　　850HP = 12 kts
　　　　　　　　　　　　　　　　　　　　P.No:　　　　　T 341

1943: L. 25 March. Built at Beverley by CWG and engined by Holmes. Completed as A/S-M/S. 1946: TIH for conversion to WDV and disarmed. Based at Sheerness.1958: Sold to mercantile on 28 May and renamed *Ulva*. Acquired by the Scottish Fisheries Inspectorate as a patrol vessel. 1971: Laid up. 1972: BU at Dalmuir.

ANTICOSTI　　　　　　　　1942/46　　　RCN
　　　　　　　　　　　　　　　　　　　　P.No:　　　　　T 274

1942: L. 1 April. Built at Ontario, Canada, by Collingwood SY. Transferred on loan to the RCN. 1945: Returned to the RN on 17 June. 1946: Sold to mercantile and renamed *Guloy*. 1948: Renamed *Barbro*. 1957: Renamed *Guiseppina*.

ARRAN　　　　　　　　　　1940/46　　　Displacement:　　452TG　142TN
　　　　　　　　　　　　　　　　　　　　Engines:　　　　850HP = 12 kts
　　　　　　　　　　　　　　　　　　　　P.No:　　　　　T 06

1940: L.16 November. Built at Beverley by CWG and Engined by Holmes. 1946: Sold to Dutch mercantile and renamed *Assan Reis*. 1952: Acquired by German owners and renamed *Proffessor Henking*. 1956: Renamed *Berta Kienass*. 1962: Mercantile Loss. Sank off the Texel whilst on passage from Amsterdam to Copenhagen with the loss of all hands.

BAFFIN	1942/45	RCN	
		P.No:	T 275

1942: L. 13 April. Built in Canada by Collingwood SY of Ontario. Transferred on loan to the RCN. 1945: Returned to the RN on 20 August. Placed on the Disposal List. Sold to mercantile in October and retained the same name. 1952: Renamed *Niedermehenen*.

BALTA	1940/46	Displacement:	452TG 142TN
		Engines:	850HP = 12 kts
		P.No:	T 50

1940: L. 2 December. Built at Beverley by CWG and engined by Holmes. Transferred on loan to the RCN. 1946: Sold to Chinese mercantile, converted to a cargo vessel and renamed *Ching Hai*. 1992: Deleted from Lloyd's Register.

BARDSEY	1943/59	P.No:	T 273

1942: Ordered on 1 January. 1943: L. 17 July. Built at Paisley by Fleming & Ferguson. 1946: Disarmed and converted to a WDV. 1950: Converted to a TCV. Based at Malta. 1959: Sold to mercantile in March and retained the same name. Acquired by Malta Dockyards (Baileys).

BENBECULA	1943/46	Displacement:	456TG 144TN
		Engines:	850HP = 12 kts
		P.No:	T 379

1942: Ordered on 13 December. 1943: L. 28 October. Built at Beverley by CWG and engined by Holmes. 1946: Transferred to Customs and Excise on 12 March and renamed *Vigilant*. 1982: Acquired by Albert Yard & Motor Packet Services of Southampton and converted to an accomodation ship.

BENBECULA as HM Customs Cutter VIGILANT. Just one of the many uses to which these sturdy vessels were put post-war. . **(MPL)**

BERN	1942/78	Displacement: Engines: P.No:	452TG 142TN 850HP = 12 kts T 294 DV 4 (WDV) A 334 (TCV)

1942: L. Built at Beverley by CWG and engined by Holmes. Completed as A/S-M/S. 1944: TPI Operation Neptune, the Normandy Landings, in June as A/S escort. 1946: Disarmed and converted to a WDV. 1956: Converted to a TCV. 1978: BU at Sittingbourne.

BIGGAL	1944/46	P.No:	T 404

1942: Ordered on 4 November. 1944: L. 4 December. Built at Port Glasgow by Ferguson Bros. 1946: Sold to mercantile in March and renamed *Frankfurt-Main*. 1961: BU at Hamburg in February.

BRESSAY	1942/46	Displacement: Engines: P.No:	452TG 142TN 850HP = 12 kts T 214

1941: Ordered on 17 May and Laid Down on 7 September. 1942: L. 20 January. Built at Beverley by CWG and engined by Amos & Smith. 1945: Paid Off and Laid Up at Portland. Placed on the Disposal List. 1946: Sold to mercantile in March. Acquired by Belgian owners.

BRORA	1940/41	Displacement: Engines: P.No:	452TG 142TN 850HP = 12 kts T 99

1940: Ordered on 6 April. L. 18 December. Built at Beverley by CWG and engined by Holmes. Completed as an A/S. 1941: LOST. Wrecked in the Hebrides on 6 September.

BRORERAY	1942/46	Displacement: Engines: P.No:	452TG 142TN 850HP = 12 kts T 246

1941: Ordered on 24 October. 1942: L. 17 June. Built at Beverley by CWG and engined by Holmes. Completed as an A/S. Renamed GWEAL in September. 1944: TPI Operation Neptune, the Normandy Landings in June as an A/S Escort. 1946: Sold to Norwegian mercantile, renamed *Velox* and converted to a cargo vessel. 1965: Acquired by China. 1991: Deleted.

BRURAY	1942/45	Displacement: Engines: P.No:	452TG 142TN 850HP = 12 kts T 236

1941: Ordered in July. 1942: L. 16 May. Built at Beverley by CWG and engined by Holmes. Completed as an A/S. 1943: Loaned to the Portuguese Navy from 8 October and renamed P1 for the duration of the loan. 1945: Returned to the RN 2 July. Laid Up. 1946: Sold to the Portuguese Navy on 11 February and renamed SAO MIGUEL. 1957: BU at Lisbon.

BRYHER	1943/47	Displacement: Engines: P.No:	456TG 144TN 850HP = 12 kts T 350

1942: Ordered in July. 1943: L. 8 April. Built at Beverley by CWG and engined by Holmes. Completed in August as an A/S. 1944: TPI Operation Neptune, the Normandy

Landings in June, as a D/L attached to the 9th M/S Flot. 1947: Sold to Norwegian mercantile and renamed *Eskimo*. 1950: Renamed *Zero*. 1960: Acquired by China. 1981: Deleted.

| BURRA | 1941/46 | P.No: | T 158 |

1940: Ordered on 6 April. 1941: L. 12 April. Built at Goole by Goole SB and engined by Amos & Smith. 1946: Sold to the Italian Navy on 22 January and renamed RD 301.

| BUTE | 1941/46 | P.No: | T 168 |

1940: Ordered on 6 April. 1941: L. 12 May. Built at Goole by Goole SB and engined by Amos & Smith. 1946: Sold to mercantile in March.

| CAILIFF | 1942/46 | P.No: | T 276 |

1942: L. 30 April. Built in Canada by Collingwood SY, Ontario. Transferred on loan to the RCN. Commissioned into the RCN on 17 September. 1943: Joined the Halifax Defence Force in December. 1945: Returned to the RN on 17 June. 1946: Sold to mercantile and renamed *Borgenes*. 1988: Purchased by a preservation group in the USA.

| CALDY | 1943/83 | P.No: | T 359 |

1942: Ordered on 4 November. 1943: L. 31 August. Built at Aberdeen by John Lewis & Sons and completed as an A/S. 1944: TPI Operation Neptune, the Normandy Landings in June. 1946: Disarmed and converted to a WDV. 1951: Converted to a TCV. 1983: BU in June.

CALVAY   1943/46   Displacement: 456TG   144TN
                                              Engines: 850HP = 12 kts
                                              P.No: T 383

1943: Ordered on 20 March. L. 29 November. Built at Beverley by CWG and engined by Holmes. 1944: Completed on 16 February. 1944: TPI Operation Neptune, the D-Day Landings in June, as a D/L attached to the 15th M/S Flot. operating off Sword Beach. 1946: Sold to mercantile in November and renamed *William Fenton*. Acquired by Humber Pilots Steam Cutter Co of Hull and registered for Pilot Service. 1975: BU at Blyth by Hughes Bolckow.

CALDY as a Wreck Disposal Vessel   **(Author's Collection)**

CAMPOBELLO   1942/43   P.No: T 278

1942: L.19 June. Built in Canada by Collingwood SY, Ontario and completed as A/S.
1943: LOST. Foundered in the North Atlantic on 16 March.

CANNA   1940/42   P.No: T 161

1940: Ordered on 6th April. L.18 November. Built at Selby by Cochrane and engined by
Holmes. 1942: LOST. Destroyed by accidental explosion at Lagos, Nigeria, on 5
December.

CAVA   1941/47   P.No: T 145

1940: Ordered on 4 May. 1941: L. 3 March. Built at Paisley by Fleming & Ferguson and
completed as an A/S. 1944: MF. Based at Malta for A/S patrols and escort duties. 1945:
Paid Off at Malta and placed on the Disposal List. 1947: Sold to Italian mercantile on 16
May and renamed *Lucia Venturi*.

COLL   1942/75   P.No: T 207

1941: Ordered on 18 January. 1942: L. 7 April. Built at Ardrossan by the Ardrossan DY
Co.Ltd. and engined by Plenty. Completed as an A/S. 1944: TPI Operation Neptune, the
D-Day Landings in June, as an A/S Escort. 1945: Converted to a WDV in December.
1950: Converted to a TCV. 1975: Employed as a target from November.

COLSAY   1943/44   Displacement: 456TG   144TN
                                              Engines: 850HP = 12 kts
                                              P.No: T 384

1943: Ordered on 20 March. L. 14 December. Built at Beverley by CWG and engined
by Holmes. 1944: Completed in March as A/S. TPI Operation Neptune, the D-Day
Landings in June, as a D/L to the 1st M/S Flot. off Sword Beach. LOST. Sunk by
German Human Torpedo off Ostende on 2 November.

COPINSAY   1940/46   Armament: 1 x 12-pdr DP; 3 x
                                                      single 20mmAA;
                                                     DCs
                                              P.No: T 147

1940: Ordered on 27 May. L. 2 December. Built at Selby by Cochrane and engined by
Amos & Smith. 1944: West African Station sweeping between Freetown and Lagos.
Credited with a 'possible' sinking of a U-Boat. 1946: Transferred to the War Dept. 1956:
Sold to Mercantile and renamed *Ion*.

CROWLIN   1943/46   Displacement: 456TG   144TN
                                              Engines: 850HP = 12 kts
                                              P.No: T 300

1942: Ordered on 13 December. 1943: L. 15 November. Built at Beverley by CWG and
engined by Holmes. 1944: Completed on 28 January. Joined the 34th M/S Flot. MF,
based at Naples. TPI Operation Dragoon the landings in S.France in August.
Transferred to Leghorn for M/S and A/S patrols. 1946: Sold to mercantile in March and
renamed *Hans Hummersund*. Acquired by Norwegian owners and converted to a cargo
vessel. 1948: Acquired by Honduras owners and renamed *Crowlin*. 1954: Vessel cap-
sized off Stavangar and was found floating upside down. All hands lost. Uprighted and
refloated. 1955: Acquired by Norwegian owners and renamed *Thermo*. 1961: Acquired
by Bulgarian owners and renamed *Chernomoretz*. 1964: Acquired by Ethiopian owners
and renamed *Axum*. 1977: Renamed *Dire Dewa*. Mercantile Loss. Sank at Massawa
Port, Ethiopa, on 4 March. 1979: Refloated and BU.

CUMBRAE   1940/46   P.No: T 154

1940: Ordered on 22 July. L. 30 December. Built at Selby by Cochrane and engined by Amos & Smith. 1942: MF. Employed on Convoy duties. Based at Haifa ICW ISLAY. 1946: Transferred to the Italian Navy on 22 January. Renamed RD 302.

DAMSAY   1942/46   P.No: T 208

1941: Ordered on 18 January. 1942: L. 27 June. Built at Greenock by George Brown and engined by Aitchison Blair. Completed as an A/S. 1944: TPI Operation Neptune, the D-Day Landings as an A/S escort. 1946: Transferred to the War Dept. as a Store Carrier. 1959: Sold to Mole & Bray of Stourport on 28 August. 1960: BU.

DOCHET   1942/47   P.No: T 286

1942: L. 26 June. Built in Canada by Davie SB & Repair of Lauzon, Quebec. 1947: Sold to mercantile and renamed *Catherine*. Subsequently purchased into the W.German Navy and renamed EIDER.

EARRAID   1941/51   P.No: T 297

1940: Ordered on 21 December as GRUNA. 1941: Renamed in November. L.18 December. Built at Sunderland by John Crown & Sons and engined by White's ME. 1946: Disarmed and converted to a WDV. 1951: Sold to mercantile on 13 March.

EDAY   1941/47   P.No: T 201

1940: Ordered on 16 November. 1941: L. 26 June. Built at Selby by Cochrane. 1944: Temporary Loan to the Norwegian Navy from August and renamed TROMOY for the duration of the loan. Returned to the RN in October. 1947: Sold to mercantile in January and renamed *Fjellberg*. 1952: Renamed *Sempach*. 1953: Mercantile Loss on 27 April.

EGILSAY   1942/46   P.No: T 215

1941: Ordered on 17 May. 1942: L. 7 February. Built at Beverley by CWG and engined by Holmes. 1946: Transferred to the Italian Navy on 22 February and Renamed RD 306.

ENSAY   1942/46   Displacement: 452TG   142TN
                                      Engines: 850HP = 12 kts
                                      P.No: T 216

1941: Ordered on 17 May. 1942: L. 5 March. Built at Beverley by CWG and engined by Holmes. Commissioned for Channel escort duties. 1946: Transferred to the Italian Navy on 16 February and renamed RD 314. 1965: Paid Off and subsequently used as a target vessel.

ERISKAY   1942/45   Armament: 1 x 12-pdr DP; 3 x
                                                       single 20mmAA; 2 x
                                                       single LG.
                                      P.No: T 217

1941: Ordered on 17 May. 1942: L. 28 August. Built at Paisley by Fleming & Ferguson. 1943: Temporary loan to the Portuguese Navy from 8 October and renamed P 8 for the duration of the loan. 1944: Returned to the RN on 26 June. Employed on Med. convoys. 1945: LOST. Foundered off Sao Jorge in the Azores on 12 November. Notes: Lewis Guns were mounted on the bridge wings.

FARNE with twin derricks aft for laying and retrieving Dan Buoys. The two forward 20mm AA guns mounted in a bandbox and pointing heavenward show the extent to which they could be elevated. **(Steve Bush Collection)**

FARA   1941/46   P.No: T 162

1940: Ordered on 27 May. 1941: L.15 January. Built at Selby by Cochrane and engined by Amos & Smith. 1946: Sold to mercantile on 12 July.

FARNE   1943/47   P.No: T 353

1942: Ordered on 7 July. 1943: L. 22 April. Built at Beverley by CWG and engined by Holmes. Completed as a M/S. 1944: Converted to a D/L. TPI Operation Neptune, the D-Day Landings in June, as a D/L attached to the 7th M/S Flot. off Juno Beach. 1947: Sold to the mercantile and retained the same name.

FETLAR   1941/60   P.No: T 202

1940: Ordered on 16 November. 1941: L.   10 July. Built at Selby by Cochrane. 1946: Disarmed and converted to a WDV. 1960: Sold. Arrived at Antwerp on 22 June to BU.

FIARAY   1942/46   P.No: T 238

1941: Ordered on 4 July. 1942: L. 13 June. Built at Goole by the Goole SB and engined by Amos & Smith. 1946: Sold to Mercantile and renamed *Atlas*. 1955: Renamed *Aris*.

FILLA   1942/46   P.No: T 212

1941: Ordered on 15 March. 1942: L. 2 April. Built at Sunderland by Crown. 1946: Transferred to the Italian Navy and renamed RD 305.

FLATHOLM   1943/60   P.No: T 354

1942: Ordered on 30 July. 1943: L. 8 May. Built at Beverley by CWG and engined by Holmes. 1946: Disarmed and converted to a WDV. 1960: Sold on 31 August and BU in Belgium.

FLINT 1942/47 P.No: T 287

1942: L.14 July. Built in Canada by George T. Davie & Sons and completed as A/S. 1944: TPI Operation Neptune, the D-Day Landings in June, as an A/S Escort. 1947: Sold to mercantile and renamed *Cornelia*. Subsequently purchased into the W.German Navy and renamed TRAVE.

FLOTTA 1941/41 P.No: T 171

1940: Ordered on 27 May. 1941: L. 14 February. Built at Selby by Cochrane. LOST. Took the ground off E. Scotland on 29 October and finally foundered on 6 November.

FOULA 1941/46 P.No: T 203

1940: Ordered on 16 November. 1941: L. 9 August. Built at Selby by Cochrane. 1946: Transferred to the Italian Navy in February and renamed RD 313.

FOULNESS 1943/71 P.No: T 342

1942: Ordered on 11 April. 1943: L. 23 February. Built at Aberdeen by John Lewis and completed as an A/S. 1944: TPI Operation Neptune, the D-Day Landings in June, as an A/S escort. 1957: Converted to a TCV. 1971: Sold out of Service.

FUDAY 1944/47 Armament: 3 x single 20mmAA
P.No: T 389

1943: Ordered on 24 March. 1944: L. 1 January. Built at Beverley by CWG and engined by Holmes. Completed as a D/L. TPI Operation Neptune, the D-Day Landings in June, as a D/L attached to the 4th M/S Flot. in Force D. 1947: Sold to mercantile and renamed *Simon de Danser*.

GAIRSAY 1942/44 P.No: T 290

1941: Ordered on 16 June. 1942: L. 28 May. Built at Ardrossan by Ardrossan SB and engined by Plenty. Completed as an A/S. 1944: TPI Operation Neptune, the D-Day Landings in June, as an A/S Escort. LOST. Sunk by an explosive MB off Normandy on 3 August.

GANILLY 1943/44 P.No: T 376

1942: Ordered on 30 July. 1943: L. 22 May. Built at Beverley by CWG and engined by Holmes. Completed as an A/S. 1944: TPI Operation Neptune, the D-Day Landings in June as an A/S Escort. LOST. Mined in the Channel on 5 July.

GATESHEAD 1942/59 P.No: T 288

1942: L. 1 August. Built in Canada by Davie SB of Quebec. Completed as an A/S. 1944: TPI Oeration Neptune, the D-Day Landings in June, as an A/S Escort. 1959: Sold. Arrived at Rotterdam on 13 October to BU.

GILLSTONE 1943/46 P.No: T 355

1943: L.19 July. Built at Selby by Cochrane and engined by Amos & Smith. 1947: Sold to mercantile and renamed *Argo*.

GORREGAN 1943/57 P.No: Y 720

1942: Ordered on 30 July. 1943: L. 30 December. Built at Ardrossan by the Ardrossan SB and engined by White. 1957: Sold and arrived at Charlestown in October to BU.

| GRAEMSAY | 1942/78 | P.No: | T 291 |

1941: Ordered on 16 June. 1942: L. 3 August. Built at Ardrossan by the Ardrossan DY Co and engined by Plenty. 1946: Dearmed and converted for Wreck Dispersal. 1957: Converted to a TCV. 1978: BU in October.

| GRAIN | 1943/46 | P.No: | T 360 |

1942: Ordered on 21 October. 1943: L. 17 August. Built at Selby by Cochrane and engined by Amos & Smith. 1946: Transferred to the Italian Navy on 16 March and renamed RD 309.

| GRASSHOLM | 1943/46 | P.No: | T 344 |

1942: Ordered on 11 April. 1943: L. 20 April. Built at Aberdeen by Lewis and completed as an A/S. 1944: TPI Opertaton Neptune, the D-Day Landings in June as an A/S escort. 1946: Sold to mercantile and retained the same name.

| GRUINARD | 1942/46 | P.No: | T 239 |

1941: Ordered in July. 1942: L. 20 November. Built at Sunderland by Crown & Sons and engined by Holmes. 1943: On temporary loan to the Portuguese Navy from October and renamed P 7 for the duration of the loan. 1944: Returned to the RN in September. 1946: Sold to mercantile in June and renamed *President F.D.Roosevelt*. 1950: Renamed *Odin*.

| GULLAND | 1943/46 | P.No: | T 365 |

1941: Ordered on 4 November. 1943: L. 5 August. Built at Beverley by CWG and engined by Holmes. Deployed to the Med and joined the 34th M/S Grp. 1944: Group based at Leghorn. 1946: Sold to mercantile in March.

| GWEAL | 1941/46 | See under BRORERAY |

| HANNARAY | 1944/47 | Armament: | 3 x single 20mmAA |
| | | P.No: | T 389 |

1943: Ordered on 20 March. 1944: L. 12 February. Built at Beverley by CWG and engined by Holmes. Completed as a D/L. TPI Operation Neptune, the D-Day Landings in June, as a D/L attached to the 6th M/S Flotilla on Force G. 1947: Sold to mercantile and renamed *Wodan*.

| HARRIS | 1944/47 | Armament: | 3 x single 20mmAA |
| | | P.No: | T 386 |

1943: Ordered on 20 March. Laid down in December as GILSAY. 1944: Renamed in January. L. 29 January. Built at Beverley by CWG and engined by Holmes. Completed in April. 1947: Sold to Norwegian mercantile on 24 March and renamed *Lyngas*. Converted to a cargo vessel. 1950: Acquired by French mercantile and renamed *Fort Malbousquet*. 1952: Acquired by Indian mercantile and renamed *Sheila Margaret*. 1964: Renamed *Ashare*. Mercantile Loss. Driven ashore in a cyclone near Bombay on 7 August. 1965: Wreck refloated and BU at Darukhana, Bombay.

| HASCOSAY | 1944/47 | Armament: | 3 x single 20mmAA |
| | | P.No: | T 390 |

1943: Ordered on 20 March. 1944: L. 28 March. Built at Beverley by CWG and engined by Holmes. Completed as a D/L. 1947: Sold to Greek mercantile, renamed *Ypapandi* and converted to a cargo vessel. 1952: Mercantile Loss. Reported missing on 17 January whilst on passage to Piraeus.

| HAYLING | 1942/46 | P.No: | T 271 |

1942: Ordered on 1 January. L.17 August. Built at Beverley by CWG and engined by Holmes. 1943: Temporary Loan to the Portuguese Navy from October and renamed P 3 for the duration of the loan. 1945: Returned to the RN in July. 1946: Sold to the Portuguese Navy on 11 June and renamed TERCEIRA.

| HELLISAY | 1944/47 | Armament: | 3 x single 20mmAA |
| | | P.No: | T 391 |

1943: Ordered on 16 April. 1944: L. 27 March. Built at Selby by Cochrane and engined by Amos & Smith. Completed as a D/L. 1947: Sold to mercantile in June and renamed *Elpis*. 1954: Renamed *Elpis II*.

| HERMETRAY | 1944/47 | Armament: | 3 x single 20mmAA |
| | | P.No: | T 392 |

1943: Ordered on 16 April. 1944: L. 11 April. Built at Selby by Cochrane and engined by Amos & Smith. Completed as a D/L. 1947: Sold to mercantile on 25 April and renamed *Coimbra*. 1952: Renamed *Furka*.

| HERSCHELL | 1942/46 | P.No: | T 289 |

1942: L. 9 November. Built in Canada by Davie of Quebec and completed as A/S. 1944: TPI Operation Neptune, the D-Day Landings in June, as an A/S Escort. 1946: Sold to mercantile and renamed *Eirikur Hin Reidi*. 1947: Renamed *Radni*.

| HILDASAY | 1941/45 | P.No: | T 173 |

1940: Ordered on 13 September. 1941: L. 10 May. Built at Beverley by CWG and engined by Amos & Smith. 1945: LOST. Wrecked off Kilindini, East Africa, on 21 June.

| HOXA | 1941/46 | P.No: | T 16 |

1940: Ordered on 27 May. 1941: L. 15 January. Built at Beverley by CWG and engined by Amos & Smith. Completed as A/S. 1944: E.I. Station. Detailed to escort salvage vessel SALVIKING from Trincomalee to Addu Atoll. Enroute the SALVIKING was torpedoed and sunk and suvivors were rescued. 1946: Sold to mercantile in July and renamed *Sung Hwei*.

| HOY | 1941/46 | P.No: | T 114 |

1940: Ordered on 27 May. 1941: L. 1 February. Built at Beverley by CWG and engined by Amos & Smith. 1946: Sold to mercantile and renamed *Dunay*.

| HUNDA | 1942/46 | P.No: | T 298 |

1941: Ordered on 18 January. 1942: L.16 February. Built at Port Glasgow by Ferguson. 1945: MF. Sailed from Malta in the spring for UK but suffered a boiler explosion shortly after sailing and was forced to return to Malta for repairs. Subsequently returned to the UK. Paid Off and placed on the Disposal List. 1946: Sold to mercantile in May.

| IMERSAY | 1944/59 | Armament: | 3 x single 20mmAA |
| | | P.No: | J 422 |

1943: Ordered on 16 April. 1944: L. 21 August. Built at Selby by Cochrane and engined by Amos & Smith. Completed as a D/L. Deployed E. of Suez and joined the EIF. Attached to the M/S Flotillas. 1959: Sold to mercantile at Malta in January.

INCHCOLM	1941/46	Displacement:	452TG 142TN
		Engines:	850IHP = 12 kts
		P.No:	T 18

1941: L. 1 March. Built at Beverley by CWG and engined by Holmes. Completed as a M/S. 1946: Transferred to the War Dept in June. Employed on Wreck Dispersal by the RASC. 1947: Converted to a cargo vessel. 1953: Acquired by GA Ferguson of Lerwick and converted to oil fuel. Subsequently acquired by Italian mercantile and renamed *Celeste Aida*. 1999: Still in mercantile service.

| INCHKIETH | 1941/58 | P.No: | T 155 |

1941: L. 24 October. Built at Aberdeen by Lewis and completed as a M/S. Transferred to the RNZN in October. 1958: Sold on 10 September to BU.

| INCHMARNOCK | 1941/46 | P.No: | T 166 |

1941: L. 25 August. Built at Aberdeen by Lewis and completed as a M/S. 1944: Temporary Loan to the Norwegian Navy and renamed KARMOY for the period of the loan. 1946: Returned to the RN in June and placed on the Disposal List. Sold to mercantile and renamed *Tilthorn*. 1952: Renamed *Nador*. 1955: Renamed *Servanaise*.

| IRONBOUND | 1942/46 | P.No: | T 284 |

1942: L.14 January. Built in Canada by Kingston of Ontario and completed as a M/S. Loaned to the RCN from October. 1945: Returned to the RN on 17 June. 1946: Sold to mercantile and renamed *Turoy*. 1949: Renamed *Christina*. 1954: Renamed *Korso*.

| ISLAY | 1941/46 | P.No: | T 172 |

1941: L. 10 April. Built at Southbank-on-Tees by Smith's Dock. Completed as A/S. 1942: Deployed to the Med. Based at Haifa ICW CUMBRAE. Sank the Italian S/M SCIRE off Haifa on 10 August. 1946: Sold to mercantile in October and renamed *Isly*. 1949: Renamed *St. Anne*. 1950: Mercantile Loss on 14 March.

| JURA | 1941/43 | P.No: | T 169 |

1940: Ordered on 22 July. 1941: L. 22 November. Built at Ardrossan by Ardrossan DY Co and engined by Plenty. 1942: Deployed to the Med. 1943: LOST. Sunk by U-371 in the W.Med. on 7 January.

| KERRERA | 1941/46 | P.No: | T 200 |

1940: Ordered on 24 October. 1941: L. 22 September. Built at Paisley by Fleming & Ferguson and completed as A/S-M/S. Joined the 8th A/S-M/S Group based at Scapa Flow. Sustained severe storm damage off the Faroes on 6/7 December. TIH for repairs. 1944: Temporary Loan to the Norwegian Navy. Renamed OKSAY for the duration of the-loan. 1946: Returned to the RN in March and placed on the Disposal List. Sold to mercantile and renamed *Jason*. 1950: Mercantile Loss on 1 March.

KILLEGRAY	1941/58	Displacement:	452TG 142TN
		Engines:	850HP = 12 kts
		P.No:	T 174

1940: Ordered on 13 September. 1941: Laid Down in January. L. 27 May. Built at

Beverley by CWG and engined by Holmes. Transferred to the RNZN in November. 1946: Paid Off and reduced to the Reserve at Auckland. 1958: Deleted in September.

KINTYRE	1941/46	P.No:	T 165

1940: Ordered on 22 July. 1941: L. 21 October. Built at Ardrossan by the Ardrossan Dyd Co and engined by Plenty. Completed as a M/S. 1946: Sold to mercantile in May.

KITTERN	1943/46	Displacement:	144TN
		Engines:	850IHP = 12 kts
		P.No:	T 302

1941: Ordered on 4 November. 1943: L. 21 August. Built at Beverley by CWG and engined by Holmes. 1946: Sold to Norwegian mercantile in April, renamed *Bonita* and converted to a cargo vessel. 1947: Converted to FO. 1968: Mercantile Loss. Wrecked in the Fox River, Canada in December.

LINDISFARNE	1943/58	Displacement:	454TG 144TN
		Engines:	850IHP = 12 kts
		P.No:	T 361

1942: Ordered on 30 July. 1943: L. 17 June. Built at Beverley by CWG and engined by Holmes. Completed in September as A/S. 1944: TPI Operation Neptune, the D-Day Landings in June, as A/S Escort. 1946: Dearmed and converted to a WDV. 1958: Sold. Arrived at Dover on 26 April to BU.

LINGAY	1944/47	Armament:	3 x single 20mmAA
		P.No:	J 423

1943: Ordered on 16 April. 1944: L. 6 September. Built at Selby by Cochrane and engined by Amos & Smith. Completed as a D/L. Deployed to the Far East and joined the BPF. Attached to the BPF M/S Flotillas. 1947: Sold to mercantile and renamed *Tulipdale*.

LINDISFARNE in her role as a WDV.   **(PRNM)**

LISCOMB	1942/46	RCN	
		P.No:	T 285

1942: L. 23 March. Built in Canada by Kingston SB, Ontario. Transferred on loan to the RCN. 1945: Returned to the RN on 17 June. 1946: Sold to mercantile and renamed *Aalesund*.

LONGA	1943/46	P.No:	T 366

1942: Ordered on 13 December. 1943: L. 15 October. Built at Selby by Cochrane and engined by Holmes. 1946: Sold to mercantile and retained the same name.

LUNDY	1942/82	Displacement:	452TG 142TN
		Engines:	850IHP = 12 kts
		P.No:	T 272
			P 46 (WDV)
			A 366 (TCV)

1942: Ordered on 1 January. L. 29 August. Built at Beverley by CWG and engined by Holmes. 1943: Completed in January. 1946: De-armed and converted to a WDV. 1956: Converted to a TCV. 1981: Laid Up at Portsmouth. 1982: Expended as a target in August.

MAGDALEN	1942/46	RCN	
		P.No:	T 279

1942: L. 7 March. Built in Canada by Midland SY. Temporary Loan to the RCN. 1945: Returned to the RN on 17 June. Laid Up. 1946: Sold to mercantile on 14 April and renamed *Maroy*. 1951: Renamed *Cinzia*.

MANITOULIN	1942/46	RCN	
		P.No:	T 280

1942: L. 23 April. Built in Canada by Midland SY . Temporary Loan to the RCN. 1945: Returned to the RN on 17 June. 1946: Sold to mercantile and renamed *Ran*. 1951: Renamed *Ran B* and then renamed *Blue Peter*.

MEWSTONE	1943/46	Displacement:	456TG 144TN
		Engines:	850IHP = 12 kts
		P.No:	T 374

1943: L. 16 September. Built at Beverley by CWG and engined by Holmes. Completed as a M/S-A/S. 1944: Joined the 34th M/S Flotilla MF and based at Naples. TPI Operation Dragoon, the Landings in S.France in August. Transferred to Leghorn for sweeping and A/S patrols. 1945: Sweeping the Anzio Beaches after Hostilities had ended. Returned to the UK. Paid Off and reduced to the Reserve. Placed on the Disposal List. 1946: Sold to mercantile in April. Acquired by B.Nesje of Bergen, Norway. Renamed *Vingtor* and converted to a cargo vessel. 1949: Mercantile Loss. Wrecked near Cap Negro, N.Africa.

MINALTO	1943/46	Displacement:	456TG 144TN
		Engines:	850IHP = 12 kts
		P.No:	T 362

1942: Ordered on 4 November. 1943: L. 3 July. Built at Beverley by CWG and engined by Holmes. 1946 Sold to mercantile. Acquired by Svorig of Bergen, Norway, renamed *Lillen* and converted to a cargo vessel. 1956: Acquired by German mercantile and renamed *Agricola*. 1964: Acquired by Yugoslavian mercantile and renamed *Perna*. 1978: BU after she had fallen off the slipway at Vranjic whilst under repair.

MINCARLO	1944/46	P.No:	T 388

1942: Ordered 30 July. 1944: L. 28 March. Built at Ardrossan by Ardrossan SB and engined by Whites. Temporary Loan to the Norwegian Navy from October and renamed TROMOY for the duration of the loan. 1946: Returned to the RN in September and placed on the Disposal List. Sold to mercantile. 1948: Renamed *Kristianborg*. 1950: Renamed *Sverrehund*.

MISCOU	1942/46	See under CAMPENIA

MOUSA	1942/46	P.No:	T 295

1941: Ordered on 16 June. 1942: L.1 June. Built at Goole by Goole SB and engined by Amos & Smith. 1946: Sold to the Italian Navy in February and renamed RD 311.

MULL	1941/46	Displacement:	452TG 142TN
		Engines:	850IHP = 12 kts
		P.No:	T 110

1940: Ordered on 22 July. 1941: L. 27 March. Built at Beverley by CWG and engined by Holmes. 1942: Joined the MF. TPI the N.African Campaign. 1945: Returned to the UK from Alexandria, a voyage which lasted 3 months owing to constant engine break-downs. 1946: Paid Off and transferred to the War Dept. in April and employed on Wreck Dispersal. 1962: Stranded in Loch Tarbert and salvaged. 1974: Placed on the Disposal List in January. Notes: The only Admiralty Built Trawler of WWII to sink a U-Boat.

RASC MULL in her role as a WDV operated by the Royal Army Service Corps. **(MPL)**

NEAVE	1942/51	Displacement: Engines: P.No:	452TG 142TN 850IHP = 12 kts T 247 A 342 (WDV)

1941: Ordered on 24 March. 1942: L. 16 July. Built at Beverley by CWG and engined by Holmes. Completed as a M/S-A/S. 1944: TPI Operation Neptune, the D-Day Landings in June, as an A/S escort. 1946: Converted to a WDV. 1951: Sold to mercantile in July and renamed *Tulipbank*. Acquired by British Wheeler Process Ltd of Liverpool. Converted to a Petrol Sludge Carrier. 1979: BU.

ORFASY	1941/43	P.No:	T 204

1940: Ordered on 21 December. 1942: L. 17 March. Built at Aberdeen by Alex Hall. 1943: LOST. Sunk off W.Africa on 22 October. Thought to have been torpedoed by a U-Boat.

ORONSAY	1943/46	P.No:	T 375

1942: Ordered on 13 December. 1943: L. 30 October. Built at Selby by Cochrane and engined by Amos & Smith. 1946: Sold to mercantile.

ORSAY	1945/57	P.No:	J 450

1943: Ordered on 16 April. 1945: L. 1 January. Built at Selby by Cochrane and engined by Amos & Smith. Completed as a D/L. 1956: Converted to a TCV. 1957: Sold on 3 September.

OXANA	1943/46	P.No:	T 296

1941: Ordered on 16 June. 1943: L. 26 January. Built at Glasgow by Inglis and engined by Aitcheson Blair. 1946: Transferred to the War Dept on 16 July and retained the same name.

PLADDA	1941/47	Displacement: Engines: P.No:	452TG 142TN 850HP = 12 kts T 144

1941: L. 16 April. Built at Beverley by CWG and engined by Holmes. 1946: Loaned to the Rangoon Port Commissioners in May. Returned to the RN at Singapore in October. Placed on the Sale List. 1947: Sold to mercantile and retained the same name. Acquired by Gythfeldt & Co of Singapore. 1949: Acquired by Siamese owners. 1950: Deleted.

PORCHER		P.No:	T 281

1941: Laid down as PROCHER. 1942: L. 26 May. Built in Canada by Midland SY. Renamed in October. 1947: Transferred to the War Dept and retained the same name. 1951: Sold to mercantile and renamed *Tulipglen*. Notes: aka PROCHER. Occasionally listed under both names.

PROCHER	1942/47		See under PORCHER

PROSPECT	1942/46	P.No:	T 282

1942: L. 16 June. Built in Canada by the Midland SY and engined by Con. Mining & Smelting. 1946: Employed on supervising the German Navy in Mine-clearance in the North Sea. Paid Off at Portland. Transferred to the War Dept. in August and retained the same name. 1959: Sold to Greek mercantile in December.

| RONALDSAY | 1941/46 | P.No: | T 149 |

1940: Ordered on 22 July. 1941: L.15 February. Built at Selby by Cochrane and engined by Amos & Smith. 1946: Sold to mercantile and renamed *Diksmuide* 7.

| RONAY | 1945/67 | Armament: | 3 x single 20mmAA |
| | | P.No: | J 429 |

1943: Ordered on 16 April. 1945: L. 15 February. Built at Selby by Cochrane and completed as a D/L. 1967: Sold and arrived Troon on 13 April to BU.

ROSEVEAN	1943/46	Displacement:	456TG 144TN
		Engines:	850IHP = 12 kts
		P.No:	T 363

1942: Ordered on 4 November. 1943: L. 17 July. Built at Beverley by CWG and engined by Holmes. 1946: Sold to mercantile in March. Acquired by Moroccon owners and renamed *El Reszk*. 1957: Mercantile Loss. Wrecked near Punta Galha on 2 May.

| ROUSAY | 1941/46 | P.No: | T 210 |

1941: Ordered on 15 March. L. 20 December. Built at Goole by Goole SB and engined by Amos & Smith. 1946: Sold to mercantile and renamed *Tova*. 1954: Renamed *Einar Hund*.

| RUSKHOLM | 1942/49 | P.No: | T 211 |

1941: Ordered on 15 March. Built at Goole by Goole SB and engined by Amos & Smith. 1949: Transferred to the Portuguese Navy in September and renamed BALDAQUE da SILVA.

| RYSA | 1941/43 | P.No: | T 164 |

1941: L. 15 March. Built at Selby by Cochrane. 1943: LOST. Mined off Maddalena, Sicily, on 8 December.

RYSA - The class sported a variety of funnel caps and hers can be clearly seen. Note the Atlantic dazzle paint. **(MPL)**

ST. AGNES   1936/46   P.No: T 352

1942: Ordered on 30 July. 1943: L. 19 May. Built at Aberdeen by Lewis. 1946: Sold to mercantile in March and renamed *Captain Arsene Blonde*. 1950: Renamed *Thor*.

SANDA   1941/58   P.No: T 160

1941: L. 28 July. Built at Goole by Goole SB and engined by Amos & Smith. 1942: Transferred to the RNZN. 1958: Sold to mercantile in September.

SANDRAY   1944/62   Displacement: 443TG   151TN
                                        Engines: 850IHP = 12 kts
                                        Armament: 3 x single 20mmAA
                                        P.No: J 424

1943: Ordered on 16 April. 1944: L. 5 October. Built at Beverley by CWG and completed as a D/L. 1945: Joined the E.I. Fleet at Trincomalee. 1960: Sold to Honduras owners, but the sale fell through. 1962: BU at Bruges, Belguim.

SCALPAY   1942/48   Displacement: 452TG   142TN
                                        Engines: 850IHP = 12 kts
                                        P.No: T 237

1941: Ordered on 2 July. 1942: Laid Down on 14 February. L. 2 June Built at Beverley by CWG and engined by Amos & Smith. 1944: TPI Operation Neptune, the D-Day Landings in June, as an A/S escort. 1946: Dearmed and converted to a WDV in March. 1948: Sold to mercantile in April and retained the same name. Acquired by W.Ripon Ltd of London and converted to a salvage vessel. 1953: Sold to Italian owners. 1967: Mercantile Loss. Wrecked near Cape Mannu and BU.

SCARAVAY   1944/46   Armament: 3 x single 20mmAA
                                        P.No: J 425

1943: Ordered on 16 April. 1944: L. 22 October. Built at Selby by Cochrane and engined by Holmes. Completed as a D/L. Deployed to the FE and joined the BPF. 1946: Sold to mercantile in November.

SCARBA   1941/58   Armament: 3 x single 20mmAA
                                        P.No: T 175

1941: L. 25 June. Built at Beverley by CWG and engined by Holmes. 1942: Transferred to the RNZN in October. Retained the same name. 1946: Reduced to the Reserve at Auckland. 1958: Sold to G.A. Sparrey 10 September and BU at Auckland.

SHAPINSAY   1941/46   P.No: T 176

1941: L. 29 March. Built at Selby by Cochrane and engined by Amos & Smith. 1946: Sold to mercantile in August and renamed *El Hascimy*. 1955: Renamed *El Fayez*.

SHEPPEY (i)   1942/42   See under BLACKBIRD

SHEPPEY (ii)   1942/46   Ex-RAASAY
                                        Displacement: 452TG   142TN
                                        Engines: 850NHP = 12 kts
                                        P.No: T 292

1941: Ordered on 16 June as RAASAY. 1942: Renamed. L. 1 April. Built at Beverley by CWG and engined by Holmes. 1943: Deployed as a M/S. 1944: Transferred to the Med.

Operated off Pireaus, Greece as a D/L. 1946: Transferred to the War Dept (RASC) and retained the same name. Employed as a WDV. 1959: BU at Plymouth.

SHIANT	1941/46	P.No:	T 170

1941: L. 9 August. Built at Goole by Goole SB and engined by Amos & Smith. 1944: Temporary Loan to the Norwegian Navy and renamed JELDY for the duration. 1946: Returned to the RN in September and placed on the Disposal List. Sold to mercantile and renamed *Ariemis*. 1960: Mercantile Loss on 31 July.

SHILLAY	1944/58	Displacement:	443TG 151TN
		Engines:	850HP = 12 kts
		Armament:	3 x single 20mmAA
		P.No:	J 426
			1947: M 426

1943: Ordered on 16 April. 1944: L. 16 April. Built at Beverley by CWG and engined by Holmes. Completed as a D/L. 1945: Deployed to the FE and joined the BPF. 1958: Paid Off. Laid up at Malta. Sold to an Italian Company to BU but resold to mercantile and renamed *Federico Bartoli* and converted to a cargo vessel. 1966: Acquired by Genoese owners and renamed Mont Blanc. Converted to a wine carrier. 1987: BU in Italy.

SKOKHOLM	1943/46	Displacement:	456TG 144TN
		Engines:	850HP = 12 kts
		P.No:	T 376

1943: L. 29 September. Built at Beverley by CWG and engined by Holmes . Completed as A/S-M/S. Based at Milford Haven after work-up at Tobermory. 1944: Deployed to the Med. Joined the 34th M/S Flotilla based at Naples. Employed on sweeping and escort duties. TPI Operation Dragoon, the Landings in S.France on 15/17 August. Based at Leghorn for A/S and M/S duties. 1945: Employed sweeping off the Anzio beaches on completion of hostilities. Returned to the UK and based at Devonport. Paid Off at Greenock on 15 December, destored and reduced to Reserve. Placed on the Disposal List. 1946: Sold to Norwegian mercantile and renamed *Skogholm*. 1948: Converted to a cargo carrier. 195? Acquired by German owners and renamed *Hochmeister*. 1958: Acquired by Greek owners and renamed *Grigorousa*. 1965: Renamed *Stelios*. 1978: Renamed *Fenia*. 1985: Mercantile Loss. Lost in the Red Sea.

SKOMER	1943/79	P.No:	T 381

1942: Ordered on 30 July. 1943: L. 17 July. Built at Aberdeen by John Lewis and completed as A/S. 1944: TPI Operation Neptune, the D-Day Landings in June as an A/S escort. 1945: Escorted a surrendered German M/S Flotilla from Jersey to Plymouth. Returned to Jersey to escort convoys of LCTs carrying German POWs. 1946: Converted to WDV. 1956: Converted to a TCV. 1979: Sold to mercantile and renamed *Latimer*.

SKYE	1942/58	P.No:	T 163

1940: Ordered on 22 July. 1942: L.17 March. Built at Leith by Robb and engined by Whites. Completed as an A/S. 1944: TPI Operation Neptune, the D-Day Landings in June, as an A/S Escort. 1958: Sold to McLellan and arrived at Bo'ness on 29 May to BU.

SLUNA	1941/46	P.No:	T 177

1940: Ordered on 13 September. 1941: L. 14 April. Built at Selby by Cochrane and engined by Amos & Smith. 1946: Sold to mercantile in July and renamed *Shun Wu*. 1948: Renamed *Haima*. 1950: Mercantile Loss on 13 October. Subsequently salvaged and BU.

STAFFA   1942/46   P.No: T 159

1940: Ordered on 22 July. 1942: L. 15 June. Built at Leith by Robb and engined by Whites ME Completed as a M/S-A/S. 1943: MF working out of N. African port. Whilst at Algiers in November she became the Flagship of the C-in-C MF, Admiral Sir John Cunningham for four days. (See Notes below). 1944: Leader of the Group which swept the channel into Heraklion, Crete, for the invasion. 1946: Transferred to the Italian Navy on January and renamed RD 304. Notes: When she was transferred to the Italian Navy the Flag of the C-in-C MF, which had been retained onboard as a keepsake, was laid up at Leiston, Suffolk, the town which had adopted her during WWII.

STEEPHOLM   1943/60   P.No: T 356

1942: Ordered on 20 July. 1943: L. 15 July. Built at Aberdeen by Lewis and completed as A/S. 1944: TPI Operation Neptune, the D-Day Landings in June, as an A/S Escort. 1960: Sold and arrived at Antwerp on 18 June to BU.

STEEPHOLM as a WDV.   **(MPL)**

STONECHAT   See under Bird Class

STROMA	1941/46	Displacement:	540T; 443TG; 151TN
		Engines:	850HP = 12 kts
		P.No:	T 150

1941: L. Built at Aberdeen by Hall Russell. 1946: Transferred to the Italian Navy in March and renamed RD 315.

STRONSAY	1942/43	Displacement:	545T; 443TG; 151TN
		Engines:	850HP = 12 kts
		P.No:	T 178

1942: L. Built at Glasgow by AJ Inglis. Completed as a M/S - A/S. Deployed to the Med. 1943: LOST. Sunk in the Western Med. on 5 February by the Italian S/M AVORIO.

| SURSAY | 1944/67 | Armament: | 3 x single 20mmAA |
| | | P.No: | J 427 |

1943: Ordered on 16 April. 1944: L.16 December. Built at Beverley by CWG and engined by Holmes. Completed as a D/L. 1951: Joined the MF based at Malta. 1953: Returned to the UK. 1966: Sold to mercantile but sale fell through. 1967: Sold. Arrived at Troon on 15 April to BU.

| SWITHA | 1942/81 | P.No: | T 179 |

1940: Ordered on 13 September. 1942: L. 13 April. Built at Glasgow by A & J Inglis and engined by Aitchison Blair. Completed as A/S. 1944: TPI Operation Neptune, the D-Day Landings in June, as an A/S Escort. 1945: Disarmed and converted to WDV. 1950: Converted to a TCV and based at Devonport. 1981: Sold to BU.

TAHAY	1944/63 Isles	Armament:	3 x single 20mmAA
		P.Nos:	J 452
			M 427 (From 1947)

1943: Ordered 16 April. 1944: L. 13 December. Built at Beverley by CWG and engined by Holmes. Completed as a D/L. 1963: Sold in July and BU at Troon.

| TEXADA | 1942/46 | P.No: | T 283 |

1942: L. 27 July. Built in Canada by Midland SY and completed as A/S. 1944: TPI Operation Neptune, the D-Day Landings in June as an A/S escort. 1946: Sold to Belgian mercantile in March.

| TIREE | 1941/60 | P.No: | T 180 |

1941: L. 6 September. Built at Goole by Goole SB and engined by Amos & Smith. Completed as A/S. 1942: Employed as escort for N.Sea Convoys. 1946: Disarmed and converted to a WDV. 1955: Employed on survey duties around UK. 1960: Sold to Belgian Breakers in August. BU at Antwerp in September.

TIREE **(A. Snowden Collection)**

TOCOGAY	1945/58	Armament:	3 x single 20mmAA
		P.Nos:	J 451
			M 81 (1947)

1943: Ordered 16 April. 1945: L. 7 February. Built at Beverley by CWG and engined by Holmes. Completed as a D/L 19 April. 1958: Sold at Malta in November to Greek owners and renamed *Anna*. Converted to a cargo vessel. 1968: Renamed *Kyriaki*. 1974: Renamed *Rino*. 1980: BU in Greece.

TRODDAY	1945/60	Armament:	3 x single 20mmAA
		P.Nos:	J 431
			1947: M 431

1943: Ordered 16 April. 1945: L. 3 March. Built at Beverley by CWG and engined by Holmes. Completed as a D/L 10 May. Deployed to the FE and joined the BPF. 1946: 11th M/S employed off Borneo. 1947: Transferred to M/S Flot in the Palestine area. 1959: Laid up at Malta in September and placed on the Disposal List. 1960: Sold in July for BU at Spezia, Italy, but resold to mercantile. 1961: Acquired by Italian owners, renamed *Nicola Jacovitti* and converted to a tanker. 1962: Renamed *Antonella*. 1971: Renamed *Nando*. 1975: Renamed *Frai*. 1977: Acquired by Tanzanian owners and renamed *Hodari*. 1994: Laid up at Dar-es-Salam.

| TRONDRA | 1941/57 | P.No: | T 181 |

1940: Ordered 7 October. 1941: L. 4 October. Built at Aberdeen by John Lewis. 1946: Converted to a WDV in January. 1957: Sold. Arrived at Charlestown in November to BU.

| ULVA | 1942/46 | P.No: | T 248 |

1941: Ordered 24 October. 1942: L. 14 April. Built at Beverley by CWG and engined by Holmes. Completed as A/S. 1944: TPI Operation Neptune, the D-Day Landings in June, as an A/S escort. 1946: Sold to mercantile and renamed *Salvo*. 1948: Acquired by Norwegian owners converted to a cargo vessel and renamed *Plico*. 1950: Acquired by Dutch owners and renamed *Surinam*. 1951: Acquired by Monrovian owners and renamed *Anne T. Williams*. 1966: Acquired by St.Lucian owners. 1977: BU.

VACEASAY- Note the sampson posts forward of the bridge. A number of the D/Ls were fitted with these in addition to the after derrick. **(PRNM)**

UNST   1942/46   P.No: T 213

1941: Ordered on 15 March. 1942: L. 28 May. Built at Port Glasgow by Ferguson Bros. 1946: Transferred to the Italian Navy in January and renamed RD 303.

VACEASAY	1945/67	Displacement:	443TG 151TN
		Engines:	850HP = 12 kts
		Armament:	3 x single 20mmAA
		P.No:	J 432

1943: Ordered on 16 April. 1945: L. 17 March. Built at Beverley by CWG and engined by Holmes. Commissioned at Hull on 23 May and completed as a D/L on 29 May. Based at Aberdeen for N.Sea Sweeping. TIH at Hull in November for refitting and conversion for Foreign Service. Detailed for Foreign Service but this was subsequently cancelled. 1946: Paid Off on 13 January. Reduced to the Reserve. 1967: Sold to Pounds of Portsmouth to BU. 1968: Resold to Belgian breakers and BU in Belgium.

VALLAY	1945/59	Displacement:	443TG 151TN
		Engines:	850HP = 12 kts
		Armament:	3 x single 20mmAA
		P.No:	J 434
			1947: M 434

1943: Ordered on 16 April. 1945: L. 10 April. Built at Beverley by CWG and engined by Holmes. Completed on 13 June as a D/L. 1959: Paid Off and laid up at Malta. Sold to mercantile in September.

VATERSAY   1943/46   P.No: T 378

1942: Ordered on 13 December. 1943: L. 13 November. Built at Selby by Cochrane and engined by Smith & Amos. 1946: Sold to mercantile in March and renamed *Vouri*. 1954: Renamed *Nam Viet*.

WALLASEA   1943/44   P.No: T 345

1942: Ordered on 20 May. 1943: L. 22 April. Built at Leith by Henry Robb and engined by Whites ME. 1944: LOST. Unbuttoning a small convoy from the Bristol Channel to Plymouth she was set upon and torpedoed by E-Boats in Mounts Bay, Cornwall, on 6 January.

WESTRAY   1941/46   P.No: T 182

1940: Ordered on 7 October. 1941: L. 4 November. Built at Aberdeen by John Lewis. 1946: Sold to mercantile in October and retained the same name.

WHALSAY   1942/46   P.No: T 293

1942: L. 4 April. Built at Beverley by CWG and engined by Holmes. 1943: Temporary Loan to the Portuguese Navy from October and renamed P 4 for the duration of the Loan. 1945: Returned to the RN in June. 1946: Sold to the Portuguese Navy in June and renamed SANTA MARIA. 1971: Deleted.

| WHITETHROAT | 1944/67 | Armament: | 1 x 20mm AA |
| | | P.No: | M 03 |

1944: L. 6 September. Built at Beverley by CWG and engined by Holmes. Completed as a Controlled M/L. Transferred to the RCN. 1960: Converted to a Survey Vessel. 1967: Sold out of Service in October.

WIAY   1945/60   Armament: 3 x single 20mm AA
                                              P.No: J 441

1943: Ordered on 16 April. 1945: L. 26 April. Built at Beverley by CWG and engined by
Holmes. Completed as a D/L. 1960: Sold out of Service in December.

WAIY with sampson posts and single derrick aft.   **(MPL)**

KIWI CLASS

In 1941 Henry Robb Ltd. of Leith built 3 trawlers for the RNZN. Large for trawlers, they were engined by Plenty and had a 2K advantage over their RN counterparts. In some listings they are referred to as Admiralty Type rather than the Kiwi Class. The only war casualty was MOA which was lost in 1943. Both survivors remained in the RNZN post war with TUI being converted to a survey vessel in 1955 and KIWI going to the breakers yard at Auckland in 1963.

Displacement:	600T
Measurements:	156ft oa 150ft pp x 30ft x 13ft
Engines:	1 shaft Reciprocating (VTE) 1,000 IHP
Speed:	14 kts
Armament:	1 x 4-inch 1 x 20mm AA
Complement:	35

Vessels in the Class:

KIWI, MOA, TUI

KIWI CLASS - NOTES

KIWI   1941/63   Armament: 1 x 4-inch; 1 x 20mm
                                                         AA; 40 x DCs
                                          P.No: T 102

1941: L. 7 July. Built at Leith by Robb and engined by Plenty. Completed as A/S-M/S. 1942: Joined the 25th M/S Flot attached to the US Pacific Fleet and based in the Solomon Islands. 1943: ICW HMNZS MOA sank a Japanese S/M off Guadalcanal on 29 January. 1963: Sold to G.Sperry of Aukland in September to BU.

MOA   1941/43   P.No: T 233

1941: L. 13 April. Built at Leith by Henry Robb and engined by Plenty. Completed as a M/S-A/S. 1942: Attached to the US Pacific Fleet with the 25th M/S Flot. Based in the Solomon Islands. 1943: ICW Sister-ship KIWI sank a Japanese S/M off Guadalcanal on 29 January. LOST. Sunk by Japanese a/c off Guadalcanal on 7 April.

TUI   1941/   P.No: T 234

1941: L. 26 August. Built at Leith by Henry Robb. Commissioned into the RNZN. 1955: Converted to a Survey Vessel.

MERSEY CLASS

Ordered in 1917, this class was built to the plans of the commercial design for the 1916 trawler *Lord Mersey*. As with other Admiralty built classes, there were a number of trawlers already on the stocks in the builders yards similar in dimensions and these were purchased as hulls, completed to Admiralty specifications and added to the Class as Non-Standard vessels. Thus there were seven Non-Standard vessels in the Class. At the cessation of hostilities there were a number of them still on the stocks and nearing readiness so were completed as fishing vessels for immediate sale to the industry. A further 44, less near to completion or not yet laid down, were cancelled. A number of the vessels sold to the mercantile after the war survived to serve in the Second World War under their civillian names.

Displacement:	438T 665T (Deep) 324TG
Dimensions:	148ft oa 138ft 6in pp x 23ft 9in x 13ft
Engines:	1 shaft Reciprocating (VTE) 600 IHP
Speed:	11 kts
Armament:	Nominally 2 x 3-inch (singles) but vessels were armed individually
Complement:	Nominally 20 but varied with role

Vessels in the Class:

ALEXANDER HILLS, ALEXANDER MACBETH, ANDREW JEWER, ANDREW KING, BENJAMIN HAWKINS, CHARLES ADAIR, CHARLES HAMMOND, CHRISTOPHER DIXON, DANIEL FEARALL, DANIEL MCPHERSON, DANIEL MUNRO, DEGARA LEROSA, EDWARD DRUCE, EDWARD MCGUIRE, EDWARD WILLIAMS, FRASER EAVES, GEORGE ANDREW, GEORGE BLIGH, GEORGE BROWN, GEORGE FENWICK, GEORGE WESTPHALL, HENRY CRAMWELL, HENRY FORD, HENRY LANCASTER, HENRY MARSH, ISAAC CHANT, JAMES ADAMS, JAMES BUCHANAN, JAMES CATON, JAMES HAYES, JAMES HULBERT, JAMES JONES, JAMES LUDFORD, JAMES MANSELL, JAMES MCDONALD, JAMES MCLAUGHLAN, JAMES WRIGHT, JAMES YOUNG, JEREMIAH LEWIS, JOHN CORMACK, JOHN COTTRELL, JOHN DUNN, JOHN DUTTON, JOHN EBBS, JOHN EDMUND, JOHN FELTON, JOHN HIGHLAND, JOHN JACOBS, JOHN JEFFERSON, JOHN JOHNSON, JOHN MANN, JOHN PASCO, JOHN QUILLIAM, JOHN WELSTEAD, JOHN YULE, JONATHAN COLLINS, JONATHON CLARKE, LANGDON MACKENNON, LEWIS MACKENZIE, LEWIS REEVES, LEWIS ROATLEY, MICHAEL CLEMENTS, MICHAEL MCDONALD, NICHOLAS COUTEUR, NICHOLAS DEAN, PATRICK MITCHELL, PETER HOFFMAN, PETER MAGEE, RICHARD BULKELEY, RICHARD COLLIVER, RICHARD JEWELL, ROBERT BARTON, ROBERT BOOKLESS, ROBERT CAHILL, ROBERT DOUBLE, ROBERT DRUMMOND, ROBERT FINLAY, ROBERT MURRAY, SAMUEL DOWDEN, SAMUEL JAMESON, SAMUEL MARTIN, SIMEON MOON, THOMAS ATKINSON, THOMAS BAILEY, THOMAS CORNWALL, THOMAS CRUIZE, THOMAS JAGO, THOMAS JARVIS, THOMAS JOHNS, THOMAS MALONEY, THOMAS MATTHEWS, THOMAS WHIPPLE, WILLIAM CHATWOOD, WILLIAM COURTNEY, WILLIAM DOAK, WILLIAM FORBES, WILLIAM FORD, WILLIAM HONNOR, WILLIAM INWOOD, WILLIAM JACKSON, WILLIAM JOHNSON, WILLIAM JONES, WILLIAM LEECH, WILLIAM RAM, WILLIAM RIVERS.

Non-Standard Vessels:

ANTHONY ASLETT, CHARLES ASTIE, CORNELIUS BUCKLEY, JOHN APPLEBY, JOHN ARTHUR, WILLIAM ABRAHAMS, WILLIAM WESTENBURGH.

Cancelled Vessels:

ALEXANDER MCDOWELL, ALEXANDER MURRAY, ANDREW MCWILLIAM, ANGUS MCDONALD, BERNARD FLYNN, DAVID MIFFON, EDWARD FLINN, EDWARD MARR, EDWARD MOONEY, EZEKIEL JOHNSON, FRANCIS FRENCH, GEORGE MARTIN, JOHN DIXON, JOHN MARSHALL, JOHN MASON, JOHN MCCONNELL JOHN MELEBURY, JOHN DETHERIDGE, JOHN DOWNIE, JOHN LEMON, JOHN LEVER, JOHN MINUTE, JOHN MONDAY, JOHN MORRIS, JOHN MOSS, JOHN MUR-PHY, JOSEPH MURRAY, OWEN MCMANNERS, PAT MERRYGAN, PETER JONES, RICHARD DORROWDALE, ROBERT DARBY, STEPHEN FOLEY, WILLIAM DON-ALDS, WILLIAM MAINLAND, WILLIAM MARSHALL, WILLIAM MORRIS, WILLIAM MORTON and WILLIAM MUCK.

ALEXANDER HILLS (as MOY) in her target-towing role post 1921, awnings spread against the Mediterranean sun. A lattice target is alongside to port. Note the little awning over the open bridge. (Steve Bush Collection)

MERSEY CLASS - NOTES

ALEXANDER HILLS	1917/46	Armament:	WWI: 1 x 12-pdr
			WWII: 1 x 12-pdr;
			1 x Italian Breda; 5 x LG
		Admty No:	3549
		P.No:	T 79

1917: L on 22 May. Built at Selby by Cochrane. 1920: Renamed MOY. 1921: Employed on target-towing. 1939: Converted to a M/S and fitted with Oropesa gear. 1941: Deployed to the Med. 1942: Operated from Tobruk for 40 weeks. TIH at Alexandria for refitting. Remained at Alexandria for sweeping the approaches to Port Said. 1943: Converted to a D/L. 1946: Sold to the mercantile in November and renamed *Coral Island*. Acquired by May FC of North Shields. PR: SN 109. 1954: Renamed *Forbes*. Note: The Italian Breda, similar to the Oerlikon, was 'won' from an abandoned Italian gun emplace-ment in the desert behind Tobruk in 1941. Also 'won' over a period of time were the 5 x LGs.

ALEXANDER McBETH   1919/19

1919: L. Built at Selby by Cochrane. Completed as a fishing vessel and sold to mercantile. Renamed *John W. Johnson*. Acquired by J.Johnson of Scarborough. PR: SH 137.

ALEXANDER McDOWELL 1918/19   Admty No: 4273

1918: Ordered from Cochrane. 1919: Cancelled.

ALEXANDER MURRAY   1918/19   Admty No: 4280

1918: Ordered from Cochrane. 1919: Cancelled.

ANDREW JEWER   1918/46

Displacement:	152TN
Engines:	87HP
Armament:	WWI: 1 x 12-pdr
	WWII: 2 x 3-inch
	(single)
Admty No:	3844
P.No:	WWII: T 47

1918: L. Built at Selby by Cochrane and delivered on 4 December. Employed as a Gunnery Tender. 1920: Renamed NITH in September. 1922: Renamed EXCELLENT in June. 1946: Sold to Mercantile and renamed *Malvern*. Acquired by Malvern FC of Aberdeen. PR: A 234. 1954: BU.

ANDREW KING   1917/41

Armament:	1 x 12-pdr
Admty No:	3545
P.No:	WWII: T 80

1917: L. 19 April. Built at Selby by Cochrane and completed as a M/S. Fitted with Listening Hydrophones. 1920: Renamed OUSE in September. 1941: LOST. Mined off Tobruk on 20 February.

ANDREW McWILLIAMS   1918/19   Admty No: 4270

1918: Ordered from Cochrane. 1919: Cancelled.

ANGUS McDONALD   1918/19   Admty No: 4279

1918: Ordered from Cochrane. 1919: Cancelled.

ANTHONY ASLETT   1917/22

Armament:	1 x 12-pdr; 1 x 7.5-inch Bomb Thrower (A/S Howitzer)
Admty No:	3579

1917: L. 22 February. Built at Selby by Cochrane and completed as a M/S. Non - Standard. 1920: Renamed ROTHER in September. 1922: Sold to Spanish Navy and renamed UAD QUERT.

BENJAMIN HAWKINS   1919/20 1933/42

Armament:	WWII: 2 x 3-inch (2 x single)
Admty No:	3858
Port Reg:	1933: H 170
P.No:	WWII: T 05

1919: L. Built at Goole by Goole SB and completed as a fishing vessel. 1920: Sold to mercantile on 17 October and renamed *Frobisher*. Acquired by the builders. Acquired by

East Riding SFC of Hull. 1933: Purchased into the RN in June. Converted to a Boom Trawler and renamed FASTNET. 1942: Transferred to the R.Neth.Navy on 20 April and retained the same name. Deployed to the East Indies. LOST. Abandoned at Batavia in April in the face of the Japanese advance.

BERNARD FLYNN	1918/19	Admty No:	4285

1918: Ordered from Cochrane. 1919: Cancelled.

BLACKWATER	1932/46	See under WILLIAM INWOOD

BOADICEA II	1919/20	See under HENRY FORD

BOYNE	1920/46	See under WILLIAM JONES

CHARLES ADAIR	1917/20	Displacement:	132TN
		Engines:	88HP
		Armament:	1 x 12-pdr AA
		Admty No:	3551

1917: L. Built at Selby by Cochrane. Fitted with Listening Hydrophones. 1920: Sold to mercantile and retained the same name. 1924: Acquired by the Boston DSF & Ice Co and renamed *Sleaford*. Acquired by French owners. 1939: Served as French SAINT BENOIT in WWII.

CHARLES ASTIE	1917/17	Armament:	1 x 12-pdr
		Admty No:	3579

1917: L. 25 January. Built at Selby by Cochrane. Non - Standard. LOST. Mined off Lough Swilly on 26 June.

CHARLES HAMMOND	1918/18	Armament:	1 x 12-pdr
		Admty No:	3830

1918: L. Built at Selby by Cochrane and delivered on 26 March. LOST. Sunk in collision with MARKSMAN off Kirkaldy on 26 March.

CHERWELL	1920/46	See under JAMES JONES

CHRISTOPHER DIXON	1917/22 1939/46	Armament:	1 x 12-pdr
		Admty No:	3563
		Port Reg:	WWII: FD 74
		P.No:	WWII: Z 111

1917: L. 4 September. Built at Selby by Cochrane. 1922: Transferred to the Irish Government and retained the same name. Acquired by J.Man of Fleetwood and renamed *Lord Gainford*. 1939: Requisitioned in December as LORD GAINFORD and converted to a BDV. 1946: Returned to owners.

COLNE	1920/49	See under ISAAC CHANT

CORNELIUS BUCKLEY	1917/21	Displacement:	248TG 96TN
		Engines:	400HP
		Armament:	1 x 12-pdr
		Admty No:	3581

1917: L. 24 February. Built at Selby by Cochrane and completed as a Non-Standard M/S. 1921: Sold to mercantile and renamed *Savaria*. Acquired by HC.Baker AO of Grimsby. PR: GY 1341.

DANIEL FEARALL	1917/46	Armament:	1 x 12-pdr; 1 x 7.5 - inch Bomb Thrower (A/S Howitzer)
		Admty No:	3571
		P.No:	WWII: FY 1592

1917: L. 2 November. Built at Selby by Cochrane. 1920: Renamed STOUR in September. 1922: Renamed PEMBROKE on 1 September. Employed as a Base Ship. 1939: Reverted to STOUR. 1946: Sold to mercantile. 1947: Renamed *Storess*.

| DANIEL McPHERSON | 1918/19 | Admty No: | 4242 |

1918: L. 5 December. Built at Selby by Cochrane. 1919: Completed as a fishing vessel and delivered on 16 August. Sold to mercantile and renamed *Havardur Isfindingur*.

DANIEL MUNRO	1919/19 1940/46	Armament:	WWII: 1 x 12-pdr
		Admty No:	4239
		Port Reg:	WWII: Portuguese
		P.No:	WWII: FY 1807

1919: L. Built at Selby by Cochrane and completed as a fishing vessel. Sold to mercantile and renamed *Estrella Do Norte*. 1940: Purchased into the RN from Portuguese owners as ESTRELLA DO NORTE and converted to a M/S. 1942: Renamed STORMCENTRE. 1946: Sold to mercantile in August.

| DAVID MIFFON | 1918/19 | Admty No: | 4266 |

1918: Ordered from Cochrane. 1919: Cancelled.

DEGARA LEROSA	1919/19	Displacement:	149TN
		Engines:	87HP
		Armament:	None
		Admty No:	4237

1919: L. Built at Selby by Cochrane. Completed as a fishing vessel and delivered on 6 June. Sold to mercantile and renamed *James Johnson*. Acquired by J.Johnson of Scarborough. PR: SH 109. 1939: Served in WWII as Greek AXIOS.

| DOON | 1920/46 | See under FRASER EAVES |

EDWARD DRUCE	1918/20 1940/47	Displacement:	130TN
		Engines:	69HP
		Armament:	1 x 12pdr
		Admty No:	3736
		Port Reg:	H 152
		P.No:	Z 186

1918: L. Built at Goole by Goole SB and delivered on 30 July. Fitted with Listening Hydrophones. 1920: Sold to mercantile and renamed *Girard*. Acquired by F & T Ross Ltd of Hull. 1940: Requisitioned in June as GIRARD and converted to a BDV. Subsequently purchased. 1947: Sold to mercantile in January.

| EDWARD FLINN | 1918/19 | Admty No: | 4288 |

1918: Ordered from Cochrane. 1919: Cancelled.

| EDWARD MARR | 1918/19 | Admty No: | 4277 |

1918: Ordered from Cochrane. 1919: Cancelled.

EDWARD McGUIRE	1919/19	1939/46	Displacement:	324TG 148TN
			Engines:	87HP
			Admty No:	4251
			Port Reg:	WWII: H 139
			P.No:	WWII: FY 79

1919: L. 17 May. Built at Selby by Cochrane and completed as a fishing vessel. Sold to mercantile and renamed *Cape St. Vincent*. Acquired by the West Riding STC of Hull. 1939: Requisitioned in September and renamed KORAWA for the RAN. Converted to a M/S. 1946: Returned to owners.

| EDWARD MOONEY | 1918/19 | | Admty No: | 4276 |

1918: Ordered from Cochrane. 1919: Cancelled.

EDWARD WILLIAMS	1917/22	1940/47	Displacement:	133TN
			Engines:	87HP
			Armament:	1 x 12-pdr; 1 x 7.5"-inch Bomb thrower (A/S Howitzer)
			Port Reg:	WWII: H 918
			P.No:	WWII: 4 190

1917: L. 8 May. Built at Selby by Cochrane and completed as a M/S. 1922: Sold to mercantile and retained the same name. Acquired by the Hudson SFC of Hull. 1923: Renamed *Cape Trafalgar*. 1940: Purchased into the RN in May as CAPE TRAFALGAR and converted to a M/S. 1941: Converted to a BDV. 1947: Sold to mercantile in January.

| ETTRICK | 1920/26 | | See under SAMUEL JAMESON |

| EXCELLENT | 1919/22 | | See under WILLIAM LEECH |

| EXCELLENT | 1922/46 | | See under ANDREW JEWER |

| EZEKIEL JOHNSON | 1918/18 | | Admty No: | 4290 |

1918: Ordered from Cochrane and subsequently cancelled.

| FASTNET | 1933/42 | | See under BENJAMIN HAWKINS |

| FOYLE | 1920/21 | 1934/46 | See under JOHN EDMUND |

| FRANCIS FRENCH | 1918/18 | | Admty No: | 4286 |

1918: Ordered from Cochrane. Cancelled.

FRASER EAVES	1917/46		Armament:	1 x 4-inch; 1 x 12-pdr AA; 1 x 7.5-inch Bomb thrower (A/S Howitzer)
			Admty No:	3567
			P.No:	WWII: T 35

1917: L. 2 October. 1920: Renamed DOON in September. 1944: TPI in Operation Neptune, the D-Day Landings in June, for Channel operations. 1946: Sold to mercantile and renamed *Donesse*.

| GEORGE ANDREW | 1917/21 | 1939/45 | Armament: | 1 x 12-pdr AA |
| | | | Admty No: | 3556 |

FRASER EAVES (as DOON) showing the turtle-back forecastle. **(PRNM)**

| | P.No: | WWII: FY 539 |

1917: L. 23 July. Built at Selby by Cochrane and completed as a M/S. 1921: Sold to mercantile and renamed *Lord Astor*. 1939: Requisitioned in August as CRANEFLY and converted to a M/S. 1945: Returned to owners

GEORGE BLIGH	1917/20 1939/46	Displacement:	132TN
		Engines:	69HP
		Armament:	1 x 12-pdr; 1 x 7.5"-inch Bomb Thrower (A/S Howitzer)
		Admty No:	3542
		Port Reg:	WWII: LO 309
		P.No:	WWII: Z 178

1917: L. 24 March. Built at Selby by Cochrane. 1920: Sold to mercantile and retained the same name. Acquired by the Ministry of Agriculture and Fisheries, London. 1939: Requisitioned in September and converted to a BDV. 1945: Returned to the Min. of Ag. and Fisheries in December.

GEORGE BROWN	1917/22	Armament:	1 x 12-pdr
		Admty No:	3548

1917: L. 10 May. Built at Selby by Cochrane. 1919: Renamed WILLIAM DOCHERTY in December. 1922: Sold to mercantile and renamed *Rosedale Wyke*.

GEORGE FENWICK	1917/22	Displacement:	132TN
		Engines:	87HP
		Armament:	1 x 12-pdr
		Admty No:	3568
		Port Reg:	H 912

1917: L. Built at Selby by Cochrane and delivered on 10 January. 1922: Sold to mercantile and renamed *Cape Otway*. Acquired by the Hudson SF Co Ltd of Hull. 1939: Served in WWII as the Greek STRYMON.

GEORGE MARTIN   1918/18   Admty No: 4257

1918: Ordered from Cochrance but later cancelled.

GEORGE WESTPHAL   1917/21   Armament: 1 x 12-pdr
                                        Admty No: 3575

1917: L. Built at Selby by Cochrane and delivered on 7 March. 1921: Sold to mercantile and renamed *Estelle Yvonne*. 1923: Mercantile Loss.

HENRY CRAMWELL   1918/22   Armament: 1 x 12-pdr
                                        Admty No: 3705

1918: L. Built at Renfrew by Lobnitz and completed as a M/S. Delivered on 24 December. 1922: Sold to Spanish mercantile and renamed *Xaun*.

HENRY FORD   1917/21   Armament: 1 x 12-pdr
                                        Admty No: 3569

1917: L. 18 October. Built at Selby by Cochrane. 1919: Renamed BOADICEA II in February. 1920: Reverted to HENRY FORD in February. 1921: Sold to French mercantile and renamed *Duperre*. 1939: Served in WWII as the French DUPERRE.

HENRY LANCASTER   1918/21   Admty No: 4231

1918: L. Built at Selby by Cochrane. 1919: Delivered on 8 April and employed as a Mark Bouy Vessel. 1921: Sold to mercantile in August and retained the same name.

HENRY MARSH   1919/19   Admty No: 4253

1919: L. 13 March. Built at Selby by Cochrane and completed as a fishing vessel. Sold to mercantile and renamed *Springbok*. Acquired by the East Riding SFC of Hull. PR: H 137.

ISAAC CHANT   1918/49   Armament: 1 x 12-pdr
                                        Admty No: 3704
                                        P.No: WWII: T 17

1918: L. Built at Renfrew by Lobnitz. Completed as a M/S and delivered on 1 October 1920: Renamed COLNE in September. 1949: Sold to mercantile in May.

JAMES ADAMS   1917/19   Armament: 1 x 12pdr; 1 x 7.5-
                                                           inch Bomb thrower
                                                           (A/S Howitzer).
                                        Admty No: 3355

1917: Launched. Built at Selby by Cochrane. 1919: Sold to Belgian mercantile and renamed *Pilote 5*. 1939: Served as Belgian PILOTE 5 in WWII.

JAMES BUCHANAN   1917/22 1940/41 Displacement: 149TN
                                        Engines: 69HP
                                        Armament: 1 x 12-pdr AA
                                        Admty No;   3565
                                        Port Reg: WWII: FD 100

1917: L. 18 September. Built at Selby by Cochrane. Fitted with Listening Hydrophones. 1922: Sold to mercantile and renamed *Stoneferry*. Acquired by City SFC of Hull. PR: H 676. Acquired by Adam SFC of Fleetwood and renamed *Force*. 1940: Requisitioned in February as FORCE and converted to a M/S. Fitted with Orepesa Gear. Joined the

An early photograph of ISAAC CHANT as she is not yet fitted for wireless (MPL)

Lowestoft M/S Group sweeping from Lowestoft to Sheringham Shoal. 1941: LOST. Sunk in an air attack whilst at anchor off Gt. Yarmouth on 27 June. Took 20 mins to sink with no loss of life.

| JAMES CATON | 1918/21 | Armament: | 1 x 12-pdr |
| | | Admty No: | 3703 |

1918: L. 26 August. Built at Renfrew by Lobnitz. 1921: Sold to French mercantile and renamed *Emilie Pierre*. 1939: Served in WWII as French ST.PIERRE D'ALCANTAR

| JAMES HAYES | 1919/19 | Admty No: | 3859 |

1919: L. Built at Goole by Goole SB and completed as a fishing vessel. Delivered on 27 June. Sold to mercantile and renamed *Viscount Grey*. Acquired by Hellyer Bros of Hull. PR: H 91. 1920: Mercantile Loss. Stranded on 11 March.

JAMES HULBERT	1919/19 1940/41	Armament:	
		Admty No:	3799
		Port Reg:	WWII: Dutch
		P.No:	

1919: L. Built at Renfrew by Lobnitz and completed as a fishing vessel. Delivered on 9 September. Sold to mercantile and renamed *M.J.Reid*. 1940: Hired in November from Dutch owners as JEAN FREDERICK. Converted to a M/S. 1941: LOST. Sunk by enemy a/c off Start Point on 1 May.

JAMES JONES	1918/46	Armament:	1 x 12-pdr
		Admty No:	3842
		P.No:	WWII: T 03

1918: L. Built at Selby by Cochrane and delivered on 9 November. 1920: Renamed

JAMES JONES (as CHERWELL)   **(PRNM)**

CHERWELL in September. 1946: Sold to mercantile and retained the same name.

JAMES LONG	1918/19

1918: L. Built at Selby by Cochrane. 1919: Sold to mercantile and retained the same name. Acquired by Hellyer Bros of Hull. PR: H 141.

JAMES LUDFORD	1919/39	Admty No:	4232
		P.No:	T 16

1919: L. Built at Selby by Cochrane and delivered on 1 May. Employed as a Mark Bouy Vessel. 1939: LOST. Mined off the Tyne on 14 December.

JAMES MANSELL	1919/19	Admty No:	4238

1919: L. Built at Selby by Cochrane and completed as a fishing vessel. Delivered on 26 June. Sold to mercantile and renamed *Snorri Sturluson*. 1922: Acquired by H.Smethurst of Grimsby and renamed *James Mansell*. PR: GY 409.

JAMES McDONALD	1919/19 1939/39	Displacement:	148TN
		Engines:	87HP
		Admty No:	4244
		Port Reg:	WWII: FD 50

1919: L. Built at Selby by Cochrane and completed as a fishing vessel. Sold to mercantile. Acquired by Crampin of Grimsby and renamed *Grand Fleet*. PR: GY 44. Acquired by Boston DS & Ice Co of Boston and renamed *Barbara Robertson*. 1939: Requisitioned as BARBARA ROBERTSON and converted to a M/S. LOST. Sunk on 23 December by gunfire from a U-Boat N. of the Hebrides.

JAMES McLAUGHLIN	1919/19 1939/46	Displacement:	129TN
		Engines:	87HP
		Admty No:	4250

			Port Reg:	WWII: H 121
			P.No:	WWII: FY 724

1919: L. 1 May. Built at Selby by Cochrane and completed as a fishing vessel. Sold to mercantile and renamed *General Birdwood*. Acquired by F. Parkes and B.A. Parkes of Cleveleys. 1939: Requisitioned in August as GENERAL BIRDWOOD and converted to an Esso. Subsequently purchased into the RN 1946: Sold to mercantile in May.

JAMES WRIGHT	1918/21	1940/46	Displacement:	130TN
			Engines:	69HP
			Armament:	1 x 12-pdr
			Admty No:	3576
			Port Reg:	WWII: H 662
			P.No:	WWII: 4 229

1918: L. Built at Selby by Cochrane and delivered on 15 March. 1921: Sold to mercantile and renamed *Lord Lancaster*. Acquired by G.Walker of Aberdeen. Acquired by Loch FC of Hull and renamed *Loch Moidart*. 1940: Requisitioned in June as LOCH MOIDART and converted to an APV. 1942: Converted to a M/S in February. Joined the 34th M/S Grp based at Grimsby. 1945: 179th M/S Grp based at Grimsby. 1946: Returned in January.

JAMES YOUNG	1919/19		Admty No:	4235

1919: L. Built at Selby by Cochrane and completed as a fishing vessel. Delivered on 8 May. Sold to mercantile and retained the same name.

JEREMIAH LEWIS	1918/20		Admty No:	4234

1918: L. Built at Selby by Cochrane and delivered on 25 March. 1920: Sold to mercantile and renamed *Field Marshal Robertson*. Acquired by Hellyer Bros of Hull. PR: H 104.

JOHN APPLEBY	1917/22	1940/44	Displacement:	286TG 112TN
			Engines:	69TN 10.5 kts
			Armament:	1 x 12-pdr
			Admty No:	3612
			Port Reg:	WWII: FD 424
			P.No:	WWII: FY 781

1916: Ordered by Great Grimsby & East Coast SFC and purchased whilst on the stocks. 1917: L. 30 January. Built at Beverley by CWG. Fitted with Listening Hydrophones. Non-Standard. 1922: Sold to mercantile and renamed *Lois*. Acquired by the Fleetwood SF Co of Fleetwood. PR: FD424. 1940: Requisitioned in February as LOIS and converted to a M/S. 1944: Returned to owners in November. 1947: Mercantile Loss. Wrecked at Grindavik, SW Iceland on 5 January.

JOHN ARTHUR	1917/22	1939/46	Displacement:	306TG 112TN
			Engines:	69HP = 10.5 kts
			Armament:	1 x 12-pdr
			Admty No:	3613
			Port Reg:	WWII: FD 423

1916: Ordered by Standard SFC of Grimsby as *Sannyrion*. Purchased by the Admiralty whilst still on the stocks. 1917: L. 10 February. Built at Beverley by CWG. Fitted with Listening Hydrophones. Non-Standard. 1922: Sold to mercantile and renamed *Gladys*. Acquired by the Fleetwood SF Co of Fleetwood. PR: FD 423. 1939: Reqisitioned in November as GLADYS and converted to a BDV. 1943: Purchased into the RN 23 November. 1946: Sold to mercantile. Acquired by J.Buckie Ship & Shipyard Co of Leith and renamed *The Bruce*. PR: LH 21. 1961: BU at Grangemouth.

JOHN CORMACK	1917/22	1940/45	Displacement:	130TN
			Engines:	87HP
			Armament:	1 x 12-pdr AA
			Admty No:	3562
			Port Reg:	WWII: H 660
			P.No:	WWII: 4 125

1917: L. 4 September. Built at Selby by Cochrane. 1922: Sold to mercantile and renamed *Lord Pirrie*. Acquired by Pickering & Haldane STC of Hull. PR: H 429. Acquired by H.Elliot & Sons of Fleetwood and renamed *Chiltern*. 1940: Requisitioned in June as CHILTERN and converted to an APV. 1945: Returned to owners.

JOHN COTTRELL	1919/19	1940/44	Admty No:	4463
			Port Reg:	WWII: FD 68
			P.No:	WWII: FY 505

1919: L. Built at Goole by Goole SB and completed as a fishing vessel. Delivered on 1 November. Sold to mercantile and renamed *St. Endellion*. Acquired by T.Hamling of Hull. PR: LO 115. Acquired by Adams SFC of Fleetwood and renamed *Blighty*. 1940: Requisitioned as BLIGHTY and converted to a M/S. Subsequently purchased into the RN. 1944: Transferred to the Polish Navy and renamed PODDLE

JOHN DETHERIDGE	1918/18		Admty No:	4489

1918: Ordered from Goole SB and subsequently cancelled.

JOHN DIXON	1918/18		Admty No:	4283

1918: Ordered from Cochrane and subsequently cancelled.

JOHN DOWNIE	1918/18		Admty No:	4491

1918: Ordered from Goole SB and subequently cancelled.

JOHN DUNN	1918/22	1940/46	Displacement:	141TN
			Engines:	69HP
			Armament:	WWI: 1 x 12-pdr.
				WWII: 2 x 3-inch (singles)
			Admty No:	3741
			Port Reg:	WWII: FD 105
			P.No:	WWII: Z 117

1918: L. 27 March. Built at Port Glasgow by Ferguson. Fitted with Listening Hydrophones. 1922: Sold to mercantile and retained the same name. Subsequently renamed *Florence Brierley*. Acquired by New Docks ST Co of Fleetwood. 1940: Requisitioned in January as FLORENCE BRIERLEY and converted to a BDV. Subsequently purchased into the RN. 1946: Sold to mercantile in August.

JOHN DUTTON	1918/22		Armament:	1 x 12-pdr
			Admty No:	3739

1918: L. 17 January. Built at Port Glasgow by Ferguson. 1922: Sold to mercantile and renamed *Karlesefni*.

JOHN EBBS	1917/20		Armament:	1 x 12-pdr; 1 x 3.5-inch Bomb Thrower (A/S Howitzer)
			Admty No:	3566

JOHN EDMUND (MPL)

1917: L. 2 October. Built at Selby by Cochrane. Fitted with Listening Hydrophones. 1920: Sold to Belgians and renamed *Pilote 4*. 1939: Belgian PILOTE 4 in WWII.

JOHN EDMUND	1918/46	Displacement:	152TN
		Engines:	69HP
		Armament:	1 x 12-pdr
		Admty No:	3738
		P.No:	WWII: T 48

1918: L. Built at Goole by Goole SB and delivered on 22 October. 1920: Renamed FOYLE in September. 1921: Temporary Loan to the SAN from September and renamed SONNEBLOM for the duration of the loan. 1934: Returned to the RN and reverted to FOYLE in June. 1946: Sold to mercantile and renamed *Cramond Island*. Acquired by Thomas H. Scales of Edinburgh. PR: GN 18

| JOHN FELTON | 1917/20 | Armament: | 1 x 12-pdr; 1 x 6-inch Bomb Thrower (A/S Howitzer) |

1917: L 1 November. Built at Selby by Cochrane. 1920: Sold to mercantile and retained the same name.

| JOHN HIGHLAND | 1918/19 | Armament: | 1 x 12-pdr |
| | | Admty No: | 3797 |

1918: L. Built at Port Glasgow by Ferguson. 1919: Sold to mercantile an renamed *Ocean Ensign*. Acquired by Bloomfields of Yarmouth. PR: YH 222.

JOHN JACOBS	1918/23 1940/46	Armament:	1 x 12-pdr
		Admty No;	3833
		Port Reg:	WWII: French
		P.No:	WWII: FY.355

1918: L. Built at Selby by Cochrane and delivered on 15 June. Fitted with Listening Hydrophones. 1923: Sold to French mercantile and renamed *Castelnau*. 1940: Hired from French owners in August as CASTELNAU and converted to A/S. 1946: Returned to owners in February.

JOHN JEFFERSON	1918/22 1939/45	Displacement:	149TN
		Engines :	96HP
		Armament:	1 x 12-pdr; 1 x 3.5-inch Bomb Thrower (A/S Howitzer)
		Admty No:	3834
		Port Reg:	WWII: H 702
		P.No:	WWII: FY 547

1918: L. Built at Selby by Cochrane and delivered on 23 April. Fitted with Listening Hydrophones. 1920: Sold to mercantile and renamed *St.Amant*. Acquired by T.Hamling of Hull. PT: H.702. Acquired by Jutland Amalgamated Trs of Hull and renamed *Lady Enid*. 1939: Requisitioned in August as LADY ENID and converted to a M/S. 1945: Returned to owners.

JOHN JOHNSON	1918/22 1940/42	Displacement:	134TN
		Engines:	69HP
		Armament:	1 x 12-pdr
		Admty No:	3832
		Port Reg:	WWII: FD 46

1918: L. Built at Selby by Cochrane and delivered on 19 April. 1922: Sold to mercantile and renamed *Cloughton Wyke*. Acquired by Dinas ST Co. of Fleetwood. 1940: Purchased into the RN in May as CLOUGHTON WYKE and converted to a M/S. 1942: LOST. Sunk by enemy a/c on 2 February off the Humber.

JOHN LEMON	1918/18	Admty No:	4223

1918: Ordered from John Lewis and subsequently cancelled.

JOHN LEVER	1918/18	Admty No:	4227

1918: Ordered from John Lewis and subsequently cancelled.

JOHN MANN	1919/19 1933/45	Admty No:	4245
		P.No:	WWII: Z 100

1919: L. Built at Selby by Cochrane and completed as a fishing vessel. Delivered on 6 September. 1920: Sold to mercantile and renamed *Earl Haigh*. Acquired by Hellyer Bros of Hull. PR: H 87. 1933: Purchased into the RN on June and converted to a BDV. Renamed BARNET. 1945: Transferred to the Turkish Navy and renamed KILYAS. 1947: Sold out of the Turkish Navy.

JOHN MARSHALL	1918/18	Admty No:	4262

1918: Ordered from Cocrane and subsequently cancelled.

JOHN MASON	1918/18	Admty No:	4260

1918: Ordered from Cocrane and subsequently cancelled.

JOHN MASON	1920/21	See under JOHN ABBOTT

| JOHN McCONNELL | 1918/18 | Admty No: | 4271 |

1918: Ordered from Cochrane and subsequently cancelled.

| JOHN MELEBURY | 1918/18 | Admty No: | 4263 |

1918: Ordered from Cochrane and subsequently cancelled.

| JOHN MINUTE | 1918/18 | Admty No: | 4259 |

1918: Ordered from Cochrane and subsequently cancelled.

| JOHN MONDAY | 1918/18 | Admty No: | 4268 |

1918: Ordered from Cochrane and subsequently cancelled.

| JOHN MORRIS | 1918/18 | Admty No: | 4264 |

1918: Ordered from Cochrane and subsequently cancelled.

| JOHN MOSS | 1918/18 | Admty No: | 4272 |

1918: Ordered from Cochrane and subsequently cancelled.

| JOHN MURPHY | 1918/18 | Admty No: | 4281 |

1918: Ordered from Cochrane and subsequently cancelled.

| JOHN PASCO | 1917/22 | Armament: | 1 x 12-pdr |
| | | Admty No: | 3544 |

1917: L. 19 April. Built at Selby by Cochrane and completed as an escort. 1922: Sold to mercantile and renamed *Arinbjorn Hersir*.

| JOHN QUILLIAM | 1917/20 | Armament: | 1 x 12-pdr |
| | | Admty No: | 3541 |

1917: L. Built at Selby by Cochrane. Fitted with Listening Hydrophones. 1921: Sold to mercantile and renamed *Dana*.

JOHN WELSTEAD	1917/22 1941/46	Armament:	1 x 12-pdr
		Admty No:	3573
		Port Reg:	Norwegian
		P.No:	WWII: FY 1784

1917: L. Built at Selby by Cochrane and delivered on 15 February. 1922: Sold to mercantile and renamed *Lord Harewood*. Acquired by Pickering & Haldane STC of Hull. PR: H 657. Acquired by Norwegian owners and re-named *Myrland*. 1940: Seized by the Germans at the fall of Norway. 1941: German MYRLAND captured by the RN at Lofoton on 6 March. Converted to a M/S and added to the Navy List. 1944: Converted to a Firefloat. 1946: Returned to Norwegian owners

| JOHN YULE | 1917/21 | Armament: | 1 x 12-pdr |
| | | Admty No: | 3543 |

1917: L. 24 March. Built at Selby by Cochrane. Fitted with Listening Hydrophones. 1921: Sold to mercantile and renamed *Notre Dame de Lorette*.

JONATHAN CLARKE   1919/19   Admty No: 4465

1919: L. Built at Goole by Goole SB and completed as a fishing vessel. Delivered on 24 March. Sold to mercantile and renamed *St. Keverne*. Acquired by Bunch SFC of Grimsby. Acquired by T.Hamling of Hull. PR: H 175.

JONATHAN COLLINS   1919/19 1939/46   Displacement: 132TN
                                             Engines: 87HP
                                             Armament: 1 x 12-pdr
                                             Admty No: 4464
                                             Port Reg: WWII: GY 458
                                             P.No: WWII: FY 725

1919: L. Built at Goole by Goole SB and completed as a fishing vessel. Delivered on 26 November. Sold to mercantile and renamed *St. Minver*. Acquired by the Boston Deep Sea Fishing & Ice Co of Fleetwood. 1939: Requisitioned in September as ST. MINVER and converted to a M/S. Subsequently purchased into the RN. 1944: Converted to an Esso in April. 1946: Sold to mercantile in May.

JOSEPH MURRAY   1918/18   Admty No: 4274

1918: Ordered from Cochrane and subsequently cancelled

LANGDON McKENNON   1919/19   Admty No: 4243

1919: L. Built at Selby by Cochrane and completed as a fishing vessel. Delivered on 21 October. Sold to mercantile and renamed *Douglas H. Smith*. 1921: Mercantile Loss.

LEWIS McKENZIE   1918/19   Admty No: 4240

1918: L. Built at Selby by Cochrane and completed as a fishing vessel. 1919: Sold to mercantile and renamed *Florence Johnson*. Acquired by J. Johnson of Scarborough. PR: SH 118.

LEWIS REEVES   1917/22   Armament: 1 x 12-pdr AA; 1 x
                                                          7.5-inch Bomb
                                                          Thrower (A/S
                                                          Howitzer)
                                       Admty No: 3553

1917: L. 23 June. Built at Selby by Cochrane. 1922: Sold to mercantile and renamed *Lord Hawke*. Mercantile Loss.

LEWIS ROATLEY   1917/22   Displacement: 133TN
                                        Engines: 69HP
                                        Armament: 1 x 12-pdr
                                        Admty No: 3554

1917: L. Built at Selby by Cochrane and completed as a M/S. 1922: Sold to mercantile and renamed *Stalwart*. Acquired by J.Wollingsworth of Hull. PR: H 720.

MICHAEL CLEMENTS   1917/18   Armament: 1 x 12-pdr AA
                                           Admty No: 3561

1917: L. 21 August. Built at Selby by Cochrane and completed as a M/S. 1918: LOST. Sunk after a collision off St.Catherine's Point on 8 August.

MICHAEL McDONALD   1919/19   Admty No: 4252

1919: L. 17 May. Built at Selby by Cochrane and completed as a fishing vessel. Sold to mercantile and renamed *Kanuck*. Acquired by East Riding SFC of Hull. PR: H 123.

NICHOLAS COUTEUR   1919/19   Admty No: 4236

1919: L. Built at Selby by Cochrane and completed as a fishing vessel. Delivered on 20 May. Sold to mercantile and renamed *Mary A. Johnson*. Acquired by J.Johnson of Scarborough. 1920: Mercantile Loss in November.

NICHOLAS DEAN   1918/21   Armament: 1 x 12-pdr; 1 x 3.5-
                                                           inch Bomb Thrower
                                                           (A/S Howitzer)
                                        Admty No: 3740

1918: L. 11 March. Built at Port Glasgow by Ferguson Bros. 1921: Sold to French mercantile and renamed *Notre Dame de France*.

NITH   1920/22   See under ANDREW JEWER

OUSE   1920/41   See under ANDREW KING

OWEN McMANNERS   1919/19   Admty No: 4258

1918: Ordered from Cochrane. 1919: Cancelled.

PAT MERRYGAN   1918/19   Admty No: 4278

1918: Ordered from Cochrane. 1919: Cancelled.

PATRICK MITCHELL   1919/19

1919: L. 16 April. Built at Selby by Cochrane and completed as a fishing vessel. Sold to mercantile and renamed *Kelvin*.

PEMBROKE   1922/39   See under ANDREW KING

PETER HOFFMAN   1919/19   Admty No: 3798

1919: L. Built at Renfrew by Lobnitz and completed as a fishing vessel. Sold to mercantile and renamed *K.M. Hardy*. Acquired by South Fleetwood FCL of London. PR: A 228. 1939: Served in WWII as the French IMBRIN.

PETER JONES   1919/19   Admty No: 4289

1918: Ordered from Cochrane. 1919: Cancelled.

PETER MAGEE   1919/19   Admty No: 4249

1919: L. 1 May. Built at Selby by Cochrane and completed as a fishing vessel. Sold to mercantile and renamed *Lord Ernle*. Acquired by Pickering & Haldane of Hull. PR: GY 109.

RICHARD BULKELEY   1917/19   Armament: 1 x 12-pdr
                                          Admty No: 3560

1917: L. 21 August. Built at Selby by Cochrane. 1918: Temporary Loan to the USN. 1919: LOST. Mined in the North Sea on 12 July whilst still serving in the USN.

| RICHARD COLLIVER | 1918/22 | Armament: | 1 x 12-pdr |
| | | Admty No: | 3701 |

1918: L. Built at Renfrew by Lobnitz and delivered on 26 February. 1922: Sold to mercantile and renamed *Laurette*.

| RICHARD DORRODALE | 1918/19 | Admty No: | 4492 |

1918: Ordered from Goole SB. 1919: Cancelled.

RICHARD JEWELL	1918/22 1940/46	Displacement:	130TN
		Engines:	87HP
		Armament:	1 x 6-pdrAA
		Admty No:	3836
		Port Reg:	WWII: GY 488
		P.No:	WWII: FY 1551(D/L)
			4 23 (APV)

1918: L. 6 August. Built at Selby by Cochrane. 1922: Sold to mercantile and renamed *Lord Knaresborough*. Acquired by Pickering & Haldane STC of Hull. PR: H 646. Acquired by Rinovia SF Co of Grimsby and renamed *Fairway*. 1940: Requisitioned in May as FAIRWAY and converted to an APV. 1941: Converted to a D/L. 1944: TPI Operation Neptune, the D-Day Landings in June. 1946: Returned to owners in March.

ROBERT BARTON	1917/22 1940/45	Displacement:	134TN
		Engines:	87HP
		Port Reg:	WWII: FD 99
		P.No:	WWII: FY 139

1917: L. 28 August. Built at Selby by Cochrane. 1922: Sold to Mercantile and renamed *Hayburn Wyke*. Acquired by Dinas ST Co of Fleetwood. 1940: Requisitioned in May as HAYBURN WYKE and converted to an APV. 1941: Converted to a M/S. 1945: LOST. Torpedoed whilst at anchor off Ostend on 21 January. Notes: aka HAYBOURN WYKE.

| ROBERT BOOKLESS | 1917/21 |

1917: L. 23 June. Built at Selby by Cochrane. 1921: Sold to mercantile and renamed *Gris Nez*.

| ROBERT CAHILL | 1920/21 1940/46 | Port Reg: | WWII: French |
| | | P.No: | WWII: FY 1994 |

1920: L. Built at Goole by Goole SB. 1921: Sold to French mercantile and renamed *Pierre-Andre*. 1940: French APV PIERRE-ANDRE seized at Southampton in Operation Grab on 3 July. Commissioned into the RN in August as an APV. 1942: Converted to a M/S in April. 1946: Returned to French in January.

| ROBERT DARBY | 1918/19 |

1918: Ordered from CWG of Beverely. 1919: Cancelled.

| ROBERT DOUBLE | 1918/22 |

1918: L. Built at Goole by Goole SB. 1922: Sold to mercantile and retained the same name.

| ROBERT DRUMMOND | 1918/22 |

1918: L 18 May. Built at Port Glasgow by Ferguson Bros. 1922: Sold to mercantile and renamed *Salmonby*.

ROBERT FINLAY 1919/19

1919: L. Built at Goole by Goole SB and completed as a fishing vessel. Sold to mercantile and renamed *Viscount Allenby*. Acquired by Hellyer Bros. of Hull. PR: H 89.

ROBERT MURRAY	1919/22 1939/47	Displacement:	148TN
		Engines:	87HP
		Port Reg:	WWII: FD 90
		P.No:	WWII: 4 106 (APV)
			FY 1561 (M/S)

1919: L. 28 June. Built at Selby by Cochrane. 1922: Sold to mercantile and renamed *Northlyn*. Acquired by T.Cardwell & RH.Bagshaw of Fleetwood. 1939: Requisitioned in October as NORTHLYN and converted to a BDV. Based at Grimsby. 1943: Purchased into the RN in December. 1947: Sold to mercantile in March.

ROTHER 1920/22 See under ANTHONY ASLETT

SAMUEL DOWDEN	1917/22 1940/45	Armament:	1 x 12-pdr; 1 x 3.5-inch Bomb Thrower (A/S Howitzer)
		Admty No:	3564
		Port Reg;	WWII: FD 92
		P.No:	WWII: FY 1610

1917: L 18 September. Built at Selby by Cochrane. Fitted with Listening Hydrophones. 1922: Sold to mercantile and renamed *Royal Regiment*. Acquired by Jutland Amalgamated Trs of Hull. PR: H 683. Acquired by Adam SFC of Fleetwood. PR: FD 92. Renamed *Duncan*. 1940: Requisitioned in February, renamed SEA MIST and converted to a M/S. Based at Grimsby (Ungrouped). 1941: Joined the 21st M/S Grp based at Grimsby. Remained with the Grp for the remainder of the war. 1945: Returned to owners in December.

SAMUEL JAMESON	1918/26 1939/46	Displacement:	149TN
		Engines:	89HP
		Armament:	1 x 12-pdr
		Admty No:	3839
		Port Reg:	WWII: FD 148
		P.No:	WWII: Z 114

1918: L. Built at Selby by Cochrane and delivered on 10 October. 1920: Renamed ETTRICK in September. 1926: Sold to mercantile and renamed *Loughrigg*. Acquired by New Docks ST Co of Fleetwood and renamed *Phyllisia*. 1939: Requisitioned in December as PHYLLISIA and converted to a BDV. 1943: Temporary Loan to the Portuguese Navy from 9 October and renamed B 1 for the period of Loan. 1945: Returned to the RN on 19 August. 1946: Returned to owners in July.

SAMUEL MARTIN 1919/20 Admty No: 4255

1919: L. 28 June. Built at Selby by Cochrane and completed as a fishing vessel. 1920: Sold to mercantile and renamed *Field Marshal Plumer*.

SIMEON MOON 1919/20 Admty No: 4254

1919: L. 31 May. Built at Selby by Cochrane and completed as a fishing vessel. 1920: Sold to mercantile and renamed *General Rawlinson*. Acquired by Hellyer Bros of Hull. PR: H 173.

STEPHEN FOLEY	1919/19	Admty No:	4287

1918: Ordered from Cochrane. 1919: Cancelled.

STOUR	1920/22 1939/46	See under DANIEL FEARALL

WILLIAM ABRAHAMS	1917/21	Armament: Admty No:	1 x 12-pdr 3580

1917: L 24 February. Built at Selby by Cochrane and completed as a M/S. Non-Standard. 1921: Sold to mercantile and renamed *Santini*. 1938: Owned by A.M. Adam of Torry, Aberdeen. PR: A 340.

WILLIAM CHATWOOD	1919/21	Admty No:	4467

1919: L. Built at Goole by Goole SB and completed as a fishing vessel. Delivered on 24th March. 1921: Sold to mercantile and renamed *Blanc Nez*.

WILLIAM COURTNEY	1920/21	Admty No:	4466

1920: L. Built at Goole by Goole SB. 1921: Completed as a fishing vessel and delivered on 2 February. Sold to mercantile and renamed *Ternoise*.

WILLIAM DOAK	1918/22	Armament: Admty No:	1 x 12-pdr 3737

1918: L. Built at Goole by Goole SB. Fitted with Listening Hydrophones. 1922: Sold to Spanish mercantile and renamed *Arcila*.

WILLIAM DOCHERTY	1919/22	See under GEORGE BROWN

WILLIAM DONALDS	1918/19	Admty No:	4490

1918: Ordered from Goole SB. 1919: Cancelled.

WILLIAM INWOOD (as BLACKWATER)　　　　　　**(Steve Bush Collection)**

WILLIAM FORBES	1919/19 1939/45	Displacement:	132TN
		Engines:	78HP
		Admty No:	3856
		Port Reg:	WWII: H 122
		P.No:	WWII: FY 1703

1919: L. Built at Goole by Goole SB and completed as a fishing vessel. Sold to mercantile and renamed *Syrian*. Acquired by Hellyer Bros of Hull. 1939: Requisitioned in October as SYRIAN and converted to an APV. 1940: Converted to an ABV in June. Renamed TYPHOON. 1942: Converted to a M/S in January. 1945: Returned to owners in May.

WILLIAM FORD	1918/19	Admty No:	4284

1918: Ordered from Cochrane. 1919: Cancelled.

WILLIAM HONNOR	1918/22	Armament:	1 x 12-pdr
		Admty No:	3796

1918: L. 26 August. Built at Port Glasgow by Ferguson and completed as an escort. 1922: Sold to mercantile and renamed *Grimurkamban*.

WILLIAM INWOOD	1918/46	Armament:	1 x 12-pdr
		Admty No:	3841
		P.No:	WWII: T 04

1918: L. Built at Selby by Cochrane and delivered on 3 October. 1920: Renamed BLACKWATER in September. 1932: TPI in the search for the missing S/M M2 in January and found the wreck in West Bay, Portland. 1946: Sold to mercantile and renamed *Splies*. 1956: Mercantile Loss on 12 February.

WILLIAM JACKSON	1918/21 1939/45	Displacement:	130TN
		Engines:	69HP
		Armament:	1 x 12-pdr
		Admty No:	3831
		Port Reg:	WWII: GY 9
		P.No:	WWII: 4 136

1918: L. Built at Selby by Cochrane and delivered on 29 March. 1921: Sold to mercantile and renamed *Lord Byng*. Acquired by Boston DSF & Ice Co of Fleetwood and renamed *Evelyn Rose*. 1939: Requisitioned in December as EVELYN ROSE and converted to an APV. 1941: Converted to a M/S. 1945: Returned to owners.

WILLIAM JOHNSON	1918/21	Armament:	1 x 12-pdr
		Admty No:	3843

1918: L. Built at Selby by Cochrane and completed as a M/S. Delivered on 22 November. 1919: Temporary Loan to the USN for mine clearance. Returned to the RN. 1921: Sold to mercantile and renamed *Lord Birkenhead*.

WILLIAM JONES	1918/46	Armament:	1 x 12-pdr
		Admty No:	3838
		P.No:	WWII: T 29

1918: L. Built at Selby by Cochrane and completed as a M/S. Delivered on 8 September. 1920: Renamed BOYNE. 1946: Sold to mercantile and renamed *Nypuberg*. 1957: BU in April.

WILLIAM JONES (as BOYNE) (MPL)

WILLIAM LEECH	1918/22	Admty No:	4233

1918: L. Built at Selby by Cochrane. 1919: Renamed EXCELLENT in February. Delivered on 12 March. 1922: Sold to mercantile and reverted to *William Leech*. 1939: Served as French EXCELLENT in WWII.

WILLIAM MAINLAND	1918/19	Admty No:	4269

1918: Ordered from Cochrane. 1919: Cancelled.

WILLIAM MARSHALL	1918/19	Admty No:	4267

1918: Ordered from Cochrane. 1919: Cancelled.

WILLIAM MORRIS	1918/19	Admty No:	4261

1918: Ordered from Cochrane. 1919: Cancelled. Notes: Also listed as WILLIAM MOIRIS.

WILLIAM MORTON	1918/19	Admty No:	4275

1918: Ordered from Cochrane. 1919: Cancelled.

WILLIAM MUCK	1918/19	Admty No:	4265

1918: Ordered from Cochrane. 1919: Cancelled.

WILLIAM RAM	1917/21	1940/46	Displacement:	133TN
			Engines:	87HP
			Complement:	30
			Armament:	WWI: 1 x 12-pdr
				WWII: 1 x 12-pdr;
				2 x LG (single); DCs
			Admty No:	3550
			P.No:	WWII: FY 1609

1917: L. 7 June. Built at Selby by Cochrane and completed as an escort. 1921: Sold to mercantile and renamed *Lord Carson*. Acquired by Harry Franklin of Grimsby and renamed *Welbeck*. 1940: Requisitioned in June as WELBECK and converted to an APV. 1941: Converted to a M/S. Fitted with an acoustic hammer and stern sweep. Based at Lowestoft/Yarmouth for E.Coast sweeping operations. 1944: Temporarily employed towing converted London barges to the S.Coast in preparation for D-Day. 1946: Returned to owners in January.

WILLIAM RIVERS	1917/21	Armament:	1 x 12-pdr
		Admty No:	3552

1917: L. 9 June. Built at Selby by Cochrane and completed as a M/S. 1921: Sold to maercantile and renamed *Mont Cassel*. 1939: Served as French MONT CASSEL in WWII.

WILLIAM WESTENBURGH	1917/21	1940/46	Displacement:	130TN
			Engines:	87HP
			Armament:	2 x 12-pdr (single)
			Admty No:	3357
			Port Reg:	WWII: GY 475
			P.No:	WWII: Z 105

1917: L. 25 January. Built at Selby by Cochrane and completed as a M/S. Non-Standard. 1921: Sold to mercantile and renamed *Lord Talbot*. Acquired by Malmata Fishing Co and renamed *Star of the Realm*. 1940: Purchased into the RN in February as STAR OF THE REALM and converted to a BDV. 1946: Sold to mercantile in June.

In 1914 the trawler builders Smiths Dock had a number of vessels on their building stocks ordered by commercial concerns. The Admiralty purchased 10 of them whilst still building and had 9 of them completed as minesweepers. They were, therefore, not a true "Class" as regards size or even appearance so could be more correctly classified as a "Group", ranging in displacement from the smallest at 206TG to the largest, BOMBARDIER at 305TG. The 10th vessel, GUNNER, was completed as a Q Ship number Q 31. Armed with 3 x 12-pdr, 3 x 6-pdr and 2 x TTs, she operated under the name of PLANUDES. The first, LANCER, was launched in December 1914 with the rest following on between January and April 1915. The last in Service was TROOPER which was completed in June 1915. Three, CARBINEER, LANCER, and SAPPER failed to survive the war, the others being sold off when the war ended.

Displacement:	206 - 305TG
Measurements:	Varied with individual vessels
Armament:	Varied with individual vessels

Vessels in the Class:

BOMBARDIER, BRIGADIER, CARBINEER, DRAGOON, FUSILIER, HIGHLANDER, LANCER, SAPPER, TROOPER, GUNNER (Q 31)

MILITARY CLASS - NOTES

BOMBARDIER	1915/20	Displacement:	305TG
		Measurements:	130ft pp x 24ft x 13ft 3in
		Armament:	1 x 12-pdr
		Admty No:	1517

1914: Purchased into the RN in December whilst on the stocks. 1915: L. Built by Smith's Dock and completed as a M/S. 1920: Sold to the Belgian Government and retained the same name.

BRIGADIER	1915/20	Displacement:	303TG
		Measurement:	130ft pp x 24ft x 13ft 3in
		Armament:	1 x 12-pdr
		Admty No:	1530

1915: L. 1 April. Built by Smith's Dock. Purchased whilst building and completed as a M/S. 1920: Renamed BUGLER in January. Sold to mercantile on 4 May and retained the same name.

BUGLER	1920/20	See under BRIGADIER above.

CARBINEER	1915/16	Displacement:	276TG
		Measurements:	130ft pp x 23ft 6in x 12ft 3in
		Armament:	1 x 3-pdr
		Admty No:	1164

1915: L. 15 February. Built by Smith's Dock. Purchased whilst building and completed as a M/S. 1916: LOST. Wrecked on Crebawethan Point on 18 May.

CARBINEER II	1919/20 1940/46	See under FUSILEER

DRAGOON	1915/19 1939/40	Displacement:	276TG
		Dimensions:	130ft pp x 23ft 6ft x 12ft 3in
		Engines:	61HP
		Armament:	WWI: 1 x 12-pdr; 1 x 7.5-inch Bomb Thrower (A/S Howitzer). WWII: 1 x 6-pdr
		Admty No:	1152
		Port Reg:	WWII: GY 1097

1914: Purchased into the RN on 11 December whilst on the stocks. 1915: L. 16 January. Built at Middlesborough by Smith's Dock. Completed as a M/S. 1919: Renamed DRUM-MER in January. Sold to mercantile in February and retained the same name. Purchased by Consolidated Fisheries of Grimsby. 1939: Requisitoned as DRUMMER in August and converted to a M/S. 1940: Converted to an APV in July. LOST. Mined off Brightlingsea, Essex, on 4 August.

DRUMMER	1919/19 1939/40	See under DRAGOON above.

FUSILIER	1915/19 1940/46	Displacement:	276TG
		Dimensions:	130ft pp x 23ft 6in x 12ft 3in
		Armament:	1 x 12-pdr
		Admty No:	1163
		Port Reg:	WWII: GY 1048
		P.No:	WWII: 4 17

1915: L. 1 February. Built by Smith's Dock and purchased into the RN whilst building. Completed as a M/S. 1919: Renamed CARBINEER II in March. 1919: Sold to mercantile on 26 February and retained the same name. Acquired by Consolidated Fisheries of Grimsby. 1940: Requisitioned in May as CARBINEER II and converted to an APV. Subsequently converted to a BDV. 1946: Returned to owners in July.

HIGHLANDER	1915/21	Displacement:	239TG
		Dimensions:	118ft pp x 22ft 6in x 12ft 6in
		Armament:	1 x 6-pdrAA
		Admty No:	1526

1915: L. 29 April. Built by Smith's Dock. Purchased whilst building and completed as a M/S. 1921: Sold to mercantile and renamed *Fregate II*.

LANCER	1914/17	Displacement:	276TG
		Dimensions:	130ft pp x 23ft 6in x 12ft 3in
		Armament:	1 x 3-pdr
		Admty No;	1151

1914: Purchased into the RN on 11 December. L. 17 December. Built at Southbank-on-Tees by Smith's Dock and completed as a M/S. 1917: Renamed LANCER II in July. 1918: LOST. Sunk in a collision off the Brighton LV on 18 July.

LANCER II	1917/18	See under LANCER above

SAPPER   1914/17   Displacement: 276TG
                                              Dimensions: 130ft pp x 23ft 6in x 12ft 3in
                                              Armament: 1 x 12-pdr
                                              Admty No: 1162

1915: L. 1 February. Built at Southbank-on-Tees by Smith's Dock. Purchased whilst
building and completed as a M/S. 1917: LOST. Foundered off the Owers LV on 29
December.

TROOPER   1915/20 1940/45 Armament: 1 x 6-pdrAA.
                                   Admty No: 1541

1915: L. 29 April. Built at Middlesborough by Smith's Dock. Purchased into the RN
whilst building and completed as a M/S. 1920: Sold to mercantile and renamed *Eider II*.
Acquired by Dutch owners. 1940: Hired from Dutch owners in June as ALMA and converted to a M/S. Commissioned with a Dutch crew. 1945: Returned to owners.

GUNNER   1914/20   Displacement: 287TG
                                              Armament: 1 x 4-inch; 3 x 12-pdr
                                                                 3 x 6-pdr; 2 x 14-inch
                                                                 TT
                                              Admty No: 1153

1915: L. 16 January. Built at Southbank-on-Tees by Smith's Dock. Purchased whilst
building and completed as a 'Q' Ship. Operated as Q 31, BORGIA and PLANUDES.
1920: Sold to mercantile and renamed *Temehani*. 1926: Renamed *Millimumul*.

MILITARY CLASS 1942-44

There were nine vessels in this class, built by CWG at Beverley in Yorkshire between 1942 and 1944 to the builders mercantile design and all engined by Holmes. With their up-to-date weaponry they were a very valuable asset to the trawler compliment of Anti-Submarine vessels. The end of the war saw them without a single loss and they spent little time on the Disposal List before they were taken up by mercantile interests in 1946.

Displacement:	750 tons
Measurements:	193ft oa 175ft pp x 30ft x 13ft
Engines:	1 shaft Reciprocating (VTE) 1,000 IHP
Speed:	11 kts
Armament:	1 x 4-inch 4 x 20mm AA
Complement:	40

Vessels in the Class:

BOMBARDIER, COLDSTREAMER, FUSILIER, GRENADIER, GUARDSMAN, HOME GUARD, LANCER, ROYAL MARINE, SAPPER

BOMBARDIER   **(P. Phelps Collection)**

155

BOMBARDIER	1943/46	Displacement:	579TG 181TN
		Engines:	1,000HP = 11 kts
		P.No:	T 304

1942: Ordered on 28 May. 1943: L. 23 January. Built at Beverley by CWG and engined by Holmes. Completed as an A/S. 1944: TPI Operation Neptune, the Normandy Landings, in June as an A/S Escort. 1946: Sold to mercantile and renamed *Norman*. Acquired by Hellyer Bros of Hull. PR: H 289. 1952: Mercantile Loss. Wrecked in thick fog near Cape Farewell, Iceland on 4 October. Only one of her crew of 21 survived.

COLDSTREAMER	1942/46	Displacement:	579TG 181TN
		Engines:	1000HP = 11 kts
		P.No:	T 337

1942: Ordered on 16 April. L. 10 December. Built at Beverley by CWG and engined by Holmes. Completed as an A/S in August. 1946: Sold to mercantile and renamed *Esquimaux*. Acquired by Hellyer Bros of Hull. PR: H 297. 1956: Acquired by West Dock SFC of Hull and renamed *Dunsley Wyke*. 1967: BU in Belgium.

GRENADIER   **(P. Phelps Collection)**

FUSILIER	1942/46	P.No:	T 305

1942: Ordered on 6 April. L. 23 December. Built at Beverley by CWG and engined by Holmes. Completed as A/S. 1944: TPI Operation Neptune, the D-Day Landings in June, as an A/S Escort. 1946: Sold to mercantile in April and renamed *Serron*. Port Reg: GY 309. 1965: BU in January.

GRENADIER	1942/46	Displacement:	207TN
		Engines:	165HP
		Armament:	1 x 4-inch; 4 x 20mm AA (4 x single); 4 x 0.303-inch Brownings (2 x twin)

1942: Ordered on 7 February. L. 26 September. Built at Beverley by CWG and engined by Holmes. Completed as an A/S. 1943: Based at Liverpool for Atlantic convoys to Newfoundland and Gibraltar. 1944: TPI Operation Neptune, the D-Day Landings in June as an A/S Escort. 1946: Sold to Mercantile and renamed *Isernia*. Acquired by the Great Grimsby and East Coast SFC of Grimsby. PR: SY 448.

GUARDSMAN	1944/46	Displacement:	228TN
		Engines:	165HP
		P.No:	T 393

1943: Ordered on 20 March. 1944: L. 7 June. Built at Beverley by CWG and engined by Holmes. Completed as an A/S. Employed in the Western Approaches. 1945: TPI the escort for a convoy of surrendered U.Boats from the Kyle of Lochailsh to Londonderry. Forced to withdraw from the escort as she was unable to keep up. Paid Off at Devonport and reduced to the Reserve. Placed on the Disposal List. 1946: Sold to mercantile and renamed *Thuringia*. Acquired by the Great Grimsby and East Coast FCL of Grimsby. PR: GY 321. 1963: Acquired by Northern Trawlers and retained the same name.

HOME GUARD	1943/46	Displacement:	262TN
		Engines:	234HP
		Port Reg:	GY.344
		P.No:	T 394

1943: Ordered on 20 March. 1944: L. 8 July. Built at Beverley by CWG and engined by Holmes. Completed as A/S. 1945: Based at Devonport and employed as a W e a t h e r Reporting Ship for the Air Ministry. 1946: Sold to mercantile in April. Acquired by the Loyal SF Co. Ltd. of Grimsby and renamed *Loyal*.

LANCER	1942/46	Displacment:	579TG 181TN
		Engines:	1000IHP = 11 kts
		P.No:	T 335

1942: Ordered on 7 February. L. 26 October. Built at Beverley by CWG and engined by Holmes. 1943: Completed on 26 February as A/S. 1944: TPI Operation Neptune, the D-Day Landings in June, as an A/S Escort. 1946: Sold to mercantile and renamed *Stella Orion*. Acquired by East Riding Trs of Hull. Port Reg: H 379. 1949: Converted to FO. 1955: Mercantile Loss. Wrecked at Maalay, Norway on 7 November. No loss of life.

ROYAL MARINE	1944/46	Displacement:	579TG 181TN
		Engines:	1000IHP = 11 kts
		P.No:	T 395

1943: Ordered on 20 March. 1944: L. 22 July. Built at Beverely by CWG and engined by Holmes. Completed as A/S. 1946: Sold to mercantile in April and renamed *Sisapon*. Acquired by the Standard SF Co of Grimsby. PR: GY 381. 1967: BU at Antwerp.

SAPPER	1942/46	Displacement:	192TN
		Engines:	132HP
		P.No:	T 336

1942: Ordered on 7 February. L. 11 November. Built at Beverley by CWG and engined by Holmes. 1943: Completed in March as A/S. 1944: TPI Operation Neptune, the D-Day Landings in June, as an A/S escort. 1946: Sold to mercantile and renamed *Cape Gloucester*. Acquired by Hudson Bros. of Hull. Port Reg: H 395. 1956: Acquired by Henriksen of Hull and renamed *Admetus*. 1966: BU at Antwerp.

PORTUGUESE CLASS

With WWII raging British yards were under enormous pressure to build tonnage for the RN and were finding the greatest difficulty in coping. Every dock and slipway was stretched to full capacity and still the Navy was hungry for more and more ships. To help ease the pressure the Admiralty turned to an old ally, Portugal, with a request to build 16 trawlers on the understanding that materials for the building would be supplied from the UK. The Class was built in two Groups, the first constructed with wooden hulls and the second with steel.

Orders for four more trawlers were placed in 1942, two with the Alfeite Company and two with Uniao Fabril. However, there were difficulties in shipping the materials to Portugal and so the Alfeite orders were cancelled and the other two were completed by Uniao Fabril as merchant vessels.

All six of the first group survived the war and were duly sold off to the mercantile in 1946.

```
Group 1.
Displacement:     525 Tons
Measurements:     139ft oa 129ft pp x 27ft 9in x 11in
Engines:          1 shaft Deisel  350 BHP
Speed:            11 kts
Armament:          1 x 12-pdr AA
Complement:       30
```

Vessels in the Class:

PRONG, PROOF, PROPERTY, PROPHET, PROTEST, PROWESS

```
Group 2.
Displacement:     550 tons
Measurements:     140ft oa 133ft pp x 27ft 9in x 11ft
Engines:          1 shaft Deisel   550 BHP
Speed:            11 kts
Armament:         1 x 12-pdr AA
Complement:       30
```

This group was of steel construction and slightly longer and heavier than their wooden hulled counterparts. However, the speed, complement and armament were the same. Two were built by Alfeite and the other four by Uniao Fabril.

All of this group also survived the war to take up an occupation in the commercial field in 1946, with the exception of PRODUCT which went to the Greek Navy.

Vessels in the Class:

PROBE, PROCTOR, PRODIGAL, PRODUCT, PROFESSOR, PROMISE

PORTUGUESE CLASS - NOTES

PRONG	1943/46	Armament:	1 x 12-pdr; 3 x single 20mm AA
		P.No:	T 190

1941: Laid Down as PORT STANLEY. 1942: L. 14 July. Built at Aveiro by A. Monica and engined by British Auxiliaries. Completed as a M/S. 1943: Renamed. Joined the 127th M/S Grp based at Grimsby. 1946: Sold to mercantile in June and renamed *Sjostkirk*. 1954: BU.

PROOF	1943/46	Armament:	1 x 12-pdr; 3 x single 20mm AA
		P.No:	T 191

1941: Laid Down as PORT ROYAL. 1942: L. 14 July. Built at Aveiro by A. Monica and engined by British Auxiliaries. 1943: Renamed. 1946: Sold to mercantile in June.

PROPERTY	1943/46	Armament:	1 x 12-pdr; 3 x single 20mm AA
		P.No:	T 192

1941: Laid Down as PORTRUSH. 1942: L. 28 August. Built at Aveiro by A. Monica and engined by British Auxiliaries. Completed as a M/S. 1943: Renamed. Joined the 127th M/S Grp based at Grimsby. 1946: Sold to mercantile in June and renamed *Portrush*. 1947: Renamed *Property*. 1955: Renamed *Vaagness*.

PROPHET	1943/46	Armament:	1 x 12-pdr; 3 x single 20mm AA
		P.No:	T 194

1941: Laid Down as PORTOBELLO. 1942: L. 2 April. Built at Aveiro by A. Monica and engined by British Auxiliaries. Completed as a M/S. Joined the 127th M/S Grp based at Grimsby. 1943: Renamed. 1946: Sold to mercantile in June.

PROTEST	1943/46	Armament:	1 x 12-pdr; 3 x single 20mm AA
		P.No:	T 195

1941: Laid Down as PORT PATRICK. L. 12 August. Built at Aveiro by M.M.B.Monica and completed as a M/S. 127th M/S Grp based at Grimsby. 1943: Renamed. 1946: Sold to mercantile in June.

PROWESS	1943/46	Armament:	1 x 12-pdr; 3 x single 20mm AA
		P.No:	T 196

1942: Laid Down as PROVOST. Renamed PORTREATH. 1943: L. 21 February. Built at Aveiro by M.M.B.Monica. Renamed. Completed as a M/S. 1946: Sold to mercantile in June.

PROBE	1942/46	Armament:	1 x 12-pdr; 3 x single 20mm AA
		P.No:	T 186

1942: Laid Down as PORTAFERRY. L. 24 October. Built at Lisbon by Alfeite DY and engined by Ruston & Hornsby. Completed as a M/S. 1943: Renamed. 1946: Sold to mercantile in June and renamed *Porto Norte*.

| PROCTOR | 1942/46 | Armament: | 1 x 12-pdr; 3 x single 20mm |
| | | P.No: | T 185 |

1942: Laid Down as PORTISHAM. Renamed PORTADOWN. L. 23 October. Built at Lisbon by Alfeite DY and engined by Ruston & Hornsby. Completed as a M/S. 1943: Renamed. 1946: Sold to mercantile and renamed *Arrabida*.

| PRODIGAL | 1943/46 | Armament: | 3 x single 20mm AA |
| | | P.No: | T 187 |

1941: Laid Down as PORTHLEVEN. 1942: L. 26 April. Built at Lisbon by Cia Uniao Fabril and completed as a M/S Repair Ship. 1943: Renamed. Deployed to the Med. 1946: Sold to mercantile in June.

| PRODUCT | 1943/46 | Armament: | 3 x single 20mm AA; 2 x single MG |
| | | P.No: | T 188 |

1940: Laid Down as PORT JACKSON. 1941: L. 12 April. Built at Lisbon by Cia Uniao Fabril. 1943: Renamed. Completed as a M/S Repair Ship. 1946: Transferred to the Greek Navy in July and renamed HERMES.

| PROFESSOR | 1943/46 | Armament: | 1 x 12-pdr; 3 x single 20mm AA |
| | | P.No: | T 189 |

1941: Laid Down as PORTMADOC. 1942: L. 28 May. Built at Lisbon by Cia Uniao Fabril and completed as a M/S. 1946: Sold to mercantile in June and renamed *Algenib*.

| PROMISE | 1943/46 | Armament: | 1 x 12-pdr; 3 x single 20mm AA |
| | | P.No: | T 193 |

1941: Laid Down as PORT NATAL. L. 20 September. Built at Lisbon by Cia Uniao Fabril and completed as a M/S. 1943: Renamed. 1946: Sold to mercantile in June and renamed *Aldebaran*.

PROMISE - Note the sweep-drum aft and the hammer gear on the bow.
(D. Brindle Collection)

160

ROUND TABLE CLASS

Based on Hall Russell's design for their 1936 *Star of Orkney*, this Class of eight trawlers were all completed in 1941/42 as Minesweepers. They were built at Aberdeen with four coming from the designer's yard and the other four from John Lewis. All successful survivors of the war they went to the mercantile post war with the last being sold out of the Service in 1947.

Displacement:	440 tons
Measurements:	137ft oa 126ft pp x 23ft 9ft x 11ft 6in
Engines:	1 shaft Reciprocating (VTE) 600 IHP
Speed:	11kts
Armament:	1 x 12-pdrAA 1 x 20mm AA 2 x LG (2 x single)
Complement:	35

Vessels in the Class:

SIR AGRAVAINE, SIR GALAHAD, SIR GARETH, SIR GERAINT, SIR KAY, SIR LAMOROCK, SIR LANCELOT, SIR TRISTRAM.

SIR TRISTRAM streaming her sweep cable aft.   (IWM Neg: A29465)

ROUND TABLE CLASS - NOTES

SIR AGRAVAINE	1942/46		
		Displacement:	104TN
		Engines:	73HP
		P.No:	T 230

1941: Ordered on 15 March. 1942: L. 18 March. Built at Aberdeen by John Lewis and completed as a M/S. 1946: Sold to mercantile in April and retained the same name. Acquired by The Gt. Western FC of Aberdeen. PR: A 276.

SIR GALAHAD	1941/46	Displacement:	103TN
		Engines:	73HP
		P.No:	T 226

1941: Ordered on 18 January. L.18 December. Built at Aberdeen by Hall Russell and engined by Hall. Completed as a M/S. 1944 Converted to a D/L. TPI Operation Neptune, the D-Day Landings in June as a D/L attached to the 14th M/S Flotilla in Force U. 1946: Sold to mercantile in April and renamed *Star of Freedom*. Acquired by The Walker STC of Aberdeen. PR: A 283. 1956 Renamed *Robert Limbrick*. 1957 Mercantile Loss in February.

SIR GARETH	1942/46	Displacement:	108TN
		Engines:	73HP
		P.No:	T 227

1941: Ordered on 18 January. 1942: L. 19 January. Built at Aberdeen by Hall Russell and engined by Hall. Completed as a M/S. 1946: Sold to mercantile in April and renamed *Star of the East*. Acquired by Walker STF of Aberdeen. PR: A 277.

SIR GERAINT	1942/46	Displacement:	103TN
		Engines:	73HP
		P.No:	T 227

1941: Ordered on 13 June. 1942: L. 15 April. Built at Aberdeen by John Lewis and completed as a M/S. 1946: Sold to Mercantile in April and renamed *Star of the South*. Acquired by Walker STF of Aberdeen. PR: A 398.

SIR KAY	1942/46	Displacement:	108TN
		Engines:	73HP
		P.No:	T 241

1941: Ordered on 24 July. 1942: L. 24 October. Built at Aberdeen by Hall Russell and engined by Hall. Completed as a M/S. 1946: Sold to mercantile in April and renamed *Star of the North*. Acquired by Walker STF of Aberdeen. PR: A 334. 1956: Renamed *Robert Crohn*.

SIR LAMORAK	1942/46	Displacement:	106TN
		Engines:	73HP
		P.No:	T 242

1941: Ordered on 2 August. 1942: L. 23 November. Built at Aberdeen by Hall Russell and engined by Hall. Completed as a M/S. Based at Aberdeen for sweeping off the NE Coast of Scotland. 1946: Sold to mercantile in April and renamed *Bracon Bank*. Acquired by Don Fishing Co of Aberdeen. 1954: Renamed *Bracon*.

SIR LANCELOT	1941/46	Displacement:	108TN
		Engines:	73HP
		P.No:	T 228

1941: Ordered on 21 January. L. 4 December. Built at Aberdeen by John Lewis and completed as a M/S. 1944: Converted to a D/L. TPI Operation Neptune, the D-Day Landings in June, as a D/L attached to the 14th M/S Flotilla in Force U. 1946: Sold to mercantile in April and retained the same name. Acquired by the Ministry of Ag. & Fish.

SIR TRISTRAM	1942/46	P.No:	T 229

1941: Ordered on 21 January. 1942: L. 17 January. Built at Aberdeen by John Lewis and completed as a M/S. 1946: Sold to mercantile in April.

SHAKESPEARIAN CLASS

The 12 vessels of this class were all ordered on 12 December 1939. With a speed of 12 knots they were among the fastest of the Admiralty built trawlers. Completed as Minesweepers, nine were launched in 1940, with the other three following on in 1941. Three, CORIOLANUS, HORATIO and LAERTES, were war casualties and of the remainder disposal post-war was FLUELLEN to the Scottish Home Dept., OTHELLO to the Italian Navy, ROSALIND to the Kenya & Zanzibar RNVR. ROMEO was sold to Belgium in 1946 and the remainder were all sold to the mercantile in 1946/7.

Displacement:	545 tons
Measurements:	164ft oa 150ft pp x 27ft 9in x 11ft
Engines:	1 shaft Reciprocating (VTE) 950 IHP
Speed:	12 kts
Armament:	1 x 12-pdr AA 3 x 20mm AA (3 x single)
Complement:	35

Vessels in the Class:

CELIA, CORIOLANUS, FLUELLEN, HAMLET, HORATIO, JULIET, LAERTES, MACBETH, OPHELIA, OTHELLO, ROMEO, ROSALIND

OTHELLO in very sharp dazzle paint.   **(MPL)**

SHAKESPEARIAN CLASS - NOTES

CELIA   1940/46   P.No: T 134

1939: Ordered on 12 December. 1940: L. 18 September. Built at Selby by Cochrane and engined by Amos & Smith. Completed as a M/S. 1946: Sold to mercantile and retained the same name.

CORIOLANUS   1940/45   P.No: T 140

1939: Ordered on 12 December. 1940: L. 2 September. Built at Selby by Cochrane and engined by Amos & Smith. Completed as a M/S. 1944: TPI Operaton Neptune the D-Day Landings. 1945: LOST. Mined in the Adriatic on 5 May.

FLUELLEN   1940/47   P.No: T 157

1939: Ordered on 12 December. 1940: L. 1 November. Built at Selby by Cochrane and engined by Amos & Smith. 1942: Involved in a collision with Flower Class Corvette GARDENIA off Oran on 9 November which resulted in the GARDENIA sinking. 1947: Transferred to the Scottish Home Dept. and retained the same name.

HAMLET   1940/47   P.No: T 167

1939: Ordered on 12 December. 1940: L. 24 July. Built at Beverley by CWG and engined by Holmes. Completed in December as A/S. 1947: Sold to Norwegian mercantile on 30 January and renamed *Eifonn*. 1950: Acquired by French mercantile, converted to a cargo vessel and renamed *Fort Lamalgue*. 1954: Acquired by Italian mercantile and renamed *Union*. 1956: Renamed *Itaca*. 1974: Acquired by Greek mercantile and renamed *Nicolas K*. 1976: Mercantile Loss. Sank after developing engine failure and leaks 90 miles W. of Tel-Aviv, Israel, whilst on passage from Limasol to Aqaba on 23 June.

HORATIO   1940/43   P.No: T 153

1939: Ordered on 12 December. 1940: L. 8 August. Built at Beverley by CWG and engined by Holmes. Completed as A/S-M/S. 1943: LOST. Sunk by an Italian MTB in the W.Med. on 7 January.

JULIET   (MPL)

JULIET   1940/47   Displacement: 452TG   142TN
                                          Engines: 950HP = 12 kts
                                          P.No: T 136

1939: Ordered on 12 December. 1940: L. 2 October. Built at Beverley by CWG and engined by Holmes. Completed as A/S-M/S. 1947: Sold to mercantile and renamed *Peterjon*. Acquired by Regent Shippers London and converted to a Deisel engined cargo vessel. 1951: Renamed *Plassy*. 1960: Mercantile Loss. Took the ground on Finnis Rock, Galway Bay on 8 March.

LAERTES	1940/42	Displacement:	452GT 142TN
		Engines:	950HP = 12 kts
		P.No:	T 137

1939: Ordered on 12 December. 1940: L. 16 October. Built at Beverley by CWG and engined by Holmes. Completed as A/S. 1941: Joined the 1st M/S-A/S Grp based at Freetown. Convoy escort. 1942: LOST. Torpedoed by U-201 off Freetown on 25 July.

| MACBETH | 1940/47 | P.No: | T 138 |

1939: Ordered on 12 December. Built at Goole by Goole SB and engined by Amos & Smith. Completed as A/S-M/S. 1947: Sold to mercantile and retained the same name. Acquired by Devon Fishing Co of Hull. Port Reg: H 113. 1950: Mercantile Loss on 10 October.

| OPHELIA | 1940/46 | P.No: | T 05 |

1939: Ordered on 12 December. 1940: L. 3 September. Built at Goole by Goole SB and engined by Amos & Smith. Completed as A/S. 1946: Sold to mercantile in August and renamed *Totton*.

| OTHELLO | 1941/46 | P.No: | T 76 |

1939: Ordered on 13 December. 1941: L. 7 October. Built at Aberdeen by Hall Russell and completed as A/S - M/S. 1946: Transferred to the Italian Navy in March and renamed RD 310.

| ROMEO | 1941/46 | Armament: | 1 x 4-inch; 3 x 20mm AA (singles) |
| | | P.No: | T 10 |

1939: Ordered on 9 September. 1941: L. 20 March. Built at Glasgow by A & J Inglis and engined by Aitchison Blair. Completed as a M/S - A/S. 1946: Sold to Belgian Mercantile.

| ROSALIND | 1941/63 | Armament: | 1 x 4-inch; 3 x 20mm AA (singles) |
| | | P.No: | T 135 |

1939: Ordered on 9 September. 1941: L. 3 May. Built at Glasgow by A & J Inglis and engined by Aithchison Blair. Completed as a M/S - A/S. 1946: Converted to an RNVR Training Ship for Kenya and Zanzibar. 1963: BU in April.

STRATH CLASS

The Strath Class was conceived as part of the Admiralty's huge trawler building programme of 1917, and orders were placed with various yards totalling 145 vessels. At the
time of ordering there were a number of vessels in builders yards under construction for
the mercantile and these were taken up by the Admiralty. Those of similar dimensions
were adopted into the Class and thus there were 24 Non-Standard Straths. These,
together with ordered vessels totalled 167 but subsequently 18 ordered vessels were
cancelled bringing the total which came into service to 149.

As in the case of the other large classes of Admiralty Trawlers those not completed by
the end of hostilities were completed as fishing vessels and sold immediately to the mercantile. Of those serving vessels sold to the mercantile after WWI a number were requisitioned for service in WWII when they served under their civillian names.

Displacement:	311T 429T (Deep) 215TG
Dimensions:	123ft oa 115ft 6in pp x 22ft x 12ft (Depth of hold)
Engines:	1 shaft Reciprocating (VTE) 430 IHP
Speed:	10.5 kts
Armament:	Nominally 1 x 3-inch and 24 mines, but see individual ships.
Complement:	Nominally 18 but varied with role.

Vessels in the Class:

AARON HUBERT, ARTHUR HERWIN, BARNARD BOYLE, BENJAMIN COLEMAN,
BRAZIL BRASBY, CHARLES BLIGHT, CHARLES CARROLL, CHARLES DOYLE,
CORNELIUS CARROLL, DANIEL DIZMONT, DANIEL HILLIER, DAVID BLAKE, DAVID
BUCHAN, DAVID CONN, EDWARD BARKER, EDWARD GREY, GEORGE BORTH-
WICK, GEORGE BURTON, GEORGE CASTLE, GEORGE CLINES, GEORGE COUL-
STON, GEORGE FRENCH, GEORGE HODGES, GEORGE IRELAND, GEORGE
LANE, HENRY BUTCHER, HENRY COLBY, HENRY FLIGHT, HENRY HARDING,
HENRY JENNINGS, ISAAC DOBSON, ISAAC HARRIS, JAMES BASHFORD, JAMES
BEAGAN, JAMES BENTOLE, JAMES BRODIGAN, JAMES CURRY, JAMES EVANS,
JAMES FEAGAN, JAMES FENNELL, JAMES GARRICK, JAMES HARTWELL, JAMES
HINES, JAMES LENHAM, JOHN BARRY, JOHN BELL, JOHN BOWLER, JOHN BRAD-
FORD, JOHN BRASKET, JOHN BRITTON , JOHN BULLER, JOHN CALLAGHAN,
JOHN CONN, JOHN COPE, JOHN CORWARDER, JOHN CURRAN, JOHN DUNKIN,
JOHN DUPUIS, JOHN EDSWORTH, JOHN FAIRMAN, JOHN FISSER, JOHN FRAN-
COIS, JOHN GRAY, JOHN HAILE, JOHN HEATH, JOHN HOWARD, JOHN HUNS,
JOHN HUNTER, JOHN JACKSON, JOHN KENNEDY, JOHN KENTALL, JOHN LANG-
SHAW, JONATHAN BAZINO, JONATHAN GREIG, JONATHAN HARDY, JOSEPH
BURGIN, JOSEPH COATES, JOSHUA BUDGET, LAWRENCE HUGHSON,
MATTHEW HARTLEY, MICHAEL BRION, PAT CAHARTY, PATRICK BORROW,
PATRICK DEVINE, PETER BARRINGTON, PETER DOBBIN, RICHARD BOWDEN,
RICHARD DRISCOLL, RICHARD HEAVER, ROBERT FARECLOTH, ROBERT GIB-
SON, ROBERT HARDING, SAMUEL BAKER, SAMUEL BARKAS, SAMUEL BENBOW,
SAMUEL GASBY, SAMUEL HAMPTON, SAMUEL LOVITT, STEPHEN KENNEY,
THOMAS BARCLAY, THOMAS BILLINGCOLE, THOMAS BIRD, THOMAS BRYAN,
THOMAS BURNHAM, THOMAS COLLARD, THOMAS COWELL, THOMAS CUR-
RELL, THOMAS DEAR, THOMAS DENNISON, THOMAS EVISON, THOMAS FOLEY,
THOMAS GOODCHILD, THOMAS GRAHAM, THOMAS HAGGERTY, THOMAS HEN-
RIX, TIMOTHY BRANNON, WILLIAM BARROW, WILLIAM BEAUMONT, WILLIAM

BENTLEY, WILLIAM BIGGS, WILLIAM BOND, WILLIAM BUTLER, WILLIAM CHALMERS, WILLIAM FALL, WILLIAM GIBBONS, WILLIAM GILLETT, WILLIAM GRIFFIN, WILLIAM HALLETT, WILLIAM HANBURY, WILLIAM HARRISON, WILLIAM HARVEY, WILLIAM HUTCHINSON, WILLIAM IVEY, WILLIAM KING.

Non-Standard Vessels:

CORNELIUS CARROLL, GEORGE COULSTON, ISRAEL ALDCROFT, JAMES ALDRIDGE, JAMES ARCHIBALD, JAMES BERRY, JAMES JOHNSON, JOHN ABBOTT, JOHN BRADFORD, JOHN CLAY, JOHN FITZGERALD, JOHN GILLMAN, JOSEPH ANNISON, MATTHEW CROOKE, RICHARD BENNETT, THOMAS ANSELL, THOMAS BUCKLEY, WILLIAM ASHTON, WILLIAM BARLOW, WILLIAM BARNETT, WILLIAM BROWNING, WILLIAM CASTLE, WILLIAM COGSWELL, WILLIAM FERRINS.

Cancelled Vessels:

CHARLES BARBER, CHARLES COUCHER, FREDERICK BOYCE, HENRY BATTERSBY, JOHN CONDON, JOHN CORBETT, JONATHAN BENJAMIN, JONATHAN BRONTON, JONATHAN COLLIS, JOSHUA CARRETTS, PERCY BRETT, SAMUEL CUNNINGHAM, THOMAS BRAUND, THOMAS CALTRAFFE, THOMAS CLAYTON, THOMAS COPSEY, THOMAS CURR, and WILLIAM BOREHAM.

RICHARD BENNETT   **(NMM Neg FFB1)**

| AARON HUBERT | 1919/19 | Admty No: | 3373 |

1919: L. Built at Paisley by Fullerton and completed as a fishing vessel. Delivered on 19 February. Sold to Mercantile. Renamed *Grafoe*. Acquired by Stringer's SFC of Boston, Lincs. PR: BN 53.

ARTHUR HERWIN	1919/20 1940/45	Displacement:	88TN
		Engines:	57HP
		Admty No:	3817
		Port Reg:	WWII: A 332
		P.No.	WWII: 4 246

1919: L.19 December. Built at Paisley by Fleming & Ferguson and completed as a fishing vessel. 1920: Delivered on 23 January. Sold to mercantile and renamed *River Lossie*. Acquired by Craig of Aberdeen. 1940: Requisitioned in June as RIVER LOSSIE and converted to an APV. 1945: Returned to owner in February.

BARNARD BOYLE	1918/21 1939/44	Displacement:	81TN
		Engines:	57HP
		Armament:	1 x 12-pdr AA
		Admty No:	3642
		Port Reg:	WWII: A 358
		P.No:	WWII: FY 826

1918: L. 13 June. Built at Aberdeen by Hall Russell. 1921: Sold to mercantile on 13 June and renamed *Dulcibelle*. Acquired by EC Matheson AO of MacDuff. 1939: Requisitioned in November as DULCIBELLE and converted to an APV. 1944: Returned to owners in November.

BENJAMIN COLEMAN	1917/21 1939/44	Displacement:	77TN
		Engines:	57HP
		Armament:	1 x 12-pdr
		Admty No:	3687
		Port Reg:	WWII: GW 37
		P.No:	WWII: 4 444

1917: L. 2 November. Built at Paisley by Fleming & Ferguson. 1921: Sold to mercantile on 16 November and retained the same name. Acquired by Mrs.I.S. Boyle of Glasgow. 1939: Requisitioned in November and converted to an APV. 1944: Converted to an Esso. Returned to owner in September.

| BRAZIL BRASBY | 1917/19 | Armament: | 1 x 12-pdr; 1 x 3.5"-inch Bomb Thrower (A/S Howitzer) |
| | | Admty No: | 3631 |

1917: L. 31 October. Built at Aberdeen by Hall Russell. Fitted with Listening Hydrophones. 1919: Sold to mercantile and renamed *Tyrwhitt*. Acquired by LC Cockrell of Wivenhoe. PR: H 67.

| CHARLES BARBER | 1918/18 | Admty No: | 4436 |

1918: Ordered from Hall Russell. Cancelled.

CHARLES BLIGHT   1919/19   Admty No: 4424

1919: L. 13 March. Built at Aberdeen by Hall Russell and completed as a fishing vessel. Sold to mercantile and renamed *Jacj Johnson*. 1920: Mercantile Loss. Mined in September.

CHARLES CARROLL   1918/19   Armament: 1 x 12-pdr
                                       Admty No: 3690

1918: L. 11 April. Built at Montrose by the Montrose SB Co. 1919: Sold to mercantile and renamed *River Ayr*. Acquired by the Montrose FCL of Montrose. PR: ME 79.

CHARLES COUCHER   1918/18   Admty No: 4437

1918: Designated to be built by Hawthorn. Cancelled.

CHARLES DOYLE   1919/19   1940/44   Displacement: 77TN
                                               Engines: 75HP
                                               Admty No: 4495
                                               Port Reg: WWII: GY 1329
                                               P.No: WWII: 4 254

1919: L. Built at Wivenhoe by Rennie Forrest. Completed as a fishing vessel and delivered on 21 November. Sold to mercantile and renamed *Sabina*. Acquired by Consolidated Fisheries of Grimsby. 1940: Requisitioned in July as SABINA and converted to an APV. 1944: Returned in September.

CHARLES LAWRENCE   1918/19   Admty No: 4226

1918: Ordered from Hall Russell. 1919: Cancelled.

CITY OF PERTH   1919/22   See under WILLIAM ASHTON

CORNELIUS CARROLL   1918/21   Displacement: 84TN
                                                 Engines: 57HP
                                               Armament: 1 x 12-pdr
                                               Admty No: 3658

1918: L. Built at Aberdeen by Hall and delivered on 19 March. Non-Standard. Fitted with Listening Hydrophones. 1921: Sold to mercantile and renamed *Boyne Braes*. Acquired by Ann Lewis of Inchgarth. PR: A 885.

DANIEL DIZMONT   1919/20   Admty No: 3734

1919: L. Built at Montrose by the Montrose SB Co. Completed as a fishing vessel and delivered on 19 August. 1920: Sold to mercantile and renamed *Patricia Scullion*. 1939: Served in WWII as the French AD 146 IBIS.

DANIEL HILLIER   1919/19   1939/45   Displacement: 88TN
                                               Engines: 75HP:
                                               Admty No: 3825
                                               Port Reg: WWII: A 233

1919: L. Built at Leith by Hawthorne. Completed as a fishing vessel and delivered on 18 March. Sold to mercantile and renamed *Ocean Fisher*. Acquired by B. Knowles of Hull. PR: H 147. Acquired by Star SFC of Aberdeen AO. PR: A 233. 1939: Requisitioned in August as OCEAN FISHER and converted for the Exam Service. 1945: Returned to owners in August.

DAVID BLAKE   1918/21   Displacement: 78TN
                                       Engines: 74HP
                                       Armament: 1 x 12-pdr
                                       Admty No: 3643

1918: L. 13 June. Built at Aberdeen by Hall Russell. 1921: Sold to mercantile and retained the same name. Acquired by JM Davidson of Glasgow. PR: LO 306.

DAVID BUCHAN   1918/19 1939/40 Displacement: 87TN
                                       Engines: 57HP
                                       Armament: 1 x 12-pdr
                                       Admty No: 3639
                                       Port Reg: WWII: A 940

1918: L. 9 April. Built at Aberdeen by Hall Russell. 1919: Sold to mercantile on 10 November and renamed *River Ness*. Acquired by H.Lewis of Pitfodels. Acquired by River Ness FCL of Aberdeen. PR: A 940. 1939: Requisitioned as RIVER NESS in November and designated as an APV. 1940: Returned to owners in February.

DAVID CONN   1918/19 1940/44 Displacement: 83TN
                                       Engines: 57HP
                                       Armament: 1 x 12-pdr
                                       Admty No: FY 1643
                                       Port Reg: WWII: A 6
                                       P.No: WWII: FY 1643

1918: L: 13 July. Built at Montrose by the Montrose SB Co. 1919: Sold to mercantile and renamed *River Spey*. Acquired by Montrose FCL of Montrose. Acquired by Boston DSF & Ice Co of Boston, Lincs. PR: A 6. 1940: Requisitioned in April as RIVER SPEY and converted to a D/L. 1941: Converted to a M/S. 1944: Returned to owners in November.

EDWARD BARKER   1918/21 1939/44 Armament: 1 x 12-pdr
                                       Admty No: 4420
                                       Port Reg: WWII: A 176
                                       P.No: WWII: FY 1642

1918: L. 21 November. Built at Aberdeen by Hall Russell. 1921: Sold to mercantile and renamed *Mirabelle*. Acquired by AA.Davidson of Aberdeen. 1939: Requisitioned in November as MIRABELLE and converted to an APV. Based at Grimsby. 1944: Converted to an Esso. LOST. Sank after being rammed on 17 November.

EDWARD GREY   1920/20 1939/40 Displacement: 75TN
                                       Engines: 57HP
                                       Admty No: 3679
                                       Port Reg: WWII: A 346

1920: L. Built at Whiteinch, Glasgow by Ritche Graham and completed as a fishing vessel. Sold to mercantile and renamed *Suzette*. Purchased by the Gorspen ST Co Ltd. of Aberdeen. 1939: Requisitioned in November as SUZETTE and converted to an APV. 1940: Returned to owners in February.

FREDERICK BOYCE   1919/19   Admty No: 4432

1918: Ordered from Hall Russell. 1919: Cancelled.

GEORGE BORTHWICK   1917/20 1939/44 Displacement: 93TN
                                       Engines: 57HP
                                       Armament: 1 x 12-pdr
                                                        1 x 7.5-inch Bomb

1917: L. 21 June. Built at Aberdeen by Hall Russell and completed as a M/S. Fitted with Listening Hydrophones. 1920: Sold to mercantile and renamed *Annabelle*. 1939: Owned by D. Wood of Aberdeen. Requisitioned in November as ANNABELLE and converted to an APV. 1941: Converted to a BBV. 1944: Returned to owner in December.

GEORGE BURTON   1917/21 1939/44 Armament: 1 x 12-pdr.

1917: L. 8 December. Built at Aberdeen by Hall Russell. 1921: Sold to mercantile and renamed *Bervie Braes*. 1939: Requisitioned in November as BERVIE BRAES and converted to an APV. 1940: Converted to a M/S. 1944: Converted to an Esso. Returned to owners in October.

GEORGE CASTLE   1919/20 1939/45
Displacement:	84TN
Engines:	75HP
Admty No:	4482
Port Reg:	GN 103
P.No:	Z 160

1919: L. Built at Workington by Williamson & Sons and completed as a fishing vessel. 1920: Sold to mercantile and retained the same name. 1928: Renamed *Lord Tennyson*. 1939: Owned by G.G.Paton of Glasgow. Requisitioned in November as RIVER ANNAN and converted to a BGV. 1945: Returned to owner in November.

GEORGE CLINES   1919/20   Admty No: 4469

1919: L. Built at Leith by Hawthorn and completed as a fishing vessel. Delivered on 13 June. 1920: Sold to mercantile and renamed *Skirbeck*. 1939: Served in WWII as French AD 119 ROCHE FRANCOIS.

GEORGE COULSTON   1918/21 1940/45
Displacement:	84TN
Engines:	57HP
Armament:	1 x 12-pdr; 1 x 3.5"-inch Bomb Thrower (A/S Howitzer)
Admty No:	3660
Port Reg:	WWII: A 881
P.No:	WWII: 4 235

1918: L. 27 April. Built at Aberdeen by Hall. Fitted with Listening Hydrophones. 1921: Sold to mercantile and renamed *Doonie Braes*. Acquired by Andrew W. King and others of Aberdeen. 1940: Requisitioned in May as DOONIE BRAES and converted to an APV. 1945: Returned to owners in January.

GEORGE FRENCH   1918/20 1940/45
Displacement:	83TN
Engines:	57HP
Armament:	1 x 12-pdr
Admty No:	3747
Port Reg:	WWII: GY 1315

1918: L. Built at Glasgow by Murdoch & Murray and delivered on 10 June. 1920: Sold to mercantile and renamed *Arlette*. 1938: Owned by Consilidated Fisheries Ltd. of Grimsby. 1940: Requisitioned as ARLETTE and converted for the Examination Service. 1945: Returned to owners.

GEORGE HODGES	1918/19	Displacement:	78TN
		Engines:	57HP
		Armament:	1 x 12-pdr
		Admty No:	3820
		Port Reg:	A 11

1918: L. Built at Leith by Hawthorn and delivered on 20 June. 1919: Sold to mercantile and renamed *Hood.* Acquired by John Craig and others of Aberdeen.

GEORGE IRELAND	1918/23	Admty No:	3846

1918: L. Built at Wivenhoe by Rennie Forrestt and delivered on 25 October. 1919: ICW Sister ship HENRY JENNINGS employed on trials. Fitted with a primitive form of jet-propulsion but the trials were unsuccessful. 1920: Renamed TEVIOT in September. 1923: Sold to mercantile and renamed *Firsby*.

GEORGE LANE	1919/20	Admty No:	4230

1919: L. Built at Bowling, Glasgow, by Scott. Completed as a fishing vessel and delivered on 19 June. 1920: Sold to mercantile and renamed *River Kelvin.*

HENRY BATTERSBY	1919/21	Admty No:	4433

1918: Ordered from Hall Russel. 1919: L. 1921: Completed as a fishing vessel and sold to mercantile without being accepted in the RN.

HENRY BUTCHER	1918/19	Displacement:	87TN
		Engines:	57HP
		Admty No:	3638

1918: L 26 March. Built at Aberdeen by Hall Russell. 1919: Sold to mercantile and renamed *River Tay.* PR: A 188. Acquired by G.G. Paton of Glasgow.

HENRY COLBY	1919/20	Admty No:	4470

1919: L. Built at Leith by Hawthorn and completed as a fishing vessel. Delivered on 10 July and placed on the Disposal List. 1920: Sold to mercantile and renamed *Freiston.* 1939: Served as the French AD 144 ROCHE GRISE in WWII.

HENRY FLIGHT	1918/21 1939/44	Displacement:	85TN
		Engines:	57HP
		Armament:	1 x 12-pdr
		Admty No:	3758
		Port Reg:	WWII: GY 1342
		P.No:	WWII: 4 442

1918: L. Built at Queensferry, Chester, by Abdela & Mitchell. 1922: Sold to mercantile and renamed *Yesso.* Acquired by Diamonds SF Co.Ltd., Grimsby. 1939: Requisitioned in November as YESSO. Converted to an APV. 1940: Converted to a BDV in June. 1943: Renamed ARABESQUE. 1944: Converted to an Esso. Returned in November.

HENRY HARDING	1918/19	Armament:	1 x 12-pdr
		Admty No:	3822

1918: L. Built at Leith by Hawthorn and delivered on 2 December. 1919: Sold to mercantile and renamed *Ocean Clipper.* Acquired by Blomfields of Yarmouth. PR: YH 223.

HENRY JENNINGS	1918/22 1940/43	Displacement:	79TN
		Engines:	59HP
		Admty No:	3848
		Port Reg:	WWII: GN 105

1918: L. Built at Wivenhoe by Rennie Forrest. 1919: Delivered on 22 July. 1920: Renamed URE. 1922: Sold to mercantile and retained the same name. 1924: Renamed *Aby*. Subsequently renamed *Moray*. 1938: Owned by A.G.Brown of Granton. 1939: Acquired by the Boston DSF & Ice Co of Boston. 1940: Requisitioned in April as MORAY and converted to a D/L. 1942: Converted to a Water Carrier. 1943: LOST. Foundered in heavy weather off Milford Haven on 13 March.

ISAAC DOBSON	1919/19 1940/43	Displacement:	88TN
		Engines:	74HP
		Admty No:	3733
		Port Reg:	WWII: SN 40
		P.No:	WWII: FY 798

1919: L. Built at Montrose by Montrose SB and completed as a fishing vessel. Delivered on 23 April. Sold to mercantile and renamed *Holland*. Acquired by A. Mitchell Jnr of Aberdeen. Acquired by the Shields Eng. & DD Co.Ltd of N.Shields and renamed *Liddock*. 1940: Requisitioned in March as LIDDOCK and converted to a D/L. Subsequently converted to an APV. 1943: Returned to owners.

| ISAAC HARRIS | 1919/19 | Admty No: | 3826 |

1919: L. Built at Leith by Hawthorn and completed as a fishing vessel. Delivered on 12 April. Sold to mercantile and renamed *Pochard II*. Acquired by Harley & Miller of Liverpool. PR: LL 21

ISRAEL ALDCROFT	1917/21 1939/44	Displacement:	80TN
		Engines:	79HP
		Armament:	1 x 12-pdr
		Admty No:	3617
		Port Reg:	WWII: SN 57
		P.No:	WWII: 4 135

1917: L. 20 June. Built at Aberdeen by Duthie. Commissioned as a Training Ship.1921: Sold to mercantile. Acquired by G.R. Purdy Trs.Ltd. of N.Shields and renamed *George R.Purdy*. 1939: Requisitioned in September as GEORGE R. PURDY and employed on the Examination Service. 1944: Returned to owners in October.

JAMES ALDRIDGE	1917/21	Displacement:	221TG 89TN
		Engines:	57HP
		Armament:	1 x 12-pdr
		Admty No:	3614

1917: L. 10 April. Built at Aberdeen by Duthie Torry and completed as a M/S. 1921: Sold to mercantile and retained the same name. Acquired by Bracken STC of Aberdeen. PR: GW 40.

JAMES ARCHIBALD	1917/21	Displacement:	210TG 78TN
		Engines:	57HP
		Armament:	1 x 12-pdr
		Admty No:	3615

1917: L. 24 April. Built at Aberdeen by Duthie Torry and completed as a M/S. 1921: Sold to mercantile and retained the same name. 1928: Renamed *Nisus*. Acquired by David Woods AO of Aberdeen. PR: A 318

JAMES BASHFORD	1919/19 1940/45	Displacement:	88TN
		Engines:	74HP
		Armament:	1 x 3-pdr
		Admty No:	4429
		Port Reg:	WWII: A 220
		P.No:	WWII: FY 1648

1919: L. 12 June. Built at Aberdeen by Hall Russell and completed as a fishing vessel. Sold to mercantile. Acquired by Aberdeen ST & FCL of Aberdeen and renamed *Strathrannoch*. 1940: Requisitioned in April as STRATHRANNOCH and converted to a D/L. Converted to an APV in August. 1943: Converted to a Mooring Vessel. 1945: Returned to owners in July.

JAMES BEAGAN	1917/21 1939/46	Displacement:	82TN
		Engines:	57TN
		Armament:	1 x 12-pdr
		Admty No:	3630
		Port Reg:	WWII: A 828
		P.No:	WWII: 4 203

1917: L. 19 October. Built at Aberdeen by Hall Russell. 1921: Sold to mercantile. Acquired by Bon Accord SF Co.Ltd. of Aberdeen and renamed *Loch Blair*. 1940: Requisitioned in June as LOCH BLAIR and converted to an APV. 1946: Returned to owners in February.

JAMES BENTOLE	1917/21 1939/45	Displacement:	82TN
		Engines:	57HP
		Armament:	WWI: 1 x 12-pdr.
			WWII: 1 x 3-pdr; 4 x 0.303-inch Hefah (2 x twin); 2 x 0.5-inch MGs (2 x twin)
		Admty No:	3622
		Port Reg:	WWII: A 878
		P.No:	WWII: FY 762

1917: L. 21 June. Built at Aberdeen by Hall Russell. Completed as a M/S in August. 1921: Sold to mercantile and renamed *Fort Robert*. Acquired by William Masson of Aberdeen. 1939: Requisitoned in November as FORT ROBERT and converted to an APV. 1940: Converted to a M/S in April. 1943: Fitted with a bow acoustic sweep. 1945: Returned to owners in August. 1960: BU.

JAMES BERRY	1917/22 1940/46	Displacement:	109TN
		Engines:	83HP
		Armament:	1 x 12-pdr
		Admty No:	3603
		Port Reg:	WWII: GY 83
		P.No:	WWII: 4 171

1917: Originally ordered by Hull Northern FCL of Hull and puchased by the Admiralty whilst on the stocks. L. 10 May. Built at Beverley by CWG. Non-Standard. 1922: Sold to mercantile. Acquired by the original owners, Hull Northern, and renamed *Montano*. PR: H 818. 1929: Acquired by Orontes SFC of Grimsby. PR: GY 83. 1932: Acquired by the Southampton SF Co.Ltd. of Grimsby. 1940: Requisitioned on 3 May as MONTANO and converted to an APV. 1942: Converted to a M/S in March. 1944: Converted to an Esso in March. 1946: Returned to owners on 2 January. 1953: BU at Granton in March. Notes: Also listed as MONTAMO

JAMES BRODIGAN   1918/19 1939/40 Displacement: 78TN
                                      Engines: 57HP
                                      Admty No: 4419
                                      Port Reg: WWII: H 142

1918: L. 21 November. Built at Aberdeen by Hall Russell and completed as a fishing vessel. 1919: Sold to mercantile and retained the same name. Acquired by Hull Northern SFC of Hull. PR: H 142. 1939: Requisitioned in November renamed WOODS and designated as an APV. 1940: Returned to owners on 31 January.

JAMES CURRY   1917/21   Armament: 1 x 12-pdr
                            Admty No: 3708

1917: L. 20 November. Built at Port Glasgow by Murdoch & Murray. 1921: Sold to mercantile and renamed *Ady*. 1939: Served in WWII as French GENEVIEVE.

JAMES EVANS   1918/22   Admty No: 3731

1918: L. Built at Queensferry, Chester, by Abdela & Mitchell. 1922: Sold to mercantile and retained the same name.

JAMES FEAGAN   1919/19   Displacement: 88TN
                             Engines: 57HP
                             Admty No: 3760

1919: L. Built at Montrose by Montrose SB and completed as a fishing vessel. Delivered on 17 December. Sold to mercantile. Acquired by GG Paton of Glasgow and renamed *River Earn*. PR: GN 36.

JAMES FENNEL   1918/20   Armament: 1 x 12-pdr
                             Admty No: 3753

1918: L. Built by Fullerton and delivered on 9 July. 1920: LOST. Wrecked at Blacknor Point, Portland, on 16 January.

JAMES GARRICK   1919/20   Displacement: 88TN
                              Engines: 75HP
                              Admty No: 3761

1920: L. Built at Montrose by Montrose SB and completed as a fishing vessel. Delivered on 16 February. 1920: Sold to mercantile and renamed *River Findhorn*. Acquired by by Consolidated Fisheries of Grimsby.

JAMES HARTWELL   1918/21 1939/46 Displacement: 81TN
                                     Engines: 57HP
                                     Armament: 1 x 12-pdr
                                     Admty No: 3693
                                     Port Reg: WWII: A 352
                                     P.No: WWII: FY 804

1918: L. Built at Hook by the Ouse SB and delivered on 11 November. 1921: Sold to mercantile. Acquired by J.C.& A.J. Spence of Aberdeen and renamed *Georgette*. 1939: Requisitioned in November as GEORGETTE and converted to a M/S. 1946: Returned to owners in May.

JAMES HINES   1919/19 1939/46 Displacement: 88TN
                                  Engines: 75HP
                                  Admty No: 3827
                                  Port Reg: WWII: A 15

1919: L. Built at Leith by Hawthorns and completed as a fishing vessel. Sold to mercantile and acquired by George Leiper AO of Aberdeen. Renamed *Northward Ho*. 1939: Requisitioned in November as NORTHWARD HO and converted to a M/S. 1946: Returned to owners in February.

JAMES JOHNSON	1917/22	Displacement:	107TN
		Engines:	61HP
		Armament:	1 x 12-pdr
		Admty No:	3506

1917: L 18 February. Built at Southbank-on-Tees by Smiths Dock. Completed as a M/S. 1919: Renamed THOMAS DEAS in December. 1922: Sold to mercantile and retained the same name. Acquired by Elizabeth A.H.Petit of Milford Haven. PR: M 253.

JAMES LENHAM	1918/18	Admty No:	4225

1918: Ordered from John Lewis and subsequently cancelled.

JOHN ABBOT	1917/21	1939/46	Displacement:	194TG 80TN
			Engines:	79HP
			Armament:	1 x 12-pdr
			Port Reg:	WWII: SN 29

1917: L. 7 August. Built at Aberdeen by Duthie and completed as a M/S. Fitted with Listening Hydrophones. Non-Standard. 1920: Renamed JOHN MASON in May. 1921: Sold to mercantile. Acquired by G.R.Purdy of N.Shields and renamed *Christania T.Purdy*. 1939: Requisitioned in November as CHRISTANIA T. PURDY. Converted to an APV. 1940: Converted to a BDV. 1946: Returned to owner in August.

JOHN BARRY	1917/21	Armament:	1 x 12-pdr
		Admty No:	3642

1917: L. 24 July. Built at Aberdeen by Hall Russell and completed as a M/S. 1921: Sold to mercantile and renamed *Christabelle*. Acquired by Consolidated Fisheries of Grimsby. PR: GY 1328. Acquired by J. Mackie of Aberdeen. Port Reg: A 360.

JOHN BELL	1918/21	Armament:	1 x 12-pdr AA
		Admty No:	3635

1918: L. 12 February. Built at Aberdeen by Hall Russell. 1923: Sold to mercantile and renamed *John Smart*.

JOHN BOWLER	1918/22	Armament:	1 x 12-pdr
		Admty No:	3637

1918: L. 12 February. Built at Aberdeen by Hall Russell. Fitted with Listening Hydrophones. 1922: Sold to mercantile and renamed *Karabigha*.

JOHN BRADFORD	1917/20	1939/42	Displacement:	78TN
			Engines:	74HP
			Armament:	1 x 12-pdr
			Admty No:	3647
			Port Reg:	WWII: A 412

1917: L. 15 July. Built at Aberdeen by Hall Russell. Fitted with Listening Hydrophones. 1920: Sold to mercantile and renamed *Dorileen*. Acquired by R.Irvin & Sons of S.Shields. PR: A 412. Renamed *Ben Ardna*. 1939: Requisitioned in August as BEN ARDNA and converted for the Examination Service. 1942: LOST. Sunk in a collision in the Tyne on 12 May.

| JOHN BRASKET | 1917/21 | Armament: | 1 x 12-pdr AA ; 1 x 7.5-inch Bomb Thrower (A/S Howitzer) |
| | | Admty No: | 3627 |

1917: L. 13 September. Built at Aberdeen by Hall Russell. 1921: Sold to mercantile and retained the same name. Mercantile Loss. Wrecked in November.

| JOHN BULLER | 1918/19 | Admty No: | 4416 |

1918: L. 11 September. Built at Aberdeen by Hall Russell. 1919: Sold to mercantile and retained the same name. Acquired by Hull Northern FC of Hull. PR: H 144. Subsequently renamed *San Pedro*.

JOHN CALLAGHAN	1917/21 1940/46	Displacement:	82TN
		Engines:	57HP
		Armament:	1 x 12-pdr
		Admty No:	3707
		Port Reg:	WWII: A 353

1917: L. 17 October. Built at Port Glasgow by Murdoch & Murray. 1921: Sold to mercantile and retained the same name. Acquired by Dinas STC of Fleetwood. PR: FD 395. Subsequently acquired by Walker STF & Co of Aberdeen and renamed *Star of Liberty*. 1940: Reqisitioned in September as STAR OF LIBERTY and fitted out for the Examination Service. 1946: Returned to owners in January.

| JOHN CONDON | 1918/18 |

1918: Ordered from Hall Russell and subsequently cancelled.

JOHN CONNE	1919/21	Displacement:	88TN
		Engines:	75HP
		Admty No:	4476

1919: L. 30 May. Built at Leith by Hawthorn and completed as a fishing vessel. 1921: Sold to mercantile and renamed *Braconbush*. Acquired by the Don FC of Aberdeen. PR: A 770.

JOHN COPE	1918/19 1939/45	Displacement:	88TN
		Engines:	57HP
		Armament:	1 x 12-pdr
		Port Reg:	WWII: A 225

1918: L. Built at Wivenhoe by Rennie Forrest and delivered on 19 November. 1919: Sold to mercantile and renamed *River Garry*. Acquired by Consolidated Fisheries of Grimsby. PR: GY 273. Acquired by John Craig AO of Aberdeen. PR: A 225. 1939: Requisitioned in August as RIVER GARRY and fitted out for the Examination Service. 1945: Returned to owners in July.

| JOHN CORBETT | 1918/18 | Admty No: | 4442 |

1918: Ordered from Hall Russell and subsequently cancelled.

JOHN CORWARDER	1917/19	Displacement:	81TN
		Engines:	57HP
		Armament:	1 x 12-pdr
		Admty No:	3685

1917: L. 20 September. Built at Paisley by Fleming & Ferguson and completed as a M/S. 1919: Sold to mercantile and renamed *River Nith*. Acquired by Consolidated Fisheries of Grimsby. PR: GY 289.

| JOHN CURRAN | 1918/22 | Armament: | 1 x 12-pdr |
| | | Admty No: | 3688 |

1918: L. Built at Montrose by Montrose SB and delivered on 8 June. Fitted with Listening Hydrophones. 1922: Sold to mercantile and renamed *Commandant Gamas*.

JOHN DUNKIN	1918/21	Displacement:	77TN
		Engines:	57HP
		Armament:	1 x 12-pdr
		Admty No:	3727

1918: L. 6 August. Built at Paisley by Fleming & Ferguson. 1919: Renamed PEKIN in March. Reverted to JOHN DUNKIN in May and temporarily loaned to the USN. Returned to the RN in August. 1921: Sold to mercantile and retained the same name. Acquired by JS.Boyle of Glasgow. PR: GW.35. 1938: Owned by Mrs. L.S.Boyle of Glasgow.

JOHN DUPUIS	1918/22	Displacement:	77TN
		Engines:	430HP
		Armament:	1 x 12-pdr
		Admty No:	3732

1918: L. Built at Queensferry, Cheshire, by Abdela Mitchell and delivered on 3 July. Fitted with Listening Hydrohones. Employed as a Training Ship. 1922: Sold to mercantile and renamed *Ravenna*. Acquired by Trawlers (White Sea & Grimsby) Ltd of Grimsby.

| JOHN DUTTON | 1918/22 | Armament: | 1 x 12-pdr |
| | | Admty No: | 3739 |

1918: L. 17 January. Built at Port Glasgow by Ferguson. 1922: Sold to mercantile and renamed *Karlesefni*.

JOHN EDSWORTH	1918/19	1939/45	Displacement:	81TN
			Engines:	57HP
			Armament:	1 x 12-pdr
			Admty No:	3744
			Port Reg:	WWII: GY 293
			P.No:	WWII: 4 51

1918: L. Built at Paisley by Fullerton and delivered on 3 June. Fitted with Listening Hydrophones. 1919: Sold to mercantile and renamed *River Leven*. Acquired by Consolidated Fisheries of Grimsby. 1939: Requisitioned in August as RIVER LEVEN, fitted out for the Examination Service and based at Grimsby. 1942: Converted to an Escort. 1944: Converted to an Esso in April. 1945: Returned to owners in March.

JOHN FAIRMAN	1918/20	1939/40	Displacement:	79TN
			Engines:	57HP
			Armament:	1 x 12-pdr
			Admty No:	3750
			Port Reg:	WWII: A 7

1918: L. Built at Wivenhoe by Rennie Forrestt. Fitted with Listening Hydrophones. 1920: Sold to mercantile and renamed *Ocean Victor*. Acquired J.Craig & Others of Aberdeen. 1939: Requisitioned in November as OCEAN VICTOR and designated as an APV. 1940: Returned to owners in February.

JOHN FISSER	1918/19 1942/48	Armament:	1 x 12-pdr
		Admty No:	3732
		P.No:	WWII: Z 57

1918: L. Built at Glasgow by Ritcie, Graham and delivered on 27 September. Fitted with Listening Hydrophones. 1919: Sold to mercantile and renamed *Joule*. Acquired by F & T Ross of Hull. PR: H 159. 1942: Requisitioned into the RAN as MART CAM and converted to a M/S. Subsequently purchased into the RAN. 1948: Sold in May.

JOHN FITZGERALD	1917/21 1941/46	Displacement:	90TN
		Engines:	57HP
		Armament:	1 x 12-pdr
		Admty No:	3754
		Port Reg:	WWII: SN 69
		P.No:	WWII: Z 149

1917: L. 14 December. Built at Aberdeen by Duthie Torry. 1919: On Temporary Loan to the USN from May. Returned to the RN in August. 1921: Sold to mercantile and retained the same name. Acquired by R.Hastie of N.Shields. 1941: Requisitioned in January and converted to a BDV. 1946: Returned in January.

JOHN FRANCOIS	1918/21 1940/45	Displacement:	79TN
		Engines:	75HP
		Armament:	1 x 6-pdr AA
		Admty No:	3748
		Port Reg:	WWII: SN 129

1918: L. Built at Port Glasgow by Murdoch & Murray. Delivered on 9 August. 1921: Sold to mercantile and renamed *Edith M. Purdy*. Acquired by Purdy Trs of N.Shields. 1940: Requisitioned in February as EDITH M. PURDY and converted to a BDV. 1945: Returned to owners in May.

JOHN GILLMAN	1917/20	Displacement:	106TN
		Engines:	78HP
		Armament:	1 x 12-pdr; 1 x 7.5-inch Bomb Thrower (A/S Howitzer)
		Admty No:	3502

1917: L. 9 January. Built at Southbank-on-Tees by Smith's Dock. 1920: Sold to mercantile and retained the same name. Acquired by N.E.Fisheries Ltd of Aberdeen. Port Reg: A 230.

JOHN GRAY	1918/20	Displacement:	89TN
		Engines:	67HP
		Armament:	1 x 12-pdr
		Admty No:	3763

1918: L. 11 April. Built at Bowling by Scott and fitted with Listening Hydrophones. 1920: Sold to mercantile and retained the same name. Acquired by Canute STC of Grimsby. PR: GY 1078 1932: Acquired by John Lewis of Aberdeen and renamed *Fort Rona*. PR: A.195.

JOHN HAILE	1918/22 1939/45	Displacement:	78TN
		Engines:	59HP
		Armament:	WWI: 1 x 12-pdr.
			WWII: 1 x 3-pdr.
		Admty No:	3819
		Port Reg:	WWII: DE 10
		P.No:	WWII: FY 850

1918: L. Built at Leith by Hawthorn and delivered on 9 May. Fitted with Listening Hydrophones. 1922: Sold to mercantile and renamed *Tumby*. Acquired by Don Fishing Co of Dundee. 1939: Requisitioned in November as TUMBY and converted to an APV. Based at Grimsby. 1942: Converted to a M/S in March. 1945: Returned to owners in April.

JOHN HEATH	1919/19 1934/45	Displacement:	87TN
		Engines:	74HP
		Admty No:	3757
		Port Reg:	WWII: A 384
		P.No:	WWII:

1919: L. Built at Hook by Ouse SB and completed as a fishing vessel. Delivered on 14th June. Sold to mercantile and renamed *Kuvera*. Acquired by R.Baxter & others of Aberdeen. 1940: Requisitioned in July as KUVERA and converted to an APV. 1945: Returned to owners in September.

JOHN HOWARD	1919/21 1939/40	Displacement:	77TN
		Engines:	430HP
		Admty No:	4203
		Port Reg:	WWII: SN 62

1919: L. Built at Wivenhoe by Rennie Forrestt and completed as a fishing vessel. Delivered on 22 July. 1921: Sold to mercantile and renamed *Evelina*. Acquired by J.Tomlinson & J.Tomlinson Jnr. of N.Shields. 1939: Requisitioned in November as EVELINA and converted to an APV. LOST. Mined off the Tyne on 16 December.

JOHN HUNS	1919/19 1940/44	Displacement:	88TN
		Engines:	75HP
		Admty No:	4273
		Port Reg:	WWII: SN 4

1919: L. Built at Paisley by Fullerton and completed as a fishing vessel. Delivered on 4 April and renamed JOHN MOSS. Sold to mercantile and renamed *Lord Allenby*. Acquired by Lowestoft SHDC of Lowestoft. PR: LT666. Acquired by G.R.Purdy Trs of N.Shields and renamed *Sarah A. Purdy*. 1940: Requisitioned in February as SARAH A. PURDY and converted to a BBV. 1944: Returned to owners in November.

JOHN HUNTER	1918/21 1940/46	Displacement:	77TN
		Engines:	57HP
		Admty No:	3777
		Port Reg:	WWII: A 182
		P.No:	WWII: 4 273

1919: L. Built at Wivenhoe by Rennie Forrest. 1921: Sold to mercantile and renamed *Delila*. Acquired by the Gorspen ST Co.Ltd of Aberdeen. 1940: Requisitioned in June as DELILA and converted to an APV. 1946: Returned to owners in January.

JOHN JACKSON	1918/21 1939/46	Displacement:	77TN
		Engines:	57HP
		Armament:	1 x 12-pdr

		Admty No:	3847
		Port Reg:	WWII: A 265
		P.No:	WWII: FY 735

1918: L. Built at Wivenhoe by Rennie Forrest and completed as a M/S. Delivered on 10 September. 1921: Sold to mercantile and retained the same name. Acquired by J.R.Bruse AO of Buckie and renamed *Inchgower*. 1939: Requisitioned in November as INCHGOWER and converted to a M/S. 1946: Returned to owners in February.

JOHN KENNEDY	1919/19 1939/45	Displacement:	94TN
		Engines:	80HP
		Admty No:	3853
		Port Reg:	WWII: SN 5
		P.No:	WWII: 4 408

1919: L. Built at Queensferry, Cheshire, by Abdela Mitchell and completed as a fishing vessel. Sold to mercantile and renamed *John Elliot*. Acquired by the Co-op Fish.Soc. of Scarborough. PR: SH.131. Acquired by Richard Irvin of N.Shields and renamed *Gillian*. 1939: Requisitioned in August as GILLIAN and fitted out for the Examination Service. 1945: Returned to owners in August.

| JOHN KENTALL | 1918/19 | Armament: | 1 x 12-pdr |
| | | Admty No: | 3850 |

1918: L. Built at Workington by Williamson and delivered on 20 September. 1919: Sold to mercantile and renamed *Wheatstone*. Acquired by F & T Ross of Hull. PR: H158

| JOHN LANGSHAW | 1919/19 | Admty No: | 4229 |

1919: L. Built at Bowling by Scott and completed as a fishing vessel. Sold to mercantile and renamed *Ethel Crawford*. Acquired by N.E. Fisheries of Aberdeen. PR: A 36.

| JOHN MASON | 1920/21 | See under JOHN ABBOTT |

| JOHN MOSS | 1919/19 | See under JOHN HUNS |

| JONATHAN BAZINO | 1919/19 | Admty No: | 4421 |

1919: L. 29 January. Built at Port Glasgow by Russell and completed as a fishing vessel. Sold to mercantile and renamed *Pitstruan*. Acquired by JS.Doig of Aberdeen. PR: A.129.

| JONATHAN BENJAMIN | 1918/18 | Admty No: | 4435 |

1918: Ordered from Hall Russell and subsequently cancelled.

| JONATHAN BRONTON | 1918/18 | Admty No: | 4431 |

1918: Ordered from Hall Russell and subsequently cancelled.

| JONATHAN COLLIS | 1918/18 | Admty No: | 4443 |

1918: Ordered from Hall Russell and subsequently cancelled.

| JONATHAN GREIG | 1919/19 | Admty No: | 4471 |

1919: L. Built at Leith by Hawthorn and completed as a fishing vessel. Delivered on 16 September. Sold to mercantile and renamed *Strathglass*. Acquired by North Star Fishing Co of Aberdeen. PR: A 62.

| JONATHAN HARDY | 1918/21 | Armament:
Admty No: | 1 x 12-pdr
3772 |

1918: L. Built by Fullerton and delivered on 7 November. 1921: Sold to French mercantile and renamed *Roche Bleue*. 1939: French AD 170 ROCHE BLEUE in WWII.

| JOSEPH ANNISON | 1917/22 1939/43 | Displacement:
Engines:
Armament:
Admty No:
Port Reg:
P.No: | 194TG 90TN
71HP
1 x 12-pdr
3619
WWII: A.24
WWII: FY 806
FY 1585 |

1917: L. 19 September. Built at Aberdeen by Duthie. 1922: Sold to mercantile and retained the same name. Acquired by Perhelion AFC of Grimsby. PR: GY 231. Acquired by Stephen Fishing Co. of Aberdeen and renamed *William Stephen*. 1939: Requisitioned in November as WILLIAM STEPHEN and converted to a M/S. 1943: LOST. Sunk by E-Boat off Cromer on 25 October.

| JOSEPH BURGIN | 1918/19 | Armament:
Admty No: | 1 x 12-pdr
3686 |

1918: L. 12 February. Built at Aberdeen by Hall Russell. 1919: Sold to mercantile and retained the same name. Acquired by Grimsby SS Co. PR: GY.887.

| JOSEPH COATES | 1918/21 | Armament:

Admty No: | 1 x 12pdr; 1 x 3.5-inch Bomb Thrower (A/S Howitzer)
3709 |

1918: L. Built at Port Glasgow by Murdoch & Murray and delivered on 30 May. 1921: Sold to mercantile and renamed *Aigrette*. Acquired by Consolidated Fisheries of Grimsby. PR: GY 1334.

| JOSHUA BUDGET | 1919/19 1939/40 | Displacement:
Engines:
Admty No:
Port Reg: | 88TN
59HP
4425
WWII: SN 42 |

1919: L. 11 April. Built at Aberdeen by Hall Russell and completed as a fishing vessel. Sold to mercantile and renamed *Mary Crowther*. Acquired by RW Crawford of Scarborough. PR: SH 99. Acquired by D.Dougal of Tynemouth & others and renamed *Olden Times*. 1939: Requisitioned in November as OLDEN TIMES and designated as an APV. 1940: Returned to owners on 20 February.

| JOSHUA CARRETTS | 1918/18 | Admty No: | 4474 |

1918: Ordered from Hawthorn and subsequently cancelled.

| LAWRENCE HUGHSON | 1919/19 | Admty No: | 4201 |

1919: L. Built at Wivenhoe by Rennie Forrest and completed as a fishing vessel. Delivered on 21 March. Sold to mercantile and renamed *Elloe*. Acquired by Stringers SFC of Boston, Lincs. PR: BN 63.

| MATTHEW CROOKE | 1917/21 1940/45 | Displacement:
Engines:
Armament: | 78TN
75HP
WWI: 1 x 12-pdr. |

1917: L. 2 October. Built at Aberdeen by Hall. 1921: Sold to mercantile and renamed *Fortrose*. Acquired by John Lewis of Aberdeen. 1940: Requisitioned in May as FORT ROSE and converted to an APV. 1945: Returned to owners.

| MATTHEW HARTLEY | 1919/19 | Admty No: | 4202 |

1919: L. Built at Wivenhoe by Rennie Forrest and completed as a fishing vessel. Sold to mercantile and renamed *Wyberton*.

MICHAEL BRION	1919/19	1939/40	Displacement:	88TN
			Engines:	74HP
			Admty No:	4430
			Port Reg:	A 219

1919: L. 12 June. Built at Aberdeen by Russell And completed as a fishing vessel. Sold to mercantile and renamed *Sturdee*. Acquired by Gorspen ST Co. Ltd of Aberdeen. 1939: Requisitioned in November as STURDEE and designated as an APV. 1940: Returned to owners in January.

PAT CAHERTY	1918/21	1940/46	Displacement:	88TN
			Engines:	430HP
			Armament:	1 x 12-pdr
			Admty No:	3860
			Port Reg:	WWII: A 162
			P.No:	WWII: FY 335

1918: L. Built at Wivenhoe by Rennie Forrest and delivered on 8 October. 1919: Temporary Loan to the USN. 1922: Sold to mercantile and renamed *Kirby*. Acquired by Consolidated Fisheries of Grimsby. PR: GY 280. Acquired by Wilson Buchan of Torry, Aberdeen and renamed *Buchans II*. 1940: Requisitioned in July as BUCHANS II and converted to an APV. 1946: Returned to owner in August.

| PATRICK BORROW | 1918/19 | | Armament: | 1 x 12-pdr; 1 x 3.5-inch Bomb Thrower (A/S Howitzer) |
| | | | Admty No: | 3689 |

1918: L. Built at Montrose by Montrose SB and delivered on 3 July. Fitted with Listening Hydrophones. 1919: Sold to mercantile and renamed *River Don*. Acquired by Consolidated Fisheries of Grimsby. PR: GY 277.

PATRICK DEVINE	1919/21	1939/40	Displacement:	77TN
			Engines:	430HP
			Admty No:	WWII:4496.
			Port Reg:	WWII: SN 12

1919: Launched. Built at Wivenhoe by Rennie Forrest and completed as a fishing vessel. Delivered 11 December. 1921: Sold to mercantile and renamed *Yolanda*. Acquired by Consolidated Fisheries of Grimsby. PR: GY 1332. Acquired by The Shields Eng. & DD Co of N.Shields and renamed *Sedock*. 1939: Requisitioned in November as SEDOCK and designated as an APV. 1940: Returned to owners in February.

| PEKIN | 1919/19 | See under JOHN DUNKIN |

PERCY BRETT   1919/19   Admty No: 4434

1918: Ordered from Hall Russell. 1919: Cancelled.

PETER BARRINGTON   1919/20   Admty No: 4423

1919: L. 13 March. Built at Aberdeen by Hall Russell and completed as a fishing vessel. 1920: Sold to mercantile and renamed *Caliama II*.

PETER DOBBIN   1917/21 1940/46   Displacement: 78TN
                                    Engines: 75HP
                                    Armament: WWI: 1 x 12-pdr
                                                      WWII: 1 x 3-pdr
                                    Admty No: 3729
                                    Port Reg: WWII: A 75

1918: L. Built at Workington by Williamson. 1921: Sold to mercantile and renamed *Phillippe*. Acquired by John Craig AO of Aberdeen. 1940: Requisitioned in April as PHILLIPPE and converted to a D/L. Converted to an APV in September. 1946: Returned to owners.

RICHARD BENNETT   1917/21 1939/40   Displacement: 237TG
                                     Armament: 1 x 12-pdr; 1 x 7.5-
                                                      inch Bomb Thrower
                                                      (A/S Howitzer)
                                     Admty No: 3649

1917: L. 17 May. Built at Aberdeen by Hall Russell. 1921: Sold to mercantile and retained the same name. Acquired by Ivey STC of Milford Haven. PR: LO 439. 1939: Requisitioned in September and designated as a M/S for the SAN. 1940: Returned to owners in May.

RICHARD BOWDEN   1919/19   Admty No: 4426

1919: L. 17 May. Built at Aberdeen by Hall Russell and completed as a fishing vessel. Sold to French mercantile and renamed *Cissie Scatchard*. 1939: Served in WWII as French AD 233 AIGRETTE.

RICHARD BRISCOLL   1918/21 1944/44   Displacement: 78TN
                                      Engines: 75HP
                                      Admty No: 4418
                                      Port Reg: WWII: A 768

1918: L. 9 October. Built at Aberdeen by Hall Russell. Completed as a M/S and employed as a Training vessel. 1921: Sold to mercantile and renamed *Braconburn*. Acquired by The Don Fishing Co of Aberdeen. 1944: Purchased into the RN as BRACONBURN and designated as a Blockship. LOST. Sank on passage to Scapa Flow on 30 July.

RICHARD DORRODALE   1919/19   Admty No: 4492

1918: Ordered from Goole SB. 1919: Cancelled.

RICHARD HEAVER   1918/20   Armament: 1 x 12-pdr
                                      Admty No: 3771

1918: L. Built at Paisley by Fullerton and delivered on 7 October. 1920: Sold to mercantile and renamed *Forthvale*. Acquired by Forth STC of Edinburgh. PR: GN 52.

ROBERT FAIRCLOTH   1918/19 1939/44 (RNZN)

1918: L. Built at Chester by Abdela Mitchell. 1919: Sold to mercantile and renamed *Humphrey*. Acquired by F & T.Ross of Hull. PR: H 160. 1939: Requisitioned in September as HUMPHREY and converted to a M/S. Commissioned into the RNZN. 1944: Returned to owners in August.

ROBERT GIBSON   1918/21

1918: L. 12 February. Built at Glasgow by Scott & Sons. 1921: Sold to mercantile and retained the same name. Acquired by CE.Curzon of Milford Haven. PR: LO 441.

ROBERT HARDING   1918/21 1939/45

Displacement:	82TN
Engines:	57HP
Port Reg:	WWII: A 205
P.No:	WWII: FY 1855

1918: L. Built at Leith by Hawthorns. 1921: Sold to mercantile and renamed *Henriette*. Acquired by J.Mackie AO of Aberdeen. 1939: Requisitioned in December as HENRI-ETTE and converted to an APV. 1940: Converted to a M/S in July and renamed ARTE-GAL. 1945: Returned in March.

SAMUEL BAKER   1917/21 1939/46

Displacement:	237TG 163TN
Engines:	79HP
Armament:	1 x 12-pdr
Admty No:	3650
Port Reg:	WWII: A 767
P.No:	WWII: FY 686

1917: L. 7 June. Built at Aberdeen by Hall Russell and completed as a M/S. 1921: Sold to mercantile and renamed *Braconmoor*. Acquired by Don SFC of Aberdeen. 1939: Requisitioned in August as BRACONMOOR and converted to a M/S. Joined the 31st M/S Grp based at Grimsby. 1946: Returned to owners in August.

SAMUEL BARKAS   1917/20

Displacement:	93TN
Engines:	57HP
Armament:	1 x 12-pdr
Admty No:	3628

1917: L. 13 September. Built at Aberdeen by Hall Russell. 1920: Sold to mercantile and retained the same name. 1926: Renamed *Inverneill*. 1938: Owned by Dryburgh of Leith. PR: GN 69.

SAMUEL BENBOW   1918/21 1940/46

Armament:	1 x 12-pdr; 1 x 6-pdr AA
Admty No:	3645
P.No:	WWII: FY 95

1918: L. 9 July. Built at Aberdeen by Hall Russell. 1921: Sold to mercantile and retained the same name. Acquired by T. Davidson of Aberdeen. PR: A 749. 1940: Purchased into the RAN and converted to a M/S. Commissioned into the RAN on 5 September. 1946: Sold to mercantile on 24 May.

SAMUEL CUNNINGHAM   1919/19

Admty No:	4444

1918: Ordered from Hall Russell. 1919: Cancelled.

SAMUEL GASBY	1920/21 1940/45	Displacement:	75TN
		Engines:	75HP
		Admty No:	3768
		Port Reg:	WWII: A 357

1920: L. Built at Whitechurch, Glasgow by Ritchie Graham. Completed as a fishing vessel. 1921: Sold to mercantile and renamed *Soubrette*. Acquired by G. Cormack AO of Aberdeen. 1940: Requisitioned in August as SOUBRETTE and converted for the Examination Service. 1945: Returned to owners in April.

| SAMUEL HAMPTON | 1919/19 | Admty No: | 3775 |

1919: L. Built at Hook by Ouse SB and completed as a fishing vessel. Sold to mercantile and renamed *Bostonian*. 1920: Mercantile Loss. Posted missing on 10 November.

| SAMUEL LOVITT | 1919/19 | Admty No: | 4224 |

1918: Ordered from John Lewis. 1919: Cancelled.

STEPHEN KENNEY	1919/19 1939/44	Displacement:	93TN
		Engines:	90HP
		Armament:	WWII:
		Admty No:	3852
		Port Reg:	WWII: GY 283
		P.No:	WWII: FY 770

1919: L. Built at Queensferry, Chester, by Abdela Mitchell. Completed as a fishing vessel and delivered on 3 April. Sold to mercantile and renamed *Witham*. Acquired by Consolidated Fisheries of Grimsby. 1939: Requisitioned in November as WITHAM and converted to a M/S. 1944: Converted to an Esso in April. Returned to owners in November.

| TEVIOT | See under GEORGE IRELAND. |

THOMAS ANSELL	1917/21	Displacement:	83TN
		Engines:	57HP
		Armament:	1 x 12pdr
		Admty No:	3616

1917: L. 21 May. Built at Aberdeen by Duthie. 1921: Sold to mercantile and retained the same name. Acquired by O.Johnson of Neyland, Pembrokeshire. Port Reg: LO.472.

| THOMAS BARCLAY | 1918/21 | Admty No: | 4417 |

1918: Launched 9 October. Built at Aberdeen by Hall Russell. 1922: Sold to mercantile, acquired by G.D. Taylor AO of Aberdeen and renamed *John Morrice*. Port Reg: A.786.

| THOMAS BILLINGCOLE | 1919/19 | Admty No: | 4428. |

1919: Launched 2 May. Built at Aberdeen by Hall Russell and completed as a fishing vessel. Sold to mercantile, acquired by Robinson & Son of Grimsby and renamed *Saltaire*. Port Reg: GY.558.

| THOMAS BIRD | 1917/19 | Armament: | 1 x 12-pdr |
| | | Admty No: | 3623 |

1917: Launched 24 June. Built at Aberdeen by Hall Russell. 1919: Sold to mercantile, acquired by G. G. Paton of Glasgow and renamed *River Tweed*. Port Reg: GN.43.

THOMAS BRAUND   1919/19   Admty No: 4438.

1918: Order placed with Hall Russell of Aberdeen. 1919: Cancelled.

THOMAS BRYAN   1917/21   Armament: 1 x 12-pdr
                                       Admty No: 3625.

1917: Launched 16 August. Built at Aberdeen by Hall Russell. Fitted with Listening Hydrophones. 1921: Sold to mercantile, acquired by Brand & Curzon of Milford Haven and retained the same name.

THOMAS BUCKLEY   1917/22 1940/46 Displacement: 249TG 109TN
                                         Engines: 480HP = 10.5 Kts
                                         Armament: 1 x 12-pdr
                                         Admty No: 3607
                                         Port Reg: WWII: GY 170
                                         P.No: WWII: FY 1853

1917: Ordered by Kingston SFC of Hull and purchased into the RN whilst on the stocks. Launched 7 July. Built at Beverley by CWG and completed in December as a M/S. 1919:Temporary loan to the USN in May for M/S operations in the N. Sea. Returned to the RN in October. 1922: Sold to mercantile, acquired by the original owners and renamed *Ceylonite*. Port Reg: H 724. 1930: Acquired by Taylor SFC of Grimsby. Port Reg: GY 170. 1939: Acquired by St. Andrews SFC of Grimsby. 1940: Requisitioned in April as CEYLONITE and converted to a M/S. 1946: Returned to owners in January. 1947: Acquired by J. Croan of Newhaven. Port Reg: LH 246. 1960: BU at Charlestown.

THOMAS BURNHAM   1918/21   Armament: 1 x 12-pdr
                                         Admty No: 4415

1918: L. 9 September. Built at Aberdeen by Hall Russell. 1921: Sold to mercantile, acquired by A.G. Brown of Granton and renamed *Floribelle*. Port Reg: GN 80.

THOMAS CALTRAFFE   1919/19   Admty No: 4477

1918: Order placed with Hawthorne of Leith. 1919: Cancelled.

THOMAS CLAYTON   1919/19   Admty No: 4478

1918: Order placed with Hawthorn of Leith. 1919: Cancelled.

THOMAS COLLARD   1917/19   Armament: 1 x 12pdr,
                                                            1 x 7.7-inch Bomb
                                                            Thrower (A/S
                                                            Howitzer).
                                         Admty No: 3686

1917: L. 11 July. Built at Paisley by Fleming & Ferguson. 1918: LOST. Sunk by German S/M off N. Rathlin Island on 1st March.

THOMAS COPSEY   1919/19   Admty No: 4441

1918: Order placed with Hall Russell of Aberdeen. 1919: Cancelled.

THOMAS CURR   1919/19   Admty No: 4439

1918: Order placed with Hall Russell of Aberdeen. 1919: Cancelled.

THOMAS CURRELL   1919/19 1939/45 Admty No: 4481

1919: Launched. Built at Workington by Williamson. Completed as a fishing vessel and delivered 8 May. Sold to mercantile, acquired by G. Sandford of Aukland, New Zealand and retained the same name. 1939: Requisitioned for the RNZN and converted to a M/S. Commissioned into the RNZN 16 October. 1945: Returned to owners in November.

THOMAS DEAR   1918/21   Armament: 1 x 12-pdr.
                                          Admty No: 3730

1918: L. 3 May. Built at Workington by Williamson. 1921: Sold to mercantile and retained the same name. Acquired by Consolidated Fisheries of Grimsby and renamed *Ninette*. Port Reg: GY 1337.

THOMAS DENNISON   1919/20 1940/45 Admty No: 3728
                                          Port Reg: WWII: GY 608
                                          P.No: WWII: FY 889

1919: L. 27 October. Built at Paisley by Fleming & Ferguson and completed as a fishing vessel. 1920: Sold to mercantile, acquired by the Tower SFC of Grimsby and renamed *The Tower*. 1939: Requisitioned in November as THE TOWER and converted to an APV. 1940: Converted to a BDV in June. 1945: Returned to owners in February.

THOMAS EVISON   1918/21 1944/44 Armament: 1 x 12-pdr
                                        Admty No: 3743
                                        Port Reg: WWII: A 826

1918: Launched. Built at Paisley by Fullerton and delivered 12 April. Fitted with Listening Hydrophones. 1922: Sold to mercantile, acquired by Harrow Robertson SFC of Aberdeen and renamed *Jeannie M. Robertson*. Port Reg: A 826. Acquired by the North Star SFC of Aberdeen and renamed *Avondee*. Same Port Reg. 1944: Requisitioned in March as AVONDEE and converted to an Esso. Returned to owners in October.

THOMAS FOLEY   1918/20 1940/45 Armament: WWI: 1 x 12-pdr, 1 x
                                                          3.5-inch Bomb
                                                          Thrower (A/S
                                                          Howitzer).
                                        Admty No: 3751
                                        Port Reg: WWII: GY 270.

1918: Launched. Built at Glasgow by Ritchie Graham and delivered 3 August. 1920: Sold to mercantile, acquired by Consolidated Fisheries of Grimsby and renamed *River Tummell*. 1940: Requisitioned as BELTON and converted for the Examination Service. Based at Grimsby. 1945: Employed on Navigating exercises at Grimsby and then returned to owners.

THOMAS GOODCHILD   1919/21 1939/40 Admty No: 3767
                                            Port Reg: WWII: GY 1290.

1919: Launched. Built at Glasgow by Richie Graham and completed as a fishing vessel. Delivered 31 October. 1921: Sold to mercantile, acquired by Trawlers (White Sea & Grimsby) and renamed *Chandos*. 1939: Requisitioned in November as CHANDOS and designated as an APV. 1940: Returned to owners in January.

THOMAS GRAHAM   1918/21 1939/44 Armament: 1 x 12-pdr
                                        Admty No: 3764
                                        Port Reg: WWII: A 221.

1918: L. 6 June. Built at Bowling by Scott. 1919: Temporary Loan to the USN in May for

M/S operations in the N.Sea. Returned to the RN in August. 1921: Sold to mercantile and retained the same name. Acquired by Baxter SFC of Aberdeen and renamed *Sunlight.* 1939: Requisitioned in November as SUNLIGHT and converted to an APV. 1940: Converted to a M/S in May. 1944: Converted to a WDV in April and based at Grimsby. Returned to owners in July.

THOMAS HAGGERTY	1918/26 1940/44 Admty No:	3756.

1918: Launched. Built at Hook by the Ouse SB Co and completed as a M/S. 1920: Renamed ITCHEN. 1926: Sold to mercantile and renamed *River Endrick.* Acquired by G.R. Purdy of North Shields and renamed *Mary A. Purdy.* 1940: Requisitioned in February as MARY A. PURDY and converted to a BDV. 1944: Returned to owners in October.

THOMAS HENRIX   1918/21 1939/40 1944/44

	Armament:	WWI: 1 x 12-pdr
	Admty No:	3821
	Port Reg:	WWII: A 160.
	P.No:	WWII: 4 435.

1918: Launched. Built at Leith by Hawthorne and delivered 13 August. 1919: Temporary loan to the USN for M/S operations in the N.Sea. Returned to the RN in August. 1921: Sold to mercantile, acquired by A. Robertson of Aberdeen and renamed *Crevette.* 1939: Requisitioned as CREVETTE and converted to an APV. 1940: Returned to owners. 1944: Requisitioned in May as CREVETTE and converted to an Esso. Returned to owners in October.

THOMAS LAVERICKS	1919/19	Admty No:	4228

1918: Order placed with John Lewis of Aberdeen. 1919: Cancelled.

TIMOTHY BRANNON	1918/19	Armament:	1 x 12-pdrAA,
			1 x 3.5-inch Bomb
			Thrower (A/S
			Howitzer)
		Admty No:	3641

1918: L. 30 April. Built at Aberdeen by Hall Russell. 1919: Sold to mercantile and renamed *Keyes.* Acquired by LC.Cockrell of Wyvenhoe. PR: H 66.

WILLIAM ASHTON	1917/22	Armament:	1 x 12-pdr
		Admty No:	3620

1917: L. 1 November. Built at Aberdeen by Duthie. 1919: Temporary Loan to the USN and renamed CITY OF PERTH. Returned to the RN. 1922: Sold to mercantile and reverted to *William Ashton.*

WILLIAM BARLOW	1917/20 1940/46	Displacement:	91TN
		Engines:	57HP
		Armament:	WWI: 1 x 12-pdr;
			1 x 7.5-inch Bomb
			Thrower (A/S
			Howitzer).
			WWII: 1 x 12-pdr
		Admty No:	3646
		Port Reg:	WWII: A 412
		P.No:	WWII: Z 148

1917: L. 25 April. Built at Aberdeen by Hall Russell. Fitted with Listening Hydrophones.

1920: Sold to mercantile and renamed *Ben Ardna*. Acquired by Irvine of N.Shields and renamed *Dorileen*. 1940: Purchased into the RN in January as DORILEEN and converted to a BDV. 1946: Sold to mercantile in May.

WILLIAM BARNETT	1917/19	Armament:	1 x 12-pdr
		Admty No:	3632

1917: L 8 December. Built at Aberdeen by Hall Russell. 1919: Sold to mercantile and renamed *Valerie W*. 1939: Served in WWII as French AD 355 ROCHE NOIRE.

WILLIAM BARROW	1918/21 1941/45	Armament:	WWI: 1 x 12-pdr; 1 x 7.5-inch Bomb Thrower (A/S Howitzer). WWII: 1 x 12-pdr
		Admty No:	3640
		P.No:	WWII: FY 1828

1918: L 30 April. Built at Aberdeen by Hall Russell. 1921: Sold to mercantile and renamed *Claribelle*. 1941: Requisitioned as CLARIBELLE and converted to a M/S. 1945: Returned to owners.

WILLIAM BEAUMONT	1918/20	Displacement:	87TN
		Engines:	57HP
		Armament:	1 x 12-pdr
		Admty No:	3644

1918: L 9 July. Built at Aberdeen by Hall Russell. 1920: Sold to mercantile and retained the same name. 1928: Acquired by Walker STF Co of Aberdeen and renamed *Star of Scotland*. PR: A.347.

WILLIAM BENTLEY	1919/19 1939/45	Displacement:	88TN
		Engines:	74HP
		Admty No:	4422
		Port Reg:	WWII: A 138

1919: L 30 January. Built at Aberdeen by Hall Russell and completed as a fishing vessel Sold to mercantile and renamed *Braconhill*. Acquired by Bracken STC of Aberdeen. 1939: Requisitioned in November as BRACONHILL and converted for Examination Service. 1945: Returned to owners in July.

WILLIAM BIGGS	1917/21 1939/45	Displacement:	80TN
		Engines:	74HP
		Armament:	1 x 12-pdr
		Admty No:	3632
		Port Reg:	WWII: GY 248
		P.No:	WWII: FY 885

1917: L 11 August. Built at Aberdeen by Hall Russell and completed as a M/S. 1921: Sold to mercantile and retained the same name. Acquired by the Queen SF Co of Grimsby and renamed *Kingscourt*. 1939: Requisitioned in November as KINGSCOURT and converted to an APV. 1940: Converted to a M/S in April. 1944: Converted to a BBV. 1945: Returned to owners in September

WILLIAM BOND	1918/19 1940/45	Displacement:	81TN
		Engines:	57HP
		Armament:	1 x 12-pdr
		Admty No:	3634
		Port Reg:	WWII: A 939

1918: L 10 January. Built at Aberdeen by Hall Russell. 1919: Sold to mercantile and renamed *River Esk*. Acquired by John Craig AO of Aberdeen. 1940: Requisitioned in June as RIVER ESK and converted to an APV. 1945: Returned to owners in July

WILLIAM BORHAM	1918/19	Admty No:	4437

1918: Ordered from Hall Russell. 1919: Cancelled.

WILLIAM BROWNING	1917/19 1940/46	Displacement:	102TN
		Engines:	57HP
		Armament:	1 x 12-pdr
		Admty No:	3648
		Port Reg:	WWII: GN 101
		P.No:	WWII: FY 784

1917: L. 17 May. Built at Beverley by CWG. Fitted with Listening Hydrophones. 1919: Sold to mercantile and renamed *Madden*. Acquired by T.L & R.D. Devlin of Granton. 1940: Requisitioned in February as MADDEN and converted to a M/S. 1944: Converted to a WDV. 1946: Returned to owners in April

WILLIAM BUTLER	1917/20	Armament:	1 x 12-pdr
		Admty No:	3629

1917: L. 18 October. Built at Aberdeen by Hall Russell. 1921: Sold to mercantile and retained the same name.

WILLIAM CASTLE	1917/21	Armament:	1 x 12-pdr
		Admty No:	3656

1917: L. 18 October. Built at Aberdeen by Hall Russell. 1921: Sold to mercantile and retained the same name.

WILLIAM CHALMERS	1919/19	Displacement:	88TN
		Engines:	75HP
		Admty No:	4472

1919: L. 30 August. Built at Leith by Hawthorn and completed as a fishing vessel. Sold to mercantile and renamed *Cradock*. 1938: Owned by Shields Eng. & DD Co of North Shields. PR: SN 8.

WILLIAM COGSWELL	1918/21	Armament:	1 x 12-pdr
		Admty No:	3659

1918: L. 10 January. Built at Aberdeen by Hall. Fitted with Listening Hydrophones. 1921: Sold to mercantile and renamed *Struan*.

WILLIAM FALL	1918/20	Displacement:	79TN
		Engines:	57HP
		Armament:	1 x 12-pdr
		Admty No:	3749

1918: L. Built at Wivenhoe by Rennie Forrestt and delivered on 29 May. Fitted with Listening Hydrophones. 1920: Sold to mercantile and renamed *Avondale*. Acquired by J.W.Tomlinson of N.Shields. PR: H 166.

WILLIAM FERRINS	1918/21	Armament:	1 x 12-pdr
		Admty No:	3755

1918: L. Built at Aberdeen by Duthie and delivered on 3 May. 1921: Sold to mercantile and retained the same name.

| WILLIAM GIBBONS | 1918/21 | Armament: | 1 x 12-pdr |
| | | Admty No: | 3770 |

1918: L. Built by Fullerton and delivered on 14 August. 1921: Sold to mercantile and renamed *Nordzeel*.

WILLIAM GILLETT (as ADASTRAL)   **(PRNM)**

| WILLIAM GILLETT | 1919/21 | Admty No: | 3766 |

1919: L. Built at Glasgow by Ritchie Graham and completed as a fishing vessel. Delivered on 5 November. 1925: Sold to mercantile and renamed *Adastral*. Notes: Reported in some lists as requisitioned in WWII as ADASTRAL. NFI.

WILLIAM GRIFFIN	1918/21	Displacement:	78TN
		Engines:	430HP
		Armament:	1 x 12-pdr
		Admty No:	3765

1918: L. Built at Bowling by Scott and delivered on 27 November. 1921: Sold to mercantile and retained the same name. 1928: Acquired by A.B.Lee of North Shields and renamed *Tynemouth Castle*.

WILLIAM HALLETT	1918/21 1939/39	Displacement:	78TN
		Engines:	430HP
		Admty No:	3776
		Port Reg:	WWII: LO 353
		P.No:	WWII: FY 534

1918: Built at Wivenhoe by Rennie Forrest. 1919: Delivered on 7 January. 1921: Sold to mercantile and retained the same name. Acquired by T.B.Bilton & Sons of North Shields. 1939: Requisitioned in November and converted to an APV. LOST. Mined off the Tyne on 13 December.

WILLIAM HANBURY   1918/21 1939/40

Displacement:	82TN
Engines:	57HP
Armament:	1 x 12-pdr
Admty No:	3824
Port Reg:	WWII: GY 1322

1918: L. Built at Leith by Hawthorn and delivered on 30 October. 1921: Sold to mercantile and retained the same name. Acquired by Taylor SF Co of Grimsby. 1939: Requisitioned in November and designated as an APV. 1940: Returned to owners in January.

WILLIAM HARRISON   1919/21

Displacment:	76TN
Engines:	430HP
Admty No:	4704

1919: L. Built at Wivenhoe by Rennie Forrest and completed as a fishing vessel. Delivered on 27 August. 1921: Sold to mercantile and renamed *Flavia*. Acquired by John Craig AO of Aberdeen.

WILLIAM HARVEY   1919/20 1939/46

Displacement:	88TN
Engines:	57HP
Admty No:	3816
Port Reg:	WWII: SN 120

1919: L. 10 November. Built at Paisley by Fleming & Ferguson and completed as a fishing vessel. 1920: Sold to mercantile and renamed *River Orchy*. Acquired by R.Hastie & Sons of N.Shields and renamed *Flixton*. 1939: Requisitioned in August as FLIXTON and converted for the Examination Service. 1946: Returned to owners in July.

WILLIAM HUTCHINSON   1918/22 1940/45

Armament:	1 x 12-pdr
Admty No:	3818
Port Reg:	WWII: French
P.No:	WWII: FY 1718

1918: L. Built at Leith by Hawthorn and completed as a M/S. Delivered on 4 April. Fitted with Listening Hydrophones. 1922: Sold to French mercantile and renamed *Roche Velan*. 1940: French M/S ROCHE VELAN seized in Operation Grab on 3 July. Commissioned into the RN in November as ROCHE VELAN. 1945: Returned to France in December.

WILLIAM IVEY   1918/21

Displacement:	81TN
Engines:	57HP
Armament:	1 x 12-pdr
Admty No:	3849

1918: L. Built at Wivenhoe by Rennie Forrest. 1921: Sold to mercantile and retained the same name. Acquired by T.B. Bilton & Sons of N. Shields.

WILLIAM KING   1918/21

Displacement:	78TN
Engines:	75HP
Armament:	1 x 12-pdr
Admty No:	3851

1918: L. Built at Workington by Williamson and delivered on 18 December. 1921: Sold to mercantile and retained the same name.

TREE CLASS

It is easy to confuse this Class with the Tree Group which comprised 20 trawlers purchased from the mercantile, 10 in 1935 and 10 in 1939. They, too, were named after trees and served throughout WWII as M/Ss

The Tree Class, also of 20 vessels, were Admiralty built trawlers, launched at various yards in 1939/40. To help the confusion along, they too were completed as M/Ss and served throughout WWII. In some lists, to avoid confusion, the previously purchased Group are referred to as the "Berberis Class"

Of the 20 vessels in this Class six, ALMOND, ASH, CHESTNUT, HICKORY, JUNIPER and PINE were lost. The 14 survivors were all sold to mercantile post-war.

Displacement:	530 tons
Measurements:	164ft oa 150ft pp x 27ft 6in x 10ft 6in
Engines:	1 shaft Reciprocating (VTE) 850 IHP = 11.5 kts
Armament:	1 x 12-pdr 2 x 0.5-inch AA (2 x single) 4 x LG (2 x twin)
Complement:	35

Vessels in the Class:

ACACIA, ALMOND, ASH, BAY, BIRCH, BLACKTHORN, CHESTNUT, DEODAR, ELM, FIR, HAZEL, HICKORY, JUNIPER, MANGROVE, OLIVE, PINE, ROWAN, WALNUT, WHITETHORN, WISTERIA

BIRCH   **(PRNM)**

ACACIA   1940/47   P.No: T 02

1940: L. 7 March. Built by the Ardrossan DY Co. and engined by Plenty. Completed as a M/S. 1944: TPI Operation Neptune, the Normandy Landings, as a unit of the 15th M/S Flot. off Sword Beach. 1947: Sold to the mercantile. Retained the same name. 1949: Renamed *Brandy*. 1953: Mercantile loss on 15 June.

ALMOND   1940/41

1940: L. 22 May. Built by the Ardrossan DY Co. and engined by Plenty. Completed as a M/S. 1941: LOST. Mined off Falmouth on 2 February.

ASH   1939/41   P.No: T 39

1939: L.13 December. Built at Selby by Cochrane and engined by Amos & Smith. Completed as a M/S. 1941: LOST. Mined in the Thames Estuary on 5 June.

BAY   1939/47   P.No: T 77

1939: L. 12 December. Built at Selby by Cochrane and engined by Amos & Smith. Completed as a M/S. 1947: Sold to mercantile and retained the same name. 1952: Renamed *Tristania*.

BIRCH   1939/47   Displacement: 452TG   144TN
                                   Engines: 850HP = 12 kts
                                   P.No: T 93

1939: L. 11 November. Built at Beverley by CWG and engined by Holmes. Completed as a M/S. Operated in the English Channel throughout the war 1944: TPI Operation Neptune, the Normandy Landings, in June as an Escort. 1947: Placed on the Disposal List. Acquired by Vospers of Portsmouth. 1952: Sold to mercantile and retained the same name. 1955: Renamed *Magnolia*. Transferred to Hull and managed by St.Andrews SFC of Hull. 1962: Acquired by Dutch mercantile and renamed *Frank*. 1964: BU.

BAY   **(PRNM)**

BLACKTHORN	1939/47	Displacement:	452TG 144TN
		Engines:	850HP = 12 kts
		P.No:	T 100

1939: L. 29 November. Built at Beverley by CWG and engined by Holmes. Completed as a M/S. 1947: Sold to mercantile and renamed *Maythorn*. Acquired by Vospers of Portsmouth, converted to a motor Trawler and based at Milford Haven. 1955: Acquired by Norwegian mercantile and renamed *Klan*. 1963: Renamed *Jan Ove*. 1971: BU.

CHESTNUT	1940/40

1940: L. 24 February. Built at Goole by Goole SB and engined by Amos & Smith. Completed as a M/S. LOST. Mined off the North Foreland on 30 November.

DEODAR	1940/47	P.No:	T 124

1940: L. 26 March. Built at Goole by Goole SB and engined by Amos & Smith. Completed as a M/S. Joined the Portland Flot. for sweeping in the Channel. 1947: Sold to mercantile and renamed *Mollex VI*. 1955: Renamed *Werner Felter*.

ELM	1939/46	P.No:	T 105

1939: L. 12 December. Built at Glasgow by A & J Inglis and engined by Aithchison Blair. 1946: Sold to mercantile and renamed *Helm*. 1950: Renamed *Magul*.

FIR	1940/47	P.No:	T 129

1940: L. 27 January. Built at Glasgow by Inglis and engined by Aitcheson Blair. 1947: Sold to mercantile and renamed *Vollen*.

HAZEL	1939/46	P.No:	T 108

1939: L. 27 December. Built at Leith by Robb and engined by Whites. Completed as a M/S. 1946: Sold to mercantile in March.

HICKORY	1940/40	P.No:	T 116

1940: L. 24 February. Built at Leith by Robb and engined by White. Completed as a M/S. LOST. Mined in the Channel on 22 October.

JUNIPER	1939/40	P.No:	T 123

1939: L. 15 December. Built at Port Glasgow by Ferguson Bros. 1940: Completed as A/S and commissioned in March. Joined the 19th A/S Strike Force based in the Orkneys. TPI the Norwegian Campaign in April-May. LOST. Escorting a tanker from Tromso on 8 June when she sighted a German Squadron comprising SCHARNHORST, GNEISENAU, ADMIRAL HIPPER and 4 Destroyers. There was no escape, but in an attempt to delay the enemy, she hoisted her Battle Ensign and sailed to meet the capital ships. She lasted an incredible 90 minutes before she sank leaving only 4 survivors.

MANGROVE	1940/46	P.No:	T 112

1940: L. 15 February. Built at Port Glasgow by Ferguson and completed as a M/S. 1943: Temporary Loan to the Portuguese Navy from 8 October and renamed P 2 for the duration of the Loan. 1945: Returned to the RN on 27 June. 1946: Sold to the Portuguese Navy on 11 February and renamed FAIAL.

OLIVE   1940/48   P.No: T 126

1940: L. 26 February. Built at Aberdeen by Hall Russell and completed as a M/S. 1946: TIH for refitting at Harwich. Transferred to Cuxhaven in March. Transferred to Flekkefjiord, Norway, supervising German Naval units which were employed in clearing minefields. Returned to Cuxhaven in August and Paid Off there. Temporary Loan to the German Navy. 1948: Returned to the RN and placed on the Disposal List. Sold to mercantile and renamed *Samba*. 1956: Mercantile Loss. Took the ground near Lerwick on 28 December.

PINE   1940/44   P.No: T 101

1940: L. 25 March. Built at Aberdeen by Hall Russell and completed as a M/S. 1944: LOST. Unbuttoning a section of convoy off Selsey Bill on 3 January when they were set upon by three E-Boat Flotillas. Her bows were blown off by a torpedo but she remained afloat with the remainder of her armament working until help arrived. Whilst in tow to Portsmouth she rolled over and sank.

ROWAN   1939/46   P.No: T 119

1939: L. 12 August. Built at Southbank-on-Tees by Smith's Dock. Completed as a M/S. 1946: Sold to mercantile and renamed *Maiken*.

WALNUT   1939/48   P.No: T 103

1939: L. 12 August. Built at Middlesborough by Smith's Dock and completed as a M/S. 1946: Converted to a D/L. 1948: Sold to mercantile.

WHITETHORN   1939/46   P.No: T 127

1939: L. 10 November. Built at Southbank-on-Tees by Smith's Dock and completed as a M/S. 1946: Sold to mercantile in March.

WISTARIA   1939/46   P.No: T 113

1939: L. 10 November. Built at Southbank-on-Tees by Smith's Dock and completed as a M/S. Joined the 11th A/S Strike Group. 1940: TPI the Norwegian Campaign in April/May. 1946: Sold to mercantile in March.

SHIP GROUPS

GEM GROUP

Purchased from trade in November 1935, Batch 1 of this Group comprising 10 vessels, displacing 568 - 641 tons, was acquired to boost the under-strength A/S capability of the Fleet. Fitted with ASDIC they served in A/S Groups in UK waters throughout the Second World War. Batch 2, comprising only 5 vessels, was purchased in January 1939, and likewise converted to A/S. At the outbreak of war they were despatched to the Mediterranean and two, AMBER and MOONSTONE, went further afield in 1940 when they served in the East Indies. Of Batch 1 there were 5 war losses, AGATE, AMETHYST, JASPER, TOPAZE and TOURMALINE. Batch 2 lost CORAL and JADE.

Batch 1 comprised:

AGATE, AMETHYST, CORNELIAN, JASPER, PEARL, RUBY, SAPPHIRE, TOPAZE, TOURMALINE, and TURQUOISE.

Batch 2 comprised:

AMBER, BERYL, CORAL, JADE and MOONSTONE

AGATE   **(Steve Bush Collection)**

AGATE   1935/41   Ex-*Mavis Rose*
                                                 Displacement: 627T 162TN
                                                 Engines: 100 HP
                                                 Armament: 1 x 4-inch
                                                 Port Reg: FD 14
                                                 P No: T 87

1934: L. as *Mavis Rose*. Built at Southbank-on-Tees by Smith's Dock. Owned by Boston DSF & Ice Co of Fleetwood. 1935: Purchased from the mercantile in November and converted to an A/S. 1941: LOST. Wrecked near Cromer on 6th August.

AMETHYST	1935/40	Ex-*Phyllis Rosalie*	
		Displacement:	627T
		Armament:	1 x 4-inch
		P.No:	T 12

1928: L. 1935: Purchased in November and converted to an A/S Trawler. 1940: LOST. Mined in the Barrow Deep on 24 November. She took 10 minutes to sink which allowed all her Company to escape safely. Notes: When the survivors were safely landed at Southend Pier they were arrested by local police as suspected enemy survivors.

CORNELIAN	1935/45	Ex-*Cape Warwick*	
		Displacement:	568TG 168TN
		Engines:	101HP
		Armament:	1 x 4-inch
		Port Reg:	H 503
		P.No:	T 15

1933: L. Built at Selby by Cochrane. Owned by the Hudson SFC of Hull. 1935: Purchased into the RN in November and converted to an A/S. Fitted with ASDIC. 1939: HF A/S Groups throughout WWII. 1944: TPI Operation Neptune, the D-Day Landings in June, as an A/S Escort. 1945: Sold to mercantile and renamed *Lincoln City*.

JASPER	1935/42	Ex-*Balthasar*	
		Displacement:	581T 381TG 151TN
		Engines:	102HP = 11.2 kts
		Armament:	1 x 4-inch
		Port Reg:	H 405
		P.No:	T 14

1932: L. Built at Beverley by CWG. Owned by Hull Northern FCL of Hull. 1935: Purchased into the RN in November and converted to A/S. 1939: Deployed in home waters. Joined the 2nd A/S Grp based at Plymouth. 1942: LOST. Torpedoed by E-Boat S 81 in the Channel on 1 December.

AMETHYST plainly showing the signs of wear and tear.　　　　　(Steve Bush Collection)

199

PEARL at full speed of 11 knots with the coal-burners plume of black smoke.   (MPL)

PEARL	1935/46	Ex-*Dervish*	
		Displacement:	649T 160TN
		Measurements:	154ft x 25ft x 12ft
		Engines:	111NHP = 11.5K
		Complement:	44 (4 + 40)
		Armament:	1 x 4-inch 2 x
			20mm AA DCs
		Port Reg:	H 8
		P.No:	T 22

1934: L. Built at Beverley by CWG. Owned by Hellyer Bros of Hull. 1935: Purchased into the RN in November having completed only 3 Arctic trips for her original owners. Converted to A/S and renamed. 1936: Employed on Weapon Trials at Gibraltar. Joined the 2nd A/S Flotilla MF at Malta as a result of the Abyssinian Crisis. Returned to the UK in October. Paid Off and reduced to the Reserve. Laid Up at Rosyth. 1939: Brought Forward. Commissioned in June and attached to HMS DEFIANCE at Devonport. Employed in A/S Groups in Home Waters throughout WWII based on Portsmouth - S.Wales convoys interspersed with A/S Loop patrols off Plymouth. 1942: Rescued 43 survivors from HMS PENYLAN off Start Point. 1943: Attached to the French DS PARIS at Devonport for the remainder of the War. 1944: TPI Operation Neptune, the D-Day Landings in June as an A/S escort attached to the US Forces escorting US assault craft from Salcombe to the Utah Beach-Head and then supply convoys from Falmouth to US bases in Brittany. Rescued 59 survivors from *SS Dumfries* off the IOW on 23 December. 1945: Attached to HMS COLOMBO. Escorting a convoy to Granvill, France, on 9 March ICW an American escort vessel. Subjected to an air attack from German a/c from the Channel Islands in which the American vessel was sunk.1946: Paid Off at Pembroke Dock on 15 February. Sold to mercantile in April. Acquired by Joseph Marr of Hull and renamed *Westella*. 1959: BU in Belgium.

RUBY	1935/46	Ex-*Cape Bathurst*	
		Displacement:	568T 420TG
		Armament:	1 x 4-inch
		Port Reg:	H
		P.No:	T 24

SAPPHIRE   **(Steve Bush Collection)**

1933: L. Built at Selby by Cochrane. Owned by Hudson SFC of Hull 1935: Purchased into the RN in November and converted to A/S. 1942: Picked up the sole survivor of the Trawler MANOR in the Channel whilst escorting Convoy WP.183 on 9 February. 1944: TPI Operation Neptune, the D-Day Landings in June, as an A/S escort. 1946: Sold to mercantile in April and renamed *Caretta*.

SAPPHIRE	1935/46	Ex-*Mildenhall*	
		Displacement:	608T 421TG 169TN
		Engines:	99HP
		Armament:	1 x 4-inch
		Port Reg:	GY 124
		P.No:	T 27

1935: L. Built at Southbank-on-Tees by Smith's Dock. Owned by Croft Baker of Grimsby Purchased into the RN in November and converted to A/S. 1946: Sold to mercantile and renamed *Dunsby*. Acquired by Boston DSF Co of Fleetwood. PR: H 306. 1953: Renamed *Findus I*. 1954: Renamed *Skaida*.

TOPAZE		Ex-*Melbourne*	
		Displacement:	608T 421TG 169TN
		Engines:	99HP
		Armament:	1 x 4-inch
		Port Reg:	GY 125
		P.No:	T 40

1935: Launched. Built at Southbank-on-Tees by Smith's Dock. Owned by Croft Baker of Grimsby. Purchased into the RN in November and converted to A/S. 1940: Based at Portland. TPI Operation Dynamo, the evacuation of Dunkirk in May/June. 1941: LOST. Sunk in a collision with HMS RODNEY in the Clyde 20 April.

TOURMALINE	1935/41	Ex-*Berkshire*	
		Displacement:	641T 430TG 168TN
		Engines:	99HP
		Armament:	1 x 4-inch

| | Port Reg: | GY 151 |
| | P.No: | T 42 |

1935: Launched. Built at Southbank-on-Tees by Smith's Dock. Owned by Berkshire FC of Grimsby (H. Markham). Purchased into the RN in November after only 8 months in the fishing trade. Converted to A/S. 1940: TIH for refitting in January. Completed refitting and employed on convoy escorts. Escorting a convoy in the Channel when she engaged two E-Boats, sinking one and badly damaging the other. 1941: LOST. Sunk by enemy a/c off the N. Foreland 5 February with the loss of three lives.

TURQUOISE		Ex-*Warwickshire*.
	Displacement:	640T 430TG 160TN
	Engines:	99HP = 7K
	Armament:	1 x 4-inch, 3 x single 20mmAA.
	Port Reg:	GY 133
	P.No:	T 45

1935: Launched. Built at Southbank-on-Tees by Smith's Dock. Owned by Warwickshire SF (H. Markham) of Grimsby. Purchased into the RN in November, renamed and converted to A/S. 1939: Based at Harwich for N.Sea convoy escorts. 1942: Engaged and sank an E-Boat off the E. Coast. 1946: Sold to mercantile and renamed *St.Oswald*. Acquired by St.Andrews SF of Hull. PR: H 335. 1950: Renamed *Woolton*. 1954: Renamed *Wyre Woolton*.

AMBER	1939/46	Ex-*Cape Barfleur*
	Displacement:	700T 457TG 185TN
	Engines:	122HP
	Armament:	1 x 4-inch
	Port Reg:	H 105
	P.No:	T 88

1934: L. Built at Selby by Cochrane. Owned by Hudon SFC of Hull. 1939: Purchased into the RN in January and converted to A/S. 1946: Sold to mercantile and renamed *Etonian*. Acquired by Eton FC of Hull. PR: H 333. 1950: Renamed *Arctic Crusader*. Acquired by the Boyd Line of Hull. Same PR. 1952: Reverted to *Etonian*. Reacquired by the Eton FC of Hull. PR: H 333. 1955: Renamed *Glenella*. Acquired by Marr of Fleetwood.

TOURMALINE   **(MPL)**

BERYL - The "Flagship of Malta" (see notes below). (MPL)

BERYL	1939/46	Ex-*Lady Adelaide*	
		Displacement:	615T 394TG 150TN
		Engines:	102HP = 11.5 kts
		Measurements:	160ft x 26ft 6in
		Armament:	1 x 4-inch
		Port Reg:	H 4
		P.No:	T 34

1934: L. Built at Beverley by CWG. Owned by the Jutland Amalgamated Trawlers of Hull. 1939: Purchased into the RN in January, renamed and converted to an A/S. 1940: Joined the 4th A/S Group. Transferred to the Med. 1941: Based at Malta during the seige. 1942: Nicknamed "The Flagship of Malta" as, for quite some time she was the only warship afloat during the seige, her sister ships having been sunk. One of her many roles was as marker-ship for the blockade-running fast M/Ls in their runs to Malta. TPI bringing the *Ohio* into Grand Harbour. The only warship to serve at Malta throughout the seige. 1943: TPI Operation Husky, the Sicily Landings in July/August. 1944: Employed on experiments with 2-man submarines at Malta. Survey vessel for hydrographical work on the Maltese Harbours. Convoy duties Malta/Italy. 1945: Returned to the UK. Paid Off and placed on the Disposal List. 1946: Acquired by Iago STC of Fleetwood in April and renamed *Red Knight*. PR: LO 445. 1962: BU at Barrow by TW. Ward. Notes: Earned the distinction of being the longest serving RN warship in the Med in WWII.

CORAL	1939/42	Ex-*Cape Duner*	
		Displacement:	705T 455TG 177TN
		Engines:	120HP
		Armament:	1 x 4-inch
		Port Reg:	H 174

1935: Built at Selby by Cochrane. Owned by the Hudson SFC of Hull. 1939: Purchased into the RN on 30 January and converted to A/S. 1940: Joined the 4th A/S-M/S Group. Transferred to the MF. 1942: LOST. Reduced to a CTL by enemy a/c at Malta in April. 1943: Wreck BU in situ.

CORAL   **(Steve Bush Collection)**

JADE   1939/42   Ex-*Lady Lillian*
                                                   Displacement: 615T 392TG 150TN
                                                   Engines: 102HP = 11.5 kts
                                                   Armament: 1 x 4-inch
                                                   Port Reg: H 467
                                                   P.No: T 56

1933: L. Built at Beverley by CWG. Owned by Jutland Amalgamated Trs of Hull. 1939: Purchased into the RN in January and converted to A/S. 1940: Deployed to the Med. and joined the 4th M/S-A/S Group based at Malta. 1941: Carrying out a search for a missing airman off Sicily in June she encountered 2 patrolling E-Boats. In a battle lasting over half an hour she damaged one and drove off the other. Battle ranges were never in excess of 400yds. 1942: LOST. Sunk by enemy a/c during an air raid on Grand Harbour at Malta on 10 April. 1943: BU in situ in December.

MOONSTONE   1939/46   Ex-*Lady Madeleine*
                                                   Displacement: 615T Original:
                                                                     390TG 145TN
                                                   Engines: 104HP = 12 kts
                                                   Armament: 1 x 4-inch   DCs
                                                   Port Reg: H 85
                                                   P.No: T 90

1934: L. Built at Beverley by CWG. Owned by Jutland Amalg. Trs of Hull. 1939: Purchased into the RN in January and converted to A/S. 1940: Joined the 4th M/S-A/S Group and deployed to the Med. Temporary detatchment away from the Group to the EI. Made the first S/M capture of the war when she took the Italian S/M GALILEO GALILEI off Aden on 19 June. Returned to the Med and based at Alexandria. 1941: Joined the Force defending Crete during the evacuation and employed on Suda Bay patrols. 1944: Employed on patrols around the Greek Islands. TPI the rescue of refugees from the Greek Civil War in December. Captured a Greek vessel employed on smuggling arms to the Greek rebels. 1946: Sold to mercantile and renamed *Red Lancer*. Acquired by the Iago ST Co of Fleetwood. PR: LO 442. 1947: Converted to Fuel Oil. 1964: BU at Glasgow.

JAPANESE GROUP

JAPANESE PURCHASED VESSELS.

During the First World War German armed raiders were successful, on occasions, in laying mines in the Indian Ocean especially around Ceylon. For most of the war sweeping these mines was competently dealt with by two harbour tugs suitably equipped. However, early in 1917, there was a considerable increase in mine reports and the local authorities were obliged to ask for additional resources for sweeping. Unable to supply this request with trawlers from the UK the Admiralty arranged for the temporary loan of three trawlers from the Italians whilst they cast around to find more permanent ships. In doing so they turned to the Japanese who, in the First World War were our allies, with the result that three trawlers were purchased on 10 March and a further three four days later. The six trawlers were quickly converted and commenced operations. In 1920 they were sold off with a number of them going to the Ceylon Government.

Vessels in the Group:

KUMARIHAMI, LAKSHMI, LANKDYS, PARVATI, RANMENIKA and SARASVATI II.

JAPANESE GROUP - NOTES

KUMARIHAMI   1917/20 RIM   Ex-*Minato Maru No.3*
                                        Displacement: 259TG
                                        Port Reg: Japanese

1913: L. Built in Japan. 1917: Purchased into the RIM in March and converted to a M/S. 1920: Sold to mercantile in March and retained the same name.

LAKSHMI   1917/20   Displacement: 249TG
                                        Port Reg: Japanese

1913: L. Built in Japan. 1917: Purchased into the RN in March and converted to a M/S. Employed in Ceylonese Waters. 1920: Sold to mercantile and renamed *Lilla*.

LANDKYS   1917/20 RIM   Ex-*Nishiso Maru No.1*
                                        Displacement: 255TG
                                        Port Reg: Japanese

1911: L. Built in Japan. 1917: Purchased into the RIM in March and converted to a M/S. Employed in Ceylonese Waters. 1920: Sold to mercantile and renamed *Lanka*.

PARVATI   1917/20   Ex-*Naniwa Maru*
                                        Displacement: 208TG
                                        Port Reg: Japanese

1912: L. Built in Japan as a Japanese fishing vessel. 1917: Purchased into the RN in March and converted to a M/S. Employed in Ceylonese waters. 1920: Sold to mercantile and retained the same name.

RANMENIKA   1917/20   Ex-*Nishisa Maru No.2*
                                        Displacement: 224TG
                                        Port Reg: Japanese

1913: L. Built in Japan as a fishing vessel. 1917: Purchased into the RN and converted to a M/S. Employed in Ceylonese waters. 1920: Sold to mercantile.

SARASVATI   1917/20   Ex-*Chokai Maru*
                                         Displacement: 204TG
                                         Port Reg: Japanese

1911: L. Built in Japan as a fishing vessel. 1917: Purchased into the RN in March and converted to a M/S. Employed in Ceylonese waters. 1920: Sold to mercantile and retained the same name.

PORTUGUESE GROUP

In September 1915 an assortment of British-built trawlers were purchased from Portuguese owners for the sum of £80,788. They were intended for conversion to M/Ss but in the event were used as APVs. ANTARES was lost in WWI but the other 8 survived to be sold out of the Service on 17th May 1919, to the Cruze Brothers of Gibraltar. Most of them returned to Portuguese ownership soon after.

Vessels in the Group:

ACHERNAR, ALGENIB, ALGOL, ALTAIR, ANTARES, ARCTURUS, CORVI, CRUCIS and CYGNI

PORTUGUESE GROUP - NOTES

ACHERNAR	1915/19	Ex-*Chire* Ex-*Hebden*	
		Displacement:	256TG.
		Armament:	1 x 6-pdr
		Admty No:	180

1908: Launched. Built at Aberdeen by Duthie. 1915: Purchased from Portuguese owners in September. Converted to an APV. 1919: Sold to the Cruze Bros at Gibraltar on 8 May and renamed *Rio Guadiana*.

ALGENIB	1915/19	Ex-*Neptuna* Ex-*Vinca*	
		Displacement:	321TG
		Armament:	1 x 6-pdr; 1 x 7.5-inch Bomb Thrower (A/S Howitzer)
		Admty No:	176.
		Port Reg:	Portuguese

1907: Launched. Built by Goole SB. 1915: Purchased from Portuguese owners and converted to an APV. 1919: Sold to Cruze Bros. of Gibraltar and renamed *Rio Douro*.

ALGOL	1915/19	Ex-*Maria Amalia* Ex-*Caithnesshire*	
		Displacement:	213TG
		Armament:	1 x 6-pdr
		Admty No:	179
		Port Reg:	Portuguese.

1901: Launched. Built by Mackie & Thompson. 1915: Purchased in September from Portuguese owners and converted to an APV. 1919: Sold to Cruz Bros. of Gibraltar on 17 May and renamed *Rio Lima*.

ALTAIR	1917/19	Ex-*Victoria Laura* Ex-*Star of Freedom*	
		Displacement:	257TG
		Armament:	1 x 6-pdr, 1 x 7.5-inch Bomb Thrower (A/S howitzer)
		Admty No:	178
		Port Reg:	Portuguese

1907: Launched. Built at Aberdeen by J.Duthie Torry SB Co. 1917: Purchased in September from Portuguese owners and converted to an APV. 1917: Renamed ALTAIR II in October. 1919: Sold to the Cruz Bros of Gibraltar on 17 May and re-named.

ALTAIR II		See under ALTAIR above.

ANTARES	1915/18	Ex-*Cabo Verde* Ex-*Benalloigan*
		Displacement: 218TG.
		Armament: 1 x 3-pdr
		Admty. No: 177
		Port Reg: Portuguese.

1906: Launched. Built at Aberdeen by J.Duthie Torry SB Co. 1915: Purchased into the RN in September from Portuguese owners. Converted to an APV. 1917: Renamed ANTARES II in October. 1918: LOST Sunk by gunfire after a collision off Gibraltar.

ANTARES II		See under ANTARES above

ARCTURUS	1915/19	Ex-*Alberia* ,ex-*Rio Tejo*
		Displacement: 337TG 125TN
		Engines: 84HP = 10.5 kts
		Armament: 1 x 6-pdr; 1 x 7.5-inch Bomb Thrower (A/S Howitzer).
		Admty No: 175
		Port Reg: Portuguese

1910: Launched. Built at Beverley by CWG. Owned by Crown SFC of Grimsby. Sold to Portuguese mercantile and re-named *Rio Tejo*. 1915: Purchased into the RN in September from Portuguese owners, converted to an APV and renamed. 1918: Renamed ARCTURUS II in June. 1919: Sold to the Cruz Bros. of Gibraltar and renamed *Alberia*. 1920: Acquired by Portuguese owners. 1978: BU in Portugal.

ARCTURUS II		See under ARCTURUS above

CORVI	1915/19	Ex-*Mindello II*
		Ex-*Baron Ruzette*
		Displacement: 216TG
		Armament: 1 x 6-pdr
		Admty No: 173

1909: L. Built at Govan by Mackie & Thompson. 1915: Portuguese trawler purchased in September. 1919: Sold to mercantile.

CRUCIS	1915/19	Ex-*Bicatho*
		Displacement: 243T
		Armament: 1 x 3-pdr
		Admty No: 172

1911: L. 1915: Portuguese fishing vessel purchased into the RN in September, renamed and converted to an APV. 1919: Sold to Cruz Bros. of Gibraltar on 17th May. Resold and renamed *Rio Minho*.

CYGNI   1915/19

Ex-*Monchique*   Ex-*Loch Laggan*
Displacement: 207TG
Armament: 1 x 6-pdr; 1 x 7.5-inch Bomb Thrower (A/S Howitzer)
Admty No: 174

1903: L. Built at Aberdeen by Hall. 1915: Portuguese fishing vessel purchased into the RN in September. Converted to an APV. 1919: Sold to Cruz Bros, of Gibraltar on 17 May. Resold and renamed *Rio Vouga*.

In 1914/15 a large number of German trawlers fell into British hands. They were taken in the North Sea by cruisers and destroyers on their routine sweeps and two, CHIRSIN and CLONSIN were seized at Aberdeen at the outbreak of hostilities in August 1914. Clearly a case of being in the wrong place at the wrong time. Of those captured at sea, some of which can be credited to individual captors, many were sunk when it was found that they were short of coal and unable to be steamed by prize crews back to the UK. Twenty-seven were brought back to the UK and, usually at Grimsby, were converted to Minesweepers for service in the Royal Navy. For some reason unknown, they were given composite names ending with the suffix "-sit" which, again for some unknown reason, was changed in 1915 to "-sin". In the main their war service was carried out in the Mediterranean where they were employed on the Patrol service.

One vessel, CORTASIN was TIH for fitting out but, before completion, was considered unfit for the punishing work of a Minesweeper and was released to the fishing industry. Renamed SKERNE it was subsequently requisitioned in 1917 as a Fishing Trawler (see Text). Two of the Group, CHARLSIN and CROWNSIN were war losses and the remainder were sold to the mercantile after the war.

Vessels in the Group:

CABALSIN, CACHOSIN, CAERSIN, CALLSIN, CALUMSIN, CAMBRISIN, CAMPSIN, CANOSSIN, CARBOSIN, CENSIN, CHARLESIN, CHECKSIN, CHIRSIN, CHURCHSIN, CLAROSIN, CLASSIN, CLEARSIN, CLONSIN, COALSIN, COOKSIN, COOMASIN, CORINSIN, CORTASIN, CRADOSIN, CRAIGSIN, CROMSIN, CROWNSIN, CUDWOSIN and CULBASIN

PRIZE GROUP - NOTES

CABALSIN	1915/20	Ex-*Burhave*	
		Displacement:	218TG
		Armament:	1 x 12-pdr
		Admty No:	1937

1904: L. German Fishing trawler built at Geestemunde by Tecklenborg. 1915: Captured by ARETHUSA in the N.Sea on 30 September. Added to the Navy List in October. 1920: Sold to mercantile. 1921: Renamed *Star of the Orient*.

CACHOSIN	1915/20	Ex-*Doktor Krugler*	
		Displacement:	218TG	87TN
		Engines:	42HP
		Armament:	1 x 12-pdr
		Admty No:	1932

1912: L. German Fishing vessel built at Geestemunde by Seebeck. 1915: Captured by UNDAUNTED in the N.Sea on 7 October. Added to the Navy List in October. 1920: Sold to mercantile and renamed *Cairnrigh*. Acquired by T. Davidson of Aberdeen. PR: A 377.

CAERSIN	1915/20	Ex-*Dora*	
		Displacement:	133TG
		Armament:	1 x 6-pdr AA
		Admty No:	1949

1892: L. German Fishing trawler built at Bremmerhaven by Wencke. 1915: Captured in the N.Sea by PENELOPE on 30 September. Added to the Navy List in October. 1920: Sold to mercantile on 17 March and retained the same name. Acquired by N. Cook & J. French of Aberdeen. PR: A 427.

CALLSIN	1915/21	Ex-*Mond*	
		Displacement:	136TG 53TN
		Engines:	37HP
		Armament:	1 x 6-pdr AA ;
			1 x 3-pdr
		Admty No:	1917

1896: L. German Fishing vessel built at Geestemunde by Tecklenborg. 1915: Captured in the N.Sea by CONQUEST on 7 August. Added to the Navy List in October. 1921: Sold to mercantile and retained the same name. Acquired by RWE. Lewis of Aberdeen. PR: A 873.

CALUMSIN	1915/21	Ex-*Wurzburg*	
		Displacement:	224TG
		Armament:	1 x 6-pdr
		Admty No:	1935

1902: L. German Fishing vessel built at Geestemunde by Seebeck. 1915: Captured in the N. Sea by RN ship. Added to the Navy List in October. 1921: Sold to mercantile on 13 December. 1922: Renamed *Bridge of Earn*. Acquired by AW. Johnson of Aberdeen. PR: A 851.

CAMBRISIN	1915/20	Ex-*Orion*	
		Displacement:	158TG 72TN
		Engines:	36HP
		Armament:	1 x 6-pdrAA
		Admty No:	1946

1891: L. German fishing trawler built at Bremmerhaven by Wencke. 1915: Captured in the N. Sea by CLEOPATRA on 10 September. Converted to a M/S and added to the Navy List in October. 1920: Sold to mercantile on 17 March and retained the same name. Acquired by N. Cook of Aberdeen. PR: A 426.

CAMPSIN	1915/20	Ex-*Adjutant*	
		Displacement:	133TG 56TN
		Engines:	42HP
		Armament:	1 x 6-pdr AA
		Admty No:	856

1894: L. German fishing trawler built at Geestemunde by Tecklenborg. 1915: Captured in the N. Sea by AURORA on 30 September. Converted to a M/S and added to the Navy List in October. 1920: Sold to mercantile on 18 February and retained the same name. Acquired by GFIP Taylor of Aberdeen.

CANNOSIN	1915/20	Ex-*Paul*	
		Displacement:	153TG
		Armament:	1 x 6-pdr
		Admty No:	1936

1894: L. German fishing vessel built at Geestemunde by Seebeck. 1915: Captured by

CLEOPATRA in the N. Sea on 7 October. Added to the Navy List in October. 1920: Sold to mercantile on 16 March and retained the same name. Acquired by RW Lewis of Aberdeen. PR: A 467.

CARBOSIN	1915/20	Ex-*Darmstadt*		
		Displacement:	158TG	66TN
		Engines:	47HP	
		Armament:	1 x 6-pdr AA	
		Admty No:	1947	

1896: L. German Fishing vessel built at Vegesack by Bremer Vulcan. 1915: Captured in the N.Sea by CLEOPATRA on 30 September. Converted to a M/S and added to the Navy List in October. 1920: Sold to mercantile on 5 October and renamed *Kieth Hall*. Acquired by J.Ellis & W.Meff of Aberdeen. 1921: Mercantile Loss on 27 November.

CENSIN	1915/20	Ex-*Burgermeister Smidt*	
		Displacement:	147TG
		Armament:	1 x 6-pdr AA
		Admty No:	857

1894: L. German fishing vessel built at Geestemunde by Seebeck. 1915: Captured in the N.Sea by CONQUEST on 30 September. Converted to a M/S and added to the Navy List in October. 1920: Sold to mercantile and renamed *Keelby*. Acquired by the Keelby SFC of Grimsby. PR: GY 1161.

CHARLSIN	1915/17	Ex-*Esteburg*	
		Displacement:	241TG
		Admty No:	1931

1907: L. German fishing vessel built at Tonning by Eiderwerft. 1915: Captured by S/M E4 in the N.Sea on 5 September. Added to the Navy List in September. 1917: LOST. Sunk by German S/M UC-74 8 miles to the N.of Murseh Matruh on 30 September.

CHECKSIN	1915/20	Ex-*Wulsdorf*		
		Displacement:	140TG	48TN
		Engines:	25HP	
		Armament:	1 x 6-pdr AA	
		Admty No:	1941	

1895: L. German Fishing vessel built at Vegasack by Bremer Vulcan. 1915: Captured in the N.Sea on 7 October and added to the Navy List. 1920: Sold to mercantile on 11 May. 1921: Renamed *George Turner*. Acquired by G.Turner of Plymouth. PR: PH 217.

CHERSIN	1914/20	Ex-*Else Kunkel*		
		Displacement:	218TG	48TN
		Engines:	25HP	
		Armament:	1 x 6-pdr AA	
		Admty No:	812	

1912: L. German fishing vessel built by Unterweser, Lehe. 1914: Detained at Aberdeen on 4 August. Converted to a M/S and added to the Navy List in December. 1920: Sold to mercantile on 16 March and retained the same name. 1922: Renamed *Star of England*.

CHURCHSIN	1915/20	Ex-*St.Georg*	ex-*Northmoor*	
		Displacement:	140TG	57TN
		Engines:	49HP	
		Armament:	1 x 6-pdr	
		Admty No:	1943	

1900: L. Built at by Smith's Dock as *Northmoor*. 1915: German Fishing vessel *St.Georg* captured in the N.Sea by CONQUEST on 30 September. Converted to a M/S and added to the Navy List in October. 1920: Sold to mercantile on 11 May and renamed *Banks o' Dee*. Acquired by W.McPherson AO of Aberdeen. PR: A 345.

CLAROSIN	1915/20	Ex-*Sophie*	
		Displacement:	159TG
		Armament:	1 x 6-pdr
		Admty No:	1942

1897: L. German fishing vessel built at Vegesack by Bremer Vulcan. 1915: Captured in the N.Sea by CONQUEST on 7 October and added to the Navy List in the same month. 1920: Sold to mercantile and renamed *Blackhall*. Acquired by W.Meff & J.Ellis of Aberdeen. PR: A 307.

CLASSIN	1915/20	Ex-*President Rose*	
		Displacement:	182TG
		Armament:	1 x 3-pdr
		Admty No:	1934

1889: L. German Fishing vessel built at Bremerhaven by Wencke. 1915: Captured in the N.Sea by ARETHUSA on 7 October. Converted to a M/S and added to the Navy List in October. 1920: Sold to mercantile on 18 February and retained the same name.

CLEARSIN	1915/20	Ex-*Resie*	
		Displacement:	155TG
		Armament:	1 x 6-pdr AA
		Admty No:	858

1891: L. German fishing vessel built at Bremmerhaven by Wencke. 1915: Captured in the N.Sea by AURORA on 7 October. Converted to a M/S and added to the Navy List the same month. 1920: Sold to mercantile on 18 February and retained the same name.

CLONSIN	1914/20	Ex-*Robitzsch*	
		Displacement:	202TG 92TN
		Engines:	39HP
		Armament:	1 x 6-pdr AA
		Admty No:	813

1911: L. German fishing vessel built at Geestemunde by Seebeck. 1914: Detained at Aberdeen on 4 August. Added to the Navy List in December. 1920: Sold to mercantile in March and renamed *Birkhall*. Acquired by W. Meff & J. Ellis of Aberdeen. PR: A 378.

COALSIN	1915/20	Ex-*Toni*	
		Displacement:	130TG 41TN
		Engines:	42HP
		Armament:	1 x 6-pdr AA
		Admty No:	859

1892: L. German Fishing vessel built at Geestemunde by Tecklenborg. 1915: Captured in the N.Sea by MENTOR on 7 October. Converted to a M/S and added to the Navy List the same month. 1920: Sold to mercantile on 5 October. 1922: Renamed *Laceby*. Acquired by WS.Crosthwaite & CW.Robinson of Middlesborough. PR: MH 138.

COOKSIN	1915/20	Ex-*Herbert*	
		Displacement:	149TG
		Armament:	1 x 6-pdr
		Admty No:	860

1896: L. German fishing vessel built at Geestemunde by Seebeck. 1915: Captured in the N.Sea on 7 October. 1920: Sold to mercantile on 17 March and renamed *Lowhar*.

COOMASIN	1915/20	Ex-*Heppens*	
		Displacement:	170TG
		Armament:	1 x 6-pdr
		Admty No:	1933

1897: German fishing vessel built at Roastock by Neptun. 1915: Captured in the N.Sea by ARETHUSA on 7 October. Added to the Navy List. 1919: Renamed CINCERIA in September. Reverted to COOMASIN in December. 1920: Sold to mercantile on 11 May. 1921: Renamed *Conovium*.

CORINSIN	1915/20	Ex-*Jutlandia*	Ex-*Stuttgart*
		Displacement:	159TG
		Armament:	1 x 6-pdr
		Admty No:	1940

1896: L. German fishing vessel built at Vegesack by Bremer Vulcan. 1915: Captured in the N.Sea by ARETHUSA on 30 September. Added to the Navy List. 1920: Sold to mercantile on 18 February and retained the same name.

CORTASIN	1915/15	Ex-*Sonntag*	Ex-*Rover*	
		Displacement:	156TG	54TN
		Engines:	45HP	

1891: L. Built at Govan by Mackie & Thompson. Iron construction. 1915: German fishing vessel *Sonntag* captured in the N.Sea on 7 October. Designated for addition to the Navy List. Started fitting out but found unsuitable. Sold to mercantile in December. Renamed *Skerne*. Acquired by HW.Barker of Billingsgate. PR: LT 412.

CRADOSIN	1915/20	Ex-*Elma*	
		Displacement:	133TG
		Armament:	1 x 12-pdr
		Admty No:	1945

1895: L. German fishing vessel built at Geestemunde by Tecklenberg. 1915: Captured in the N.Sea by ARETHUSA on 7 October. Added to the Navy List in the same month. 1920: Sold to mercantile on 5 October. 1925: Renamed *Jeannie Annette*.

CRAIGSIN	1915/20	Ex-*Blumenthal*	
		Displacement:	141TG
		Armament:	1 x 6-pdr AA
		Admty No:	861

1895: L. German fishing vessel built at Vegesack by Bremer Vulcan. 1915: Captured in the N.Sea on 7 October. Converted to a M/S and added to the Navy List in the same month. 1920: Sold to mercantile on 5 October. 1921: Renamed *Floric*. Acquired by HGR.Gibbons AO of Hull. PR: GY 1204.

CROMSIN	1915/20	Ex-*Ost* Ex-*Alderney*	
		Displacement:	138TG	57TN
		Engines:	40HP = 9.5 kts
		Armament:	1 x 6-pdr
		Admty No:	1881

1895: L. Built at Hull by CWG as *Alderney*. Owned by Hull SF & Ice Co of Hull. 1914: Acquired by Putz & Co of Geestamunde, Germany and renamed *Ost*. 1915: German fishing vessel captured in the N.Sea by HMS/M S1 on 24 June. Converted to a M/S and added to the Navy List in the same month and renamed CROMSIT. Renamed CROM-SIN in November. 1920: Sold to mercantile on 11 May and renamed *Aro*. Acquired by A.Robertson of Aberdeen. PR: A 333. 1936: BU.

CROWSIN	1915/16	Ex-*Varel*	
		Displacement:	137TG
		Admty No:	1950

1895: L. German fishing vessel built at Geestemunde by Tecklenborg. 1915: Captured in the N.Sea by ARETHUSA in 7 October. Added to the Navy List in the same month. 1916: Transferred to the MF. LOST. Mined off Malta on 4 May.

CUDWOSIN	1915/20	Ex-*West*	
		Displacement:	112TG
		Armament:	1 x 6-pdr
		Admty No:	1944

1907: L. German fishing vessel built at Rostock by Neptun. 1920: Captured in the N.Sea by MANLY on 7 October. Added to the Navy List in the same month. 1920: Sold to mercantile in March and retained the same name. 1921: Renamed *Karl Grammersdorf*.

CULBASIN	1915/20	Ex-*Nereus*	
		Displacement:	133TG 54TN
		Engines:	47HP
		Armament:	1 x 6-pdr AA
		Admty No:	1948

1893: L. German fishing vessel built at Geestemunde by Tecklenborg. 1915: Captured in the N.Sea on 7 October and added to the Navy List in the same month. 1920: Sold to mercantile on 5 October. 1921: Renamed *Lieth Hall*. Acquired by J.Ellis & W.Meff of Aberdeen. PR: A 632.

TREE GROUP

This Group was purchased from Trade in two batches each of ten vessels. The first, displacing 548 - 649T was purchased in November 1935 and converted to Minesweepers. The second batch, purchased in February 1939 were also converted to sweepers.

During WW2 they mostly served in UK waters although four of their number ventured abroad, HOLLY to West Africa, MAGNOLIA to the Indian Ocean and MAPLE and REDWOOD to Freetown and thence into the Mediterranean in 1941. Remarkably, every vessel in the 1st Batch survived the war, but the 2nd Batch was not so lucky. ALDER, BEECH, MYRTLE and TAMARISK succumbed to hostilities. All the Group survivors were sold to the mercantile post-war. To avoid confusion with the later built Tree Class this Group were referred to in some lists as Berberis Group

The first batch comprised:

CEDAR, CYPRESS, HAWTHORN, HOLLY, LAUREL, LILAC, MAGNOLIA, SYCAMORE, SYRINGA, and WILLOW.

The second batch comprised:

ALDER, BEECH, BERBERIS, HORNBEAM, LARCH, MAPLE, MYRTLE, OAK, REDWOOD and TAMARISK.

SYCAMORE   **(MPL)**

ALDER 1939/41 ex-*Lord Davidson*

Displacement:	560T 346TG 135TN
Engines:	96HP
Port Reg:	H 57
P.No:	T 84

1929: L. Built at Selby by Cochrane. Owned by Pickering & Haldane's SFC of Hull. 1939: Purchased in February and converted to a M/S. Based at Grimsby (ungrouped). 1941: LOST. Took the ground off the East Coast of Scotland on 22 October and wrecked.

BEECH 1939/41 ex-*Lord Dawson*

Displacement:	540TG 135TN
Engines:	96HP
Port Reg:	H 140
P.No:	T 44

1929: L. Built at Selby by Cochrane. Owned by Pickering and Haldane's SFC of Hull. 1939: Purchased into the RN in February and converted to a M/S. 1940: Joined the 18th M/S Group based at Grimsby. 1941: LOST. Sunk by enemy a/c off N.Scotland on 22 June.

BERBERIS 1939/46 ex-*Lord Hewart*

Displacement:	134TN
Engines:	96HP
Armament:	1 x 12-pdr
Port Reg:	H 475
P.No:	T 46

1935: L. Built at Selby by Cochrane. Owned by Pickering & Haldane's STC of Hull. 1939: Purchased into the RN in February and converted to a M/S. 1946: Sold to Mercantile and renamed *Bergen*.

CEDAR (MPL)

HAWTHORN (PRNM)

CEDAR 1935/46 ex-*Arab*

Displacement:	649TG 422TG 162TN
Engines:	111HP = 11.4 kts
Armament:	1 x 12-pdr
Port Reg:	H 516
P.No:	T 01

1933: L. Built at Beverley by CWG. Owned by Hellyer Bros. of Hull. 1935: Purchased into the RN in November and converted to a M/S and renamed. 1939: Served in Home waters throughout WWII. 1946: Sold to mercantile and renamed *Red Gauntlet*. Acquired by the Iago STC of Fleetwood. 1947: Mercantile Loss. Wrecked on a reef near Spitzbergen on 10 August. No loss of life.

CYPRESS 1935/46 ex-*Cape Finesterre*

Displacement:	500TG 145TN
Engines:	96HP
Armament:	1 x 12-pdr
Port Reg:	H 310
P.No:	T 09

1930: L. Built at Selby by Cochrane. Owned by the Hudson SFC of Hull. 1935: Purchased into the RN in November and converted to a M/S. 1939: Home Waters throughout WWII. 1946: Sold to mercantile in March and renamed *Vardberg*.

HAWTHORN 1935/47 ex-*Cape Guardafui*

Displacement:	593TG
Armament:	1 x 4-inch
P.No:	T 32

1930: L. 1935: Owned by Hudson Bros of Hull. Purchased into the RN in November and converted to a M/S. 1947: Sold to mercantile in July and renamed *Havborgin*.

HOLLY	1935/46	ex-*Kingston Coral*	
		Displacement:	590TG
		Armament:	1 x 12-pdr
		P.No:	T 19

1930: L. Built at Beverley by CWG. Owned by Kingston STC, Hull. 1935: Purchased into the RN in November and converted to a M/S. 1940: Deployed to the MF. 1941: Transferred to Freetown. 1944: Paid Off and Laid up at Freetown. 1946: Sold to mercantile and renamed *Dragaberg*. 1956: BU.

HORNBEAM	1939/46	ex-*Lord Trent*		
		Displacement:	530TG	135TN
		Engines:	96HP	
		Armament:	1 x 12-pdr	
		Port Reg:	H 116	
		P.No:	T 53	

1929: L. Built at Selby by Cochrane. Owned by Pickering & Haldane's ST Co.Ltd. of Hull 1939: Purchased into the RN in March and converted to a M/S. Served in Home Waters throughout WWII. 1944: TPI Operation Neptune, the D-Day Landings in June as a D/L attached to the 18th M/S Flot. in Force G. 1946: Sold to mercantile in April and renamed *Rankin*.

LARCH	1939/46	ex-*St. Alexandra*		
		Displacement:	550T	359TG
			156TN	
		Engines:	96HP = 10.8 kts	
		Armament:	1 x 12-pdr	
		Port Reg:	H 373	
		P.No:	T 96	

1928: L. Built at Beverley by CWG. Owned by Thomas Hamling & Co of Hull. 1939: Purchased into the RN on 11 March and converted to a M/S. Served in Home Waters throughout WWII. 1946: Sold to mercantile. Acquired by Westholme FCL of Milford

LAUREL　　　　　　　　　　　　　　　　　　**(Steve Bush Collection)**

Haven. PR: M 138. 1947: Acquired by JC Llewellyn of Milford Haven but remained at Hull. Renamed *Westhill.* PR: H 470. 1950: Acquired by Marr of Hull. 1952: BU at Sunderland.

LAUREL	1935/47	ex-*Kingston Cyanite*	
		Displacement:	590T 365TG
			137TN
		Engines:	96NHP = 11 kts
		Armament:	1 x 4-inch
		Port Reg:	H.
		P.No:	T 29 (M/S)
			4 417 (WDV)

1930: L. Built at Beverley by CWG. Owned by Kingston STC of Hull. 1935: Purchased into the RN on 25 November and converted to a M/S. 1944: De-armed and converted to a WDV in April. 1947: Sold to mercantile and renamed *Strathyre.* Acquired by Granton TCL. PR: GN 46. 1951: Renamed *Patricia Hague* PR: FD 58. 1955: BU at Troon.

LILAC	1935/47	ex-*Beachflower*	
		Displacement:	593TG 140TN
		Engines:	96HP
		Armament:	1 x 4-inch
		P.No:	T 26

1930: L. Built at Selby by Cochrane. 1935: Purchased into the RN in November and converted to a M/S. 1939: Employed in sweeping in Home Waters throughout WWII. 1947: Sold to mercantile and renamed *Robert Hewitt.* Acquired by Great Northern FC of London. PR: LO 427.

MAGNOLIA	1935/47	ex-*Lord Brentford*	
		Displacement:	557TG
		Armament:	1 x 4-inch
		P.No:	T 31

1930: L. 1935: Built at Selby by Cochrane. Owned by Pickering & Haldane STC of Hull. Purchased into the RN in November and converted to a M/S. 1942: Joined the EIF at Colombo. 1947: Sold at the Cape in January to BU at Mombasa. 1948: Resold to mercantile and renamed *Oranjezicht.*

MAPLE	1939/46	ex-*St. Gerontius*	
		Displacement:	550T 357TG
			155TN
		Engines:	96HP = 10.9 kts
		Armament:	1 x 4-inch
		Port Reg:	H 69
		P.No:	T 38

1929: L. Built at at Beverley by CWG. Owned by T. Hamling & Co of Hull. 1939: Purchased into the RN in February, renamed and converted to a M/S. 1940: Based at Freetown, W. Africa. 1941: Transferred to the MF. 1946: Sold to Dutch mercantile and renamed *Sumatra.* 1956: BU in Holland.

MYRTLE	1939/40	ex-*St. Irene*	
		Displacement:	550T 357TG
			154TN
		Engines:	96HP = 10.6 kts
		Armament:	1 x 12-pdr
		Port Reg:	H 472
		P.No:	T 91

1928: L. Built at Beverley by CWG. Owned by Thos. Hamling & Co of Hull. 1939: Purchased into the RN in February and converted to a M/S. 1940: LOST. Mined in the Thames Estuary on 14 June.

OAK	1939/46	ex-*St. Romanus*	
		Displacement:	545T 357TG 154TN
		Engines:	96HP = 10.7 kts
		Armament:	1 x 4-inch
		Port Reg:	H 426
		P.No:	T 54

1928: L. Built at Beverley by CWG. Owned by T. Hamling & Co of Hull. 1939: Purchased into the RN in March and converted to a M/S. 1946: Sold to mercantile in March and renamed *St. Stephen*. PR: H 299. 1949: Renamed *Lady June*. 1950: Renamed *Recepto*. PR: GY 254. 1956: BU at Bruges in Belguim.

REDWOOD	1939/45	Ex-*St. Rose*	
		Displacement:	555TG 154TN
		Engines:	96HP = 10.6HP
		Armament:	1 x 4-inch
		Port Reg:	H 492
		P.No:	T 86

1928: L. Built at Beverley by CWG as *St. Rose*. Owned by T. Hamling & Co of Hull. 1939: Purchased into the RN in March and converted to a M/S. Renamed. 1945: Sold to mercantile. Acquired by Dutch owners nad renamed *Mary*. 1956: BU.

SYCAMORE	1935/46	ex-*Lord Beaverbrook*	
		Displacement:	573T 362TG
		Engines:	
		Armament:	1 x 4-inch
		Port Reg:	
		P.No:	T 37

1930: L. 1935: Built at Selby by Cochrane. Owned by Pickering & Haldane STC of Hull.

SYRINGA (PRNM)

Purchased into the RN in November and converted to a M/S. 1945: Converted to a D/L. 1946: Sold to mercantile in July and renamed *Drattur*.

SYRINGA	1935/46	ex-*Cape Kanin*		
		Displacement:	574TG	152TN
		Engines:	96HP	
		Armament:	1 x 4-inch	
		Port Reg:		
		P.No:	T 55	

1930: L. Built at Selby by Cochrane. 1935: Purchased into the RN in November and converted to a M/S. 1939: M/S Groups in Home Waters throughout WWII. 1946: Placed on the Disposal List. 1947: Sold to mercantile and renamed *Davarr Island*. Acquired by T.H.Scales & Sons of Edinburgh. 1948: Reverted to original name *Cape Kanin*. 1954: BU.

WILLOW	1935/46	ex-*Cape Spartivento*	
		Displacment:	574T 347TG
		P.No:	T 66

1930: L. 1935: Built at Selby by Cochrane. Owned by Hudson SFC of Hull. Purchased into the RN in November and converted to a M/S. 1939: Sweeping in Home waters throughout WWII. 1945: Converted to a D/L. 1946: Sold to mercantile in June and renamed *Trondur-I-Gottu*.

ABBREVIATIONS

AMC	Armed Merchant Cruiser		MBE	Member of the British Empire
AA	Anti Aircraft		MF	Mediterranean Fleet
ABV	Armed Boarding Vessel		MG	Machine Gun
a/c	Aircraft		M-i-D	Mentioned in Despatches
Aka	Also known as		M/L	Mine Layer
AO	And Others		MRV	Mine Recovery Vessel
APV	Auxiliary Patrol Vessel		M/S	Mine Sweeper
A/S	Anti Submarine		M/W	Mine Wiping
ASR	Air Sea Rescue			
			NFI	No Further Information
BBV	Barrage Balloon Vessel		NS	Nova Scotia
BDV	Boom Defence Vessel		NSW	New South Wales
BGV	Boom Gate Vessel			
BPF	British Pacific Fleet		oa	Overall
BU	Broken Up			
			pdr	Pounder
CWG	Trawler Builders Cook Welton &		pp	Between perpendiculars
	Gemmell		PR	Port Registration
C-in-C	Commander in Chief			
			RAN	Royal Australian Navy
D & E	Docking & Engineering		RCN	Royal Canadian Navy
DC	Depth Charge		RIM	Royal Indian Marine
DCR	Depth Charge Rails		RIN	Royal Indian Navy
DCT	Depth Charge Thrower		RN	Royal Navy
D/L	Dan Layer		RNH	Royal Naval Hospital
DG	Degaussing		RNR	Royal Naval Reserve
Dk	Docking		RNVR	Royal Naval Volunteer Reserve
DP	Dual Purpose (Surface and Anti		RNZN	Royal New Zealand Navy
	Aircraft)			
DSC	Distinguished Service Cross		SAN	South African Navy
DSF	Deep Sea Fishing Company		SB	Ship Building
DSM	Distinguished Service Medal		SF	Steam Fisheries
DY	Dockyard		SFC	Steam Fishing Company
			S/M	Submarine
EI	East Indies		SS	Steam Ship
			ST	Steam Trawlers
FC	Fishing Company		STC	Steam Trawler Company
FCL	Fishing Company Limited		STL	Steam Trawlers Limited
FE	Far East		SY	Ship Yard
FO	Furnace Oil			
			T	Tons
HF	Home Fleet		TC	Trawler Co
HP	Horse Power		TCL	Total Constructural Loss
			TCV	Tank Cleaning Vessel
IHP	Indicated Horse Power		TIH	Taken in hand
ICW	In Company With		TG	Tons Gross
			TN	Tons Nett
K	Knot(s)		TPI	Took Part In
			TRV	Torpedo Recovery Vessel
L	Launched		TT	Torpedo Tubes
LA	Low Angle			
LE	Locally Entered		USN	United States Navy
LG	Lewis Gun			
LV	Light Vessel		VC	Victoria Cross
MB	Motor Boat		WDV	Wreck Dispersal Vessel

PORT REGISTRATIONS

A	Aberdeen		INS	Inverness
AA	Alloa			
AB	Aberystwyth		J	Jersey
AH	Arbroath			
AR	Ayr		K	Kirkwall
			KY	Kirkaldy
B	Belfast			
BA	Ballantrae		L	Limerick
BCK	Buckie		LH	Leith
BD	Bideford		LK	Lerwick
BE	Barnstaple		LL	Liverpool
BF	Banff		LN	Kings Lynn
BK	Berwick		LO	London
BL	Bristol		LK	Lancaster
BM	Brixham		LT	Lowestoft
BN	Boston		LY	Londonderry
BO	Barrowstowness			
BRD	Broadford		M	Milford Haven
BS	Beaumaris		ME	Montrose
BW	Barrow		MH	Middlesborough
			ML	Methil
C	Cork			
CA	Cardigan		N	Newry (Ireland)
CE	Coleraine (Ireland)		NE	Newcastle
CF	Cardiff		NN	Newhaven
CH	Chester		NT	Newport (Gwent)
CK	Colchester			
CN	Campbeltown		OB	Oban
CO	Cararvon			
CS	Cowes		P	Portsmouth
CT	Castletown IOM		PD	Peterhead
CY	Castle Bay		PEH	Perth
			PH	Plymouth
D	Dublin		PL	Peel (IOM)
DE	Dundee		PN	Preston
DK	Dundalk		PW	Padstow
DO	Douglas IOM		PZ	Penzance
DR	Dover			
			R	Ramsgate
F	Faversham		RO	Rothesay
FD	Fleetwood		RR	Rochester
FE	Folkestone		RX	Rye
FH	Falmouth		RY	Ramsay (IOM)
FR	Fraserburgh			
FY	Fowey		S	Skibbereen
			SA	Swansea
G	Galway		SC	Scilly
GK	Greenock		SD	Sunderland
GN	Granton		SH	Scarborough
GU	Guernsey		SM	Shoreham
GW	Glasgow		SN	N.Shields
GY	Grimsby		SO	Sligo
			SR	Stranraer
H	Hull		SS	St.Ives
HH	Harwich		SSS	S.Shields
HL	West Hartlepool		ST	Stockton
			SU	Southampton

SY	Stornaway	WA	Whitehaven
		WD	Wexford
T	Tralee	WH	Weymouth
TN	Teignmouth	WK	Wick
TT	Tarbert	WO	Workington
		WT	Westport
UL	Ullapool		
		YH	Yarmouth (Great)
W	Waterford		

ACKNOWLEDGEMENTS

It is with the greatest of pleasure and gratitude that I acknowledge the many people who have helped me with the assembling of the information on the Trawlers which served in the Royal Navy and which is, with their permission, reproduced in this book.

Firstly, those members of the Royal Naval Patrol Service, hardy warriors of the Second World War, who were kind enough to write in response to my calls for help, and who came up with fascinating information about their service in the Second World War.

Shipmates:

R.W. Atkinson, George Brown, H.F. Baldwin, Alan Clark, B.D.Clark, J.F.O. Connor, Geoff Dormer, Philip Dormer, Douglas Grace, F.G. Harris, P. Horne, Jim T. Hyman, Ron Lawrence, J. Lichters, William Moore, John Mulligan, A. Murray, T. Pendock, C.F. Piggin, H. Roach, M.G. Robinson, J. Shirron, G. Taylor, F. Towler, G.W.H. Wilson, J. Wilson, E. Yates, Lt.Cdr Geoff Lancashire, RN (Retd), Lt.Cdr. F. Strickland RN (Retd)

Others, not of the RNPS, but who had valuable information for me were:

D. Andrews, Henry Bett, Bill Dalton, D. Heywood, James Miller, John McKenzie, Miss A. McKay, E.J. Riseborough, Mrs. G. Robinson, A.A. Snowden, John Solway, Walter Spalding, J. Spencer, and F. Troughton.

My thanks too, to Craig Lazenby, the manager of the National Fishing Heritage Centre at Grimsby and his staff and to Roy Roberts a researcher at the Centre.

There are four authors to whom I am exceedingly grateful. Jimmy Brown author of *Harry Tate's Navy*, Maurice Cocker author of *Mine Warfare Vessels*, Colin Warwick the CO of HMT ST. LOMAN and author of *Really Not Required*, and John Winton, author of *The Victoria Cross at Sea*. All these gentlemen have kindly allowed me to pick their brains and/or their books which I consider uncommonly civil and generous of them.

Bob Roach of Grimsby has been my faithful correspondent all through my research. The amount of information he has supplied and the research he has undertaken for me is inestimable and I owe him a huge debt of gratitude.

Mrs. I.E. Wilson of Grimsby. The "E" in her initials stands for EQUATOR, her father's Trawler command in the First World War. He loved his ship sufficiently to name his daughter after EQUATOR and Mrs. Wilson is very proud of the fact. Her beautiful letters brought home to me the great sense of pride and warmth that not only the men of the Trawlers, but their families too, of both World Wars, had in their cranky little vessels.

Finally, my step daughter Penny Sutton-Woods who initiated me into the mysteries and witchcraft of computers and who never failed to answer my frequent calls for help and the most important person of all, my long-suffering wife, Myrna, who, for so long has been a "computer widow".

BIBLIOGRAPHY

1. LILLIPUT FLEET
   A. Cecil Hampshire
   New English Library
   338, Euston Rd.,
   LONDON.
   NW1 3BH

2. HARRY TATE'S NAVY
   Jimmy Brown.

3. REALLY NOT REQUIRED
   Colin Warwick
   The Pentland Press Ltd.,
   1, Hutton Close, South Church,
   Bishop Auckland, Durham

4. THE VICTORIA COSS AT SEA
   John Winton
   SCC Library No. 30105 0 06677471

5. MINE WARFARE VESSELS
   M.P.Cocker
   Airlife Publishing Ltd
   101, Longden Rd.,
   Shrewsbury.

6. COOK, WELTON & GEMMELL
   Shipbuilders of Hull and Beverley
   Michael Thompson, Dave Nerwton,
   Richard Robinson and Tony Lofthouse
   Hutton Press Ltd.,
   130, Canada Drive
   Cherry Burton,
   BEVERLEY,
   East Yorkshire
   HU17 7SB

7. SHIPS OF THE ROYAL NAVY
   (VOLUME TWO)
   J.J. Colledge
   Greenhill Books
   Lionel Levanthal Ltd.,
   Park House,
   1, Russell Gardens,
   LONDON
   NW11 9NN